Controlling
Mental Chaos

CONTROLLING MENTAL CHAOS

Harnessing the Power of the Creative Mind

JAIME A. PINEDA

ROWMAN & LITTLEFIELD
Lanham • Boulder • New York • London

Published by Rowman & Littlefield
An imprint of The Rowman & Littlefield Publishing Group, Inc.
4501 Forbes Boulevard, Suite 200, Lanham, Maryland 20706
www.rowman.com

86-90 Paul Street, London EC2A 4NE

British Library Cataloguing in Publication Information Available

Library of Congress Cataloging-in-Publication Data

978-1-5381-7980-2 (cloth)
978-1-5381-7981-9 (electronic)

I dedicate this book to those who wish to live a full life;
A life filled with curiosity, creativity, peace, and joy.

"There is no greater enemy than the uncontrolled mind."
—BHAGAVAD GITA

CONTENTS

ACKNOWLEDGMENTS

I WROTE THIS BOOK FOLLOWING MY PERSONAL JOURNEY FROM HAVING a mind that was troubled and uncontrolled to a more peaceful and "controlled" chaos that reminded me of the mind I had when I was young. That journey became possible because of many teachers, friends, and supporters who were there at the beginning and throughout my odyssey. Many of these individuals appeared when I most needed them. My heartfelt thanks go to colleagues and students in the Cognitive Science Department at the University of California, San Diego, who inspired, questioned, and made my learning of cognitive neuroscience a challenging, yet fruitful and joyful adventure. I am grateful as well for those who appeared in my parallel spiritual journey and played a similar, helpful role. My heart is full for having met and studied with Joko Beck, an extraordinary Zen Master whose naturalness and insights are still guiding me.

I extend my everlasting appreciation to Marcy Llamas Senese, PhD, my first developmental editor. She is an excellent teacher, knowledgeable writer, and insightful person who provided considerable guidance and feedback. The experience was enjoyable, interesting, and gratifying. I am equally grateful to Claire Winters, writer, editor, and content strategist, who provided an editorial assessment of an initial draft of the book. The assessment was honest and pointed without being discouraging. It made me aware of the weaknesses I needed to address. Most of all, it gave me a template for how to organize the story to maximize its teaching effectiveness. I also am fortunate to have had several individuals read earlier drafts of chapters and provide me with much-needed feedback and common sense. I appreciate their heartfelt efforts. Among them are Nour Al-Timimi, Maria Bordyug, Carissa

Cesena, Karishma D'Lima, Shari Galve, Jady Hong, Jade Hookham, Dorothy Parker, Jane Pineda, Leanne Sturman, and Iris Ulloa. Finally, I am forever grateful to my wife, Jane, who patiently and without complaint made it possible for me to retire from an academic career to follow my writing passion. Her love and encouragement allowed me to overcome many dry spells and other challenges, not the least being the COVID-19 pandemic that began in early 2020.

INTRODUCTION

THE POEM "I CARRY YOUR HEART WITH ME" BY E. E. CUMMINGS expresses beautifully how one can live creatively and function well in the world. It says that when you carry the heart of the other, of the world, or of God within your own heart, life becomes "the wonder that's keeping the stars apart." Carrying the heart of the other, being in the shoes of the other, expressing empathy and compassion are manifestations of our being that connect us, but also keep us apart. That we are individuals living in unity is the wonder of the world.

Living in peaceful unity seems like an ideal because who has not occasionally strayed from that to experience worries, anxiety, uninhibited thoughts, overwhelming feelings, and seeing no way out of difficult circumstances? When the effects of these life experiences persist and change our mood, rational deliberation, and behavior, they disrupt the normal flow, joy, and unity of life. They obscure its wonder. When this disruption turns unmanageable, it becomes the basis for physical and mental disorders, both autoimmune and emotional, heart problems, addictive behaviors, and suicidal ideation. Even worse, if negative ideations become a recurring issue, psychopathology is the inevitable consequence.

While the pressures of life exacerbate such difficulties, over millennia, many have recognized that the root of the problem is our fearful and uncontrolled mind, one centered on ego-based rumination. Indeed, in a not very flattering description, Siddhartha Gautama, the historical Buddha (ca. 5th to 4th century BCE), recognized this core predicament as the singular psychological basis for human suffering 2,500 years ago. He used the term *kapicitta*, meaning "monkey-like mind," to describe it. He said, "just as a monkey swinging through the trees grabs one branch and lets it go only to seize another, so too, that which is called thought, mind or consciousness arises and disappears continually both day and night." Siddhartha was a gifted and insightful psychologist who recognized the problem of the obsessive mind, diagnosed the source, and provided insights to its solution.

My professional and personal life experiences have given me a solid education, grounding, and a measure of understanding of this problem of the mind. I received a PhD in neuroscience in 1987 and became professor of cognitive science and neuroscience at the University of California, San Diego (UCSD). For twenty-eight years, I directed the Cognitive Neuroscience Laboratory, where I studied the relationship between mind and brain. As a scientist and then spiritual seeker for many years, I searched for answers to the uncontrolled mind conundrum and the problems it raised in my life. The combined wisdom from these two aspects of my life finally helped me understand the problem and how to overcome it. I encountered wisdom accumulated over centuries, although not everyone is privy to it, nor has the time or inclination to learn from it.

Controlling Mental Chaos: Harnessing the Power of the Creative Mind recognizes the problem in its modern context, in which we use science as the language of investigation, knowledge, and understanding. I combine this scientific understanding with a more personal understanding of the mind based on my encounter with Zen Buddhism. I studied Zen with Joko Beck, an American teacher and the author of the books *Everyday Zen: Love and Work* and *Nothing Special: Living Zen*. Beck founded the Ordinary Mind Zen School where she taught to find the Absolute in each moment regardless of its content, and not to turn practice into a search for extraordinary experiences.

Thus, I assume that recognizing and understanding the problem from these two perspectives makes it easier to become open to balancing and implementing solutions to the problem. The outcome for me was a recovery and nourishing of my Original Mind, what Buddhists understand as the mind at birth, which has an attitude of openness, eagerness, and lack of preconceptions. Such a mind helped me step into creative living. The solutions I present in this book are those I learned— easy to understand and available to everyone. Yet they are difficult to put into action, as they call for a genuine change in perception and awareness that comes about not only through gaining knowledge and understanding of the problem, but through a passionate commitment to resolving the problem. I hope that for you, reading the psychological and neuroscientific explanations, along with case studies and reflections on my personal experiences, will give you a deeper understanding of what is at issue and provide the motivation for the required changes.

I include body and mind exercises throughout the book to help you bring about this change. I call the first set of exercises *Questions to Ponder*. These are open-ended questions to give you the chance to pause, probe deeper, and consider the evidence further. There are no answers, since they are meant to expand the limits of your thinking. *Self-Parenting the Mind* is the second class of exercises to discipline the uncontrolled mind. The goal here is to learn to love your mind, as a parent loves a child, a necessary step to setting the stage for the ultimate transformation. *Stop Monkey Mind* is the third set of exercises focusing on the practice of reducing and stopping obsessive mind ruminations. It is the transformative step. The optimal way to achieve this outcome is by focusing on the present moment. Unlike secular-based meditation programs that focus mainly on stress reduction, the more comprehensive insights of Buddhism and mindfulness provide a greater ethical context and target the roots of suffering, including the stickiness of thought. This leads to deeper and longer-lasting experiences of inner freedom. Practicing present moment awareness is a mindfulness technique that changes the expectations concerning the mind's rumination process. This approach literally stops anxious, unmanageable thoughts in their tracks. Its effect is immediate and, with practice, long lasting. Finally, the last series of exercises presented is *How to Cultivate an Unencumbered Mind*. The focus is intuition, which is the interface, or direct access, to the vast intelligence of Original Mind. Cultivating this access, following transformation of uncontrolled mind to Original Mind, helps one make better decisions and provides the confidence needed to move forward. These exercises offer opportunities to transform the obsessive energy into the very positive energy of the controlled, fearless, and creative mind.

I divided the book into two parts. Part I describes the journey from extraordinary Original Mind, as reflected by your mind at birth, to when this mind recedes into the background as the uncontrolled mind grows in strength, to finally how you can recover this treasure. This part of the book discusses my personal journey of discovery and freedom. It describes two parts to address the uncontrolled mind problem and recovery of Original Mind. The first part involves self-parenting, which means consciously choosing the relationship you want to have with yourself, as if with a loving parent. The second part is learning to live in the present moment. Both parts require practice, practice, practice, until the behavior becomes habitual and natural—just like any skill you have learned in life.

Part II of the book describes the program in more detail, including the four stages necessary for a deeper dive into the how you can control the chaos and harness the creative power inherent in the mind. This involves: **R**ecognizing the problem; **U**nderstanding the solution; Finding **B**alance; and **I**mplementing answers. For readers who take this deeper dive into **RUBI**, the potential reward is a resolution that can range from temporary to permanent, depending on your level of commitment. After going through the book and doing the exercises, you will experience the positive benefits of what many have experienced. The uncontrolled or monkey mind will give way to Original Mind and you will live more joyfully and productively. But only if you make the commitment to changing perception and awareness—the easiest and hardest things a person can do. So, read on, follow the suggested practices, and enjoy life.

The insights and solutions proposed have a basis in science and in personal experience. I have tested them in the clinic and in actual life, and they have proven results. Each chapter will help you understand and maintain control of your mind to live a creative life, which means a life lived with conscious and curious awareness and as the most natural state of being. Living in this state will bring joy to the rest of your life, unburdened by fear and anxiety and in touch with a source of infinite wisdom. Regaining your Original Mind is the straightforward part. Getting rid of the bad habits of monkey mind is where the hard work takes place. Good luck on the journey toward an enlightened self, and may you come out of this process happier and wiser than you have ever been.

PART I

From Original Mind to Uncontrolled Mind and Back

Your Amazing Original Mind

*Buddhists think of Original Mind, the mind that humans are
born with, as a clear mirror, pure and unencumbered, without shape,
form, or color, with nothing in it whatsoever. More than that,
it is a mind without birth and death, neither male nor female, not young
or old; not intelligent, not stupid; not rich, not poor. It shows no dualism,
no separation, and accepts everything as one unified whole.[1]*

—SHODO HARADA ROSHI

Your Mind at Birth Is Original Mind

*Danielle knew immediately that her intuition about her baby had been right.
When Stephanie was born, she had the most beautiful smile and twinkling
eyes, and gurgled more than she cried. When baby Stephanie looked at Danielle, her penetrating gaze made her feel calm and flooded her heart and mind
with an overwhelming sense of love. Stephanie was the most extraordinarily
normal child, always active, adaptable, energetic, curious, and endlessly creative. She met all her developmental milestones, and when Stephanie was old
enough to walk and talk, Danielle noticed a kindness exuding toward others,
including animals. Stephanie displayed a no-nonsense sensibility and a
toughness beyond her years. For Danielle, every day during Stephanie's rapid
development brought astonishing insights into her wonderfully developing
persona. There was deep intelligence at work as she attended school and developed friendships. As a child, she embraced a sensibility for events happening
in the moment and rarely reflected on the past or future, even as her thinking*

appeared deep and "forward-looking." Stephanie rarely got upset or angry and quickly became known as a peacemaker among her peers. Everyone liked and respected her and wanted to be near her, to be her friend.

Stephanie is a fictionalized character who, at least during childhood, has held onto the extraordinary identity that is given to each one of us. Knowing that you once held such a treasure differs from never having had possession of this unique identity and are longing and searching for it. So, above all else, the path to transforming uncontrolled fears and anxiety into creativity requires the conviction that what you seek is real, since you once had it. Your mind at birth was Original Mind, an active, adaptable, energetic, curious, creative mind; one unencumbered by problems and with an attitude of openness, eagerness, and lack of preconceptions. While you may no longer identify with such a mind, you have not lost this treasure completely, and it is possible to recover it. This is the journey you are starting.

Leonardo was illegitimate, gay, left-handed, a bit of a heretic, and a misfit. He lived in Florence, Italy, which in the late 1400s was a very progressive and wealthy city. As a boy, he had no formal education but received instruction at home in reading, writing, Latin, geometry, and mathematics. Leonardo spent most of his childhood outdoors. Because of his lack of formal schooling, many contemporaries overlooked or ignored his later scientific contributions. Everyone, however, recognized his astounding powers of observation even in childhood; his unusual talent for making connections between unique areas of interest; a skeptical mind with a readiness to challenge dogma and contemporary beliefs; and a preternatural ability to appreciate and imagine the future.

Today, we know Leonardo da Vinci as the epitome of the creative Renaissance man. We consider him a painter, artist, engineer, architect, scientist, inventor, cartographer, anatomist, botanist, and writer. His active imagination conceptualized the tank, the helicopter, the flying machine, the parachute, and the self-powered vehicle. He was a man ahead of his time and many of his visionary inventions became real only centuries later.

Much of this reality is mixed with mythology since Leonardo created an endless succession of untested contraptions, unpublished studies, and unfinished artworks. His uncontested genius, however, rests on several personality attributes. Foremost among these was curiosity, his defining trait. It seemed *everything* interested Leonardo. As an engineer, he saw more than most about how the design of machines informed by mathematical laws of physics is better than those relying simply on practice. He was the first to design separate interchangeable components deployed in a variety of complex devices. And no one drew machines with more attention to detail and reality. His insatiable curiosity about nature drove his efforts to devise flying machines. He sought not to imitate a flying bird, but to understand and apply the principles of bird flight to endow man with the ability to fly on his own. His genius lay in his mastery of engineering principles, design, and natural law.

Walter Isaacson, author of *Leonardo da Vinci*, describes the following about his unique subject:

> Leonardo spent many pages in his notebook dissecting the human face to figure out every muscle and nerve that touched the lips. On one of those pages you see a faint sketch at the top of the beginning of the smile of the Mona Lisa. Leonardo kept that painting from 1503, when he started it, to his deathbed in 1519, trying to get every aspect exactly right in layer after layer. During that period, he dissected the human eye on cadavers and was able to understand that the center of the retina sees detail, but the edges see shadows and shapes better. If you look directly at the Mona Lisa smile, the corners of the lips turn downward slightly, but shadows and light make it seem like it's turning upwards. As you move your eyes across her face, the smile flickers on and off.[2]

From iconic paintings, including the *Mona Lisa* and *The Last Supper*, designs for flying machines, and ground-breaking studies on optics and perspective, Leonardo da Vinci fused science with art. He created works that have become aspects of the human story. We consider him the ultimate expression of an intuitive, unencumbered Original Mind.

As Shodo Harada Roshi describes it, Original Mind is "neither male nor female." Indeed, it finds expression in both genders. Jennifer was born in Washington, D.C., in 1964 but grew up in Hilo, Hawaii. When she was in the sixth grade, her father gave her a copy of James Watson's 1968 book on the discovery of the structure of DNA, *The Double Helix*, which became a major inspiration. Her interest in science was further nurtured by her tenth-grade chemistry teacher, Ms. Jeanette Wong, whom Jennifer routinely cites as a significant influence in sparking her scientific curiosity.

Jennifer can pinpoint the moment that helped put her on the path to becoming a Nobel Prize–winning biochemist. When she was in high school, a scientist gave a presentation about cancer research to her class—and the scientist was a woman. Until then, Jennifer had imagined that all scientists were men. Or, as she has explained, "my image of a scientist was the classic photograph of Albert Einstein or cartoons of mostly older White men who were in lab coats with black-rimmed glasses and crazy hair."[3] The notion that women were just as capable of studying science as men opened the door for her to pursue her curiosity about the way life worked. It was this insatiable curiosity that would lead her to the discovery of a method for gene editing.

In 2012, Jennifer Doudna, an American biochemist, and Emmanuelle Charpentier, a French professor and researcher in microbiology, developed a way to edit genes with high precision. Genes comprise deoxyribonucleic acid, or DNA, which controls life processes in most living organisms. These two researchers took advantage of the immune defenses of bacteria, which disable viruses by cutting their DNA up with a type of genetic scissors. By extracting and simplifying the molecular components of the genetic scissors, the two made a tool that could cut any DNA molecule at a predetermined site. The clustered regularly interspaced short palindromic repeats, or CRISPR/Cas9 gene scissors, made new scientific discoveries, better crops, and new weapons in the fight against cancer and genetic diseases possible. Scientists have called the discovery one of the most significant in the history of biology. For their extraordinary work, as well as other fundamental contributions in biochemistry and genetics, Drs. Doudna and Charpentier received the Nobel Prize in Chemistry in 2020. Dr. Jennifer Doudna became one of the *Time 100* most influential people in 2015 (along with Charpentier). They listed her as a runner-up for *Time Person of the Year* in

2016 alongside other CRISPR researchers. Like Leonardo da Vinci, Jennifer Doudna is a modern example of an intuitive, unencumbered Original Mind.

How to Cultivate an Unencumbered Mind: Encourage Curiosity

Being like Leonardo da Vinci, Jennifer Doudna, or like a child means encouraging your curiosity—about everything. This curiosity, however, has no other goal than the pleasure of knowing. The answer is its own satisfaction.

How do you cultivate this? For starters, ask "Why?" questions. Ask "Why not?" questions. Challenge your beliefs and assumptions.

Begin by focusing on a problem. Use your creative imagination to visualize the problem. Write the hunches, insights, instincts, answers to your questions your mind conjures up. Writing things down strengthens the connection to the intuition interface. Focus on the wonder inherent in the process and not on the outcome.

Here is another exercise to try: As you go to work or to the store, or any of your routine stops, pay attention and notice how many other things you had not noticed before. Try to see something new every day on the same route. Ask yourself why you didn't notice this "thing" before and why you are only noticing it now.

The Mind at Birth

Modern science is converging with Buddhist thought on the special nature of Original Mind, the mind at birth. Both perspectives recognize that this mind is an extraordinary living entity. They agree it can produce wondrous accomplishments when unencumbered, as exemplified by Leonardo da Vinci or Jennifer Doudna, and that we are all recipients of this amazing gift.

Over the past few decades, developmental psychologists have created new and better ways to study how and what newborns know. The general conclusion is that babies know much more than most of us realize, and science is only now discovering this wealth of skills. In 1890, a mere 133 years ago, the science luminary and founder of American Psychology, William James, concluded erroneously that infants experience a "blooming, buzzing confusion." We now know better. Accounts during the last decade by scientists, developmental psychologists, and science reporters tell an unfamiliar story. Their accounts, based on the recounting of controlled scientific studies, describe the amazing skills newborns display.[4]

A few months after birth, babies show an unusual grasp of the basic rules of the physical world. They intuitively understand that unsupported objects will fall, an important principle of gravity. More interesting is that before three months, babies lack a sense of object permanence. At that age, an object that is no longer visible ceases to exist, and young minds assume its location is in several places at a time.

Experiments using "Peekaboo" games show that newborns assume that a hidden or unobserved object can be anywhere. Most adults do not realize or understand that this notion is a fundamental principle of quantum physics. The newborn's intuition for the theoretical basis of modern physics is accidental or remarkable. Seth Lloyd, an expert on quantum computing and professor of mechanical engineering at the Massachusetts Institute of Technology, claims newborns are the only people alive who intuitively understand quantum mechanics.[5] Unfortunately, we lose that intuition early on, chiefly because that specific knowledge is unnecessary for us to live in the normal Newtonian (and not quantum) environment.

Similar reasoning explains the assortment of unique and automatic reflexes that, as a newborn, you bring into the world, only to lose them later in development. That you keep only what is useful in your specific environment is a sign of the high adaptability of your mind. An interesting example is the "diving reflex" or "bradycardia response" seen in seals and other aquatic animals. This reflex occurs when the face of an infant touches chilly water. That experience triggers the baby to inhibit or slow down the drive to breathe. Their heart rate slows and blood circulation to the extremities reduces. This diving reflex, which serves as a defense mechanism when you lose oxygen, diminishes with increasing age and disappears by about six months of age. The "diving reflex" may be a vestige of our marine origins, but is unnecessary because we don't live in water.[6]

The same is true for other aquatic skills, including the dolphin's ability to sleep one brain hemisphere at a time. Dolphins are mammals and, like us, need to breathe. Thus, they sleep with only one hemisphere at a time to swim to the surface and take a breath now and then; otherwise, they would drown. In a land environment, this skill is unnecessary and thus, both hemispheres are engaged in sleep-related processes at the same time. Recent research shows, however, that humans can revert to dolphin-like sleep, meaning an uncoupling of the hemispheres, when experiencing troubled sleep in a new location, called the "first night effect."[7] What this emergent phenomenon suggests is that adapting to our specific environment of living on land does not mean losing innate skills, such as those needed for living in water. The unneeded skills are simply masked, but when necessary, we can recover them, or at least some aspects of those behaviors.

Along with the unusual physical skills you lose because they become unnecessary in your environment, you learn an extraordinary number of new *cognitive* skills because of the needs that arise. Many of these cognitive skills appear early in development, between four to six months of age. Babies, for example, detect differences in facial expressions, reacting to sadness, anger, joy, interest, and excitement. These varying facial expressions result from the forty-three muscles in the face and the infinite combination of how these muscles activate to produce unique expressions. As an infant, you analyze this combinatorial explosion with amazing accuracy—a computational accomplishment that is remarkable. However, the relationship between facial expression and emotion is variable and complex.[8]

During the same developmental time frame, you pay attention to and track the eye and hand movements of others. You respond to your own name and appear attuned to higher pitched, sing-song voices. A recent study looked at emotion recognition of four-month-old infants. In this study, infants saw a face with either mutual gaze, one that looked at the infant, or averted gaze. Another face followed this with an eyebrow raised and an accompanying smile. With the help of near infrared light, researchers took images of the infants' brains. What they found was that infants use the same brain regions that adults do when they look at the gaze of another. This ability to detect emotions is foundational for social interactions and critical for social development.[9]

At about ten months, babies understand social hierarchies and know that size can determine who is in charge. In one study,[10] for example, infants watched cartoon movies in which two different-size blocks, each having an eye and a mouth, bounced toward each other from opposite directions. The babies watched the blocks collide and then back up several times as if contending for the right to pass. Then, one block moved out of the way while the other continued its trajectory. Infants showed surprise when the bigger block "surrendered"—as if this action was an unexpected outcome. They seemed to sense that "might makes right," at least as a matter of size, and expected the smaller block to surrender to the larger block. The implication of this response is that the rules of social interaction may be present very early on. In fact, understanding such a complex set of relationships occurs before language develops, and suggests that these rules of social behavior may be innate to the human brain.

Before you learn to speak, you learn to decipher emotions in sounds, including the tone of voice. Scientists in one study[11] showed infants an emotionally neutral face while music played. As soon as the baby looked away from the face, the music stopped. The time a baby looked at the face served as a measure of how interested they were in the music. Infants heard five happy and five sad songs. The results showed that babies that noticed a switch from happy to sad, or vice versa, stared at the face three to four seconds longer because of their heightened interest. Five-month-old newborns could thus distinguish an upbeat from a gloomy tune. And by nine months, babies identify the mournful sound of Beethoven's Seventh Symphony from a lineup of more upbeat music.

While these sight and sound capabilities are remarkable, so are motor development and movement. Babies move in rhythm with the beat of the music, something only a handful of other animals can do. Entrained motor rhythmicity suggests that entrainment to music is a complex phenomenon requiring a special brain. Perhaps rhythmic abilities that produce dancing are intrinsic and serve a special but still unspecified role.

Based on these early aptitudes and competencies, newborns respond and adapt to their environment and interact with life in remarkable, exquisite, and creative ways, discarding irrelevant behaviors and building upon socially and intellectually relevant ones. They enter the world with an exceptional mind chock-full of talent and potential. Shodo Harada Roshi describes this as "a mind that is unencumbered, without shape, form, or color, with nothing in it whatsoever, no dualism, no separation, and accepting everything as one unified whole."

Overcoming the Odds

On the night of December 8, 1995, Jean-Dominique Bauby had a stroke and went into a coma. Bauby was the fashion editor-in-chief of French *Elle*, a magazine considered the ultimate insider's guide to Paris chic. He was a forty-four-year-old man known and loved for his wit, flair, and impassioned approach to life. He was also the father of two young children. Bauby awakened from the coma twenty days after the stroke, aware of his surroundings but unable to move, except for turning his head. He soon realized that only his left eye was functional, allowing him to see and, by blinking, to make clear to others that his mind remained unimpaired. A darkness engulfed his once wide-open vista of life, with the most minuscule of openings still accessible to him. Bauby hoped against hope to regain abilities, like the ability to communicate.

Throughout the course of the first year following the stroke, Bauby consulted with many medical specialists, yet the strangeness and permanency of his situation took a while to sink in. During the twenty weeks after arriving at the hospital, Bauby lost sixty pounds. He could eat only through a tube connected to his stomach, and therefore his taste of food had become only a memory. After a time, he knew he had been the victim of the rarest of strokes to the brainstem. This region of the brain is continuous with the spinal cord, and the stroke left him immobilized in a condition known as "locked-in syndrome." The condition meant that Bauby could only move the muscles controlling his eyes (and only the left eye, at that). But despite this paralysis, his intellect, imagination, memories, and spirit remained intact.

A year after the stroke, Bauby found himself in room 119 at the Maritime Hospital at Berck-sur-Mer in Pas-de-Calais in northern France, waiting for an emissary from his publisher. With the help of a speech therapist, Bauby had opened a larger window into his alternative world. He had discovered how to express himself in the richest detail as he communicated with others. Sandrine, his therapist, developed a simple communication code. The method involved having visitors read the French alphabet slowly and repeatedly to him, with the letters ordered from the most common to the least. When Bauby heard the letter he wanted, he blinked his left eye so readers could write it down. In this way, slowly and methodically, he communicated. In no time, he was writing daily messages, letters to friends and family, and composing a book describing his unusual condition. The story took ten months to write, with Bauby working four hours a day along with several readers. The effort required about 200,000 blinks, with an average word taking two minutes to complete. A year after the stroke, Bauby waited for the literary agent who would help publish his extraordinary achievement.

In the book *The Diving Bell and the Butterfly*,[12] Bauby described himself as trapped in his body. He compared this trapped feeling to being inside an old-fashioned deep-sea diving outfit with a brass helmet, called a *scaphandre* in French. In contrast, his friends saw his spirit, still alive, comparable to a "butterfly." For them, this butterfly was the unrestrained antithesis of the constricting diving suit. In this story, recaptured in his amazing book, the power of Bauby's Original Mind, imagination, and creativity transcend the confines of the most stifling and challenging of conditions. Bauby's story, of a mind encumbered by circumstances but overcoming great odds, is an inspirational story.

Adapting to Circumstances

When Original Mind, the mind at birth, is unencumbered and allowed to flourish, the outcome is a Leonardo da Vinci or a Jennifer Doudna. When encumbered by tragedy, as reflected in Jean-Dominique Bauby's story, the mind can still work to overcome its extraordinary circumstances. These very human stories show how the mind adapts to significantly different circumstances.

That the mind and the brain adapt and change with experience goes back to William James. In 1890, he conceived of the nervous systems as "endowed with a very extraordinary *plasticity*."[13] Plasticity, or neuroplasticity, is the brain's remarkable ability to change and adapt its physical nature because of experience. This ability means that seeing, hearing, touching, smelling, feeling, and thinking affect the brain's hardware in significant ways. Brain activity itself creates changes in the wiring of the circuits, the actual anatomy that connects sensory experience to emotions and actions. Thus, just like water takes the shape of the container into which we pour it, a developing brain will take the shape dictated by the environment in which it lives. It assumes the richness or poverty of stimulation that the environment provides (see Figure 1.1). An enriched environment in which music, laughter, conversation, love, toys, and other people interact will produce a healthy, curious, energetic, da Vinci- or Doudna-type brain. An impoverished environment where many of these things are absent will not.

Neuroplasticity means that the brain develops and programs the skills needed to accommodate to the specific environment, and loses inborn skills unnecessary for that environment. This human malleability and adaptability make us totally different from computers, whose physical components or hardware are unchangeable. Likewise, the extensive neuroplasticity that occurs in primates makes us different from many other animals.

Until the 1960s, neuroscientists assumed that neuroplastic changes in the brain could only take place during infancy and childhood. And that by early adulthood, the brain's physical structure could no longer change. They believed that the only effect possible at that point was for cells and their connections to die. Modern research has upended this doctrine by showing that the brain continues to create new connections and new pathways, even into late adulthood. Rewiring of existing circuits is continuous throughout life, as the brain adapts to unfamiliar experiences, new learning, fresh memories, injuries, and other kinds of changes. In fact, specific areas of the adult brain make new cells, or neurons, in a process called neurogenesis.

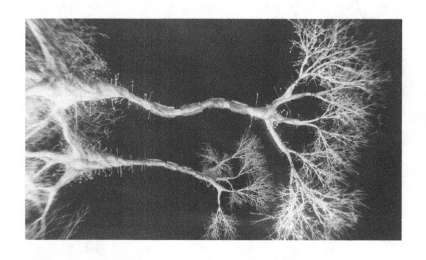

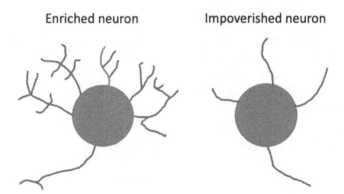

Enriched neuron   Impoverished neuron

An enriched environment produces thicker and more numerous dendrites in rat neurons

Figure 1.1 and 1.2 Normal human neuron and a schematized representation of neural plasticity. *Source:* iStock.

Modern dogma, therefore, views the brain as possessing a remarkable ability to rewire and reorganize pathways, producing changes in the connections between functionally distinct areas. An adaptive brain creates new connections that did not exist before, loses connections no longer needed, and sometimes produces new cells. In older adults who have suffered massive strokes, the brain can recover and regain function by rewiring itself. This neuroplasticity suggests that the brain remains malleable throughout life and that the mental abilities you are born with do not limit function—an important feature in shaping your identity. Reminding ourselves that limits on this malleability exist is important, since the brain's plasticity is not infinite, just extraordinarily malleable. Attempts to learn unfamiliar languages, for example, become more difficult for an adult than for a child, and recovery from a stroke is sometimes only a partial recovery.

Scientists have discovered that the primary way plasticity, malleability, and adaptability occur is through changes in the point-to-point connections between cells, in what neuroscientists call *synapses*. These are the focal points of brain communication, the gaps between cells where information transfers from one cell to the next through chemical neurotransmitters. When information activates or stimulates a synapse, the interaction *strengthens* the pathway between the two cells, and this increase lasts longer than normal. The enhanced communication results from many factors, including more neurotransmitters made and delivered across the synaptic gap, or additional physical connections or bridges between the two cells. Neuroscientists have concluded that this strengthening process, lasting an extended period, is one basis for memories. And that the longer the strengthening lasts, the longer the memory lasts.

Neuroplasticity increases the strength between synapses to increase memories but can also decrease *or weaken* the strength between them, sometimes because of lack of stimulation and communication to decrease memories. When the reduction in strength is substantial, it leads to the removal or pruning of the physical connections, which may lead to greater memory disruptions. Mechanisms are engaged to remove the physical pathway, much like a broken tree branch shriveling and falling off. Thus, pruning of neural branches may underlie the basis for forgetting. Both the strengthening and weakening of synaptic connections are active, continuous processes as the brain dynamically responds to stimulation and adapts to changes in the environment.

Many factors in the internal and external environment affect neuroplasticity. Age and genetics play a role, as does the interaction with the world. Because of the sheer volume of information that you learn and remember as you age, the increased processing load leads to a natural reduction in overall plasticity. Thus, a younger brain is more plastic than an older brain. But aging does not mean that the brain loses the ability to change and adapt. Older brains still keep the ability to learn new skills, or languages, into advanced old age, although not as quickly or efficiently as before. The reduction in ability may result from the larger volume of information accumulated.

It would be unrealistic if neuroplasticity always led to a positive outcome. Unfortunately, it is possible to associate and learn the wrong or inappropriate thing, which is what happens in addiction. We consider addiction to be an aberrant learning process in which an individual will make and learn inappropriate associations. They may learn, for example, that stealing money helps them buy the drugs that produce pleasurable effects. At the level of neurons, the associations between stealing and pleasure strengthen and reinforce the negative outcome, ultimately helping to maintain the addiction. The bottom line is that, from an ethical perspective, this unique feature of the brain is a *neutral* process, for the brain learns both positive and negative associations. Our genetic profiles establish the basic structure of our brain, the rules of learning, and how we remember and associate events. But how this learning unfolds and how neuroplasticity shapes the brain rely on the interaction between the genetic code and the environment in which we find or create for ourselves.

How to Cultivate an Unencumbered Mind: Nurture Creativity

Intuition is the secret ingredient in creativity. However, you must be intentional about strengthening this ability. Start with a creative endeavor and set your intention. For example, if you are a writer, you might aim to come up with fresh story ideas.

Still your mind, relax, and become attentive to inspiration. Focus on thoughts that arise. If a particular thought captures your imagination, turn the thought over in your mind. What is this thought telling you? To what other thoughts does it lead? Let your mind guide you down the path of inspiration. Try not to control the outcome; simply be open to whatever comes up.

Explosive Unfoldment

Infancy, childhood, and early adolescence bring forth an explosive flourishing of Original Mind. While we can apply many general descriptions to this mind, I describe it as an active, adaptable, energetic, curious, and creative (AAECC) impulse. The AAECC impulse drives the brain to respond, process, and learn an enormous amount of information in a brief amount of time. Infants, for example, learn to crawl, walk, and talk. They learn to control their bladder and bowels, feed themselves, discern sounds, recognize themselves and others, learn a language or two, manipulate and control the environment, and understand the world. This set of skills is nothing less than a prodigious amount of proficiencies, and it only partially describes what we can do during those early years. Child development experts have described this amazing, creative unfolding as occurring within unique and distinct set of stages. Sometimes the stages overlap and include actions like babbling, talking, crawling, grasping, playing, and interacting with surrounding objects.

Jean Piaget (1896–1980), a Swiss psychologist and genetic epistemologist, ushered in a revolutionary understanding in child development in the 1930s.[14] He described stages that children undergo while developing cognitive abilities (see Table 1.1). Prior to Piaget, psychologists saw children as mini-adults. But Piaget's insight was that children deliberate in very distinct ways from adults, and that adult judgment emerges over a series of developmental stages.

Piaget described object permanence, for example, as occurring during an early sensorimotor stage. This stage lasts between zero to two years old and has many substages. His primary insight was that children take an active role in cognitive development during this time by *building knowledge while interacting with the world*. In the sensorimotor stage, the interaction is through abilities with which we are born,

Table 1.1 Piaget's Stages of Cognitive Development

Stage	Age Range	Functional Changes
Sensorimotor	0–2 years old	Coordination of senses with motor and curiosity about the world. Language used for demands and cataloging. Object permanence develops.
Preoperational	2–7 years old	Symbolic thinking, use of proper syntax and grammar to express concepts. Imagination and intuition are strong, but complex abstract thoughts are still underdeveloped. Conservation is developed.
Concrete operational	7–11 years old	Concepts attached to concrete situations. Time, space, and quantity are understood and can be applied, but not as independent concepts.
Formal operational	11 years old and older	Theoretical, hypothetical, and counterfactual thinking. Abstract logic and reasoning. Strategy and planning are possible. Concepts learned in one context applied to another.

including sight, hearing, smell, taste, and touch. These sensory abilities combine with other physical skills, like the ability to move while continuing to develop. This combination of skills allows us to interact and build awareness of ourselves and what is around us.

At the end of the sensorimotor stage, children develop symbols to represent events or objects. They move toward understanding the world through mental operations, such as symbolic thinking, combined with physical actions. During this preoperational stage lasting between two to seven years, we develop and use language. In the course of what Piaget called the concrete operational stage between seven to eleven years, we reason more abstractly and more often about objects, time, space, and numbers. We form mental images. The last stages of development are the formal operational stages (beyond eleven years). At this stage, we develop the ability to think in abstract terms, to use scientific and philosophical lines of reasoning. Strategy and planning for the future become possible.

In sum, at least from this Piagetian perspective, although other child development perspectives agree, the astonishing, developing, and creative mind produces miraculous-like behaviors when allowed to develop uninterrupted. This development occurs in periods of explosive unfoldment that happen in an organized and predetermined fashion. Original Mind learns and carries out a significant number of operations, including attending to many things, selecting objects of relevance, making inferences, and establishing patterns and memories. The amazing thing about this extraordinary unfoldment is that it occurs mostly without overt control and below the level of conscious awareness.

Creative Living

The extraordinary yet normal unfolding of the mind that starts in infancy, carries into adolescence, and continues into adulthood is the essence of *creative living*. I define creative living as unencumbered being and doing. The process is not a fixed state of mind, but an attitude and actions arising from those attitudes in response to living. Creative living does not end in infancy or childhood, but continues throughout our lifetime. The interactive unfolding of nature and nurture becomes playtime with the world of things, and flourishes in the creativity, love, and meaning that fill our being. Creative living defines the core of who we are when living a natural and authentic life. It does not apply just to the arts or any particular outcomes. Without a nimble, curious, Original Mind, normal development and normal enjoyment of life become problematic. When development is unsuccessful or incomplete, and circumstances encumber the mind, the outcomes are dissatisfying. They impede aspects of creative living. But like the story of Jean-Dominique Bauby, we can still overcome even extreme circumstances.

Questions to Ponder

Recall a time when you were a very young child and playing with friends or siblings. Can you recall your most vivid memory of that time? What was uppermost in your mind? What do you consider extraordinary about your mind at that age?

Key Takeaways

- Original Mind is an extraordinary living entity—Active, Adaptable, Energetic, Curious, and Creative. It comes with a wealth of skills, including an intuitive grasp of the basic rules of the physical world and curiosity as a character trait.
- During development, you lose many innate sensorimotor and emotional skills and gain others relevant to the environment in which you live. You maintain this remarkable adaptability/neuroplasticity to change and adapt because of experiences.
- Neuroplasticity does not always lead to positive outcomes, since you can associate with and learn the wrong or inappropriate things.
- Development of your personality occurs within unique and distinct set of stages, while building knowledge through interaction with the world. This unfoldment occurs mostly without overt control and below the level of conscious awareness. It is the singular characteristic of creative living.

Next chapter: What makes things go awry?

Birth of the Uncontrolled Mind

Resistance to change is a psychological and normal
reaction to the need to protect a fragile ego.

Dark Night of the Soul

Stephanie didn't know what the word meant, so kept walking, trying to
get away from them. But they followed her, and after several pushes from
behind, she took off running. Stephanie had become vulnerable to such taunt-
ing since her mother had moved the family from Chicago to Los Angeles to
pursue a better job. For Stephanie, it meant losing the relatives, friends, and
culture she had adapted to back East. Los Angeles made her feel adrift, alone,
angry, and vulnerable. While these taunting episodes were short-lived and
mild, they made her aware of a dark side of growing up that temporarily
colored her positive perspective, expectations, and sense of self as she started
high school. Stephanie's confidence eroded quickly amid the new environ-
ment. She no longer commanded respect from friends and classmates. She
was an outsider, taunted and scorned. Her peers did not see her as a leader.
Coupled with the hormonal changes flooding her adolescent mind, her quiet-
ness gained a tinge of low self-esteem and fearfulness, and she became pain-
fully shy and insecure by the time she finished high school. Her sense of worth
had disappeared completely, and she now judged herself relative to others,
with a sense of lack and an increasingly self-critical attitude. Her increased
self-consciousness revolved around the loss of trust in the reality around her

and of control she thought she had as a child. By the time Stephanie finished high school, the curiosity and creativity of infancy and childhood had transformed into fear and anxiety.

The thinnest of mental boundaries separate the darkest from the brightest thoughts. The mind can travel enormous psychological distances in the blink of an eye within its imaginary space. From imagining murder or suicide to planning a wedding or feeding the baby. It's a dizzying crisscrossing of thoughts that can occur nearly instantaneously, with no impediment or remorse. You can feel sorry for yourself and fuel your anxiety and depression or reach out your hand to help those in greater need. The amazing thing is that within this chaotic thought stream, you *have* the choice of which ones to attend, and each produces a different mental experience. Choice becomes harder when pleasure, pain, or other emotions overwhelm your rational mind. You can even reach a point where you see no apparent alternative and no escape. In such a place, you experience being closed off to other thought streams, and the only path seems to be an end to life. But even then, you have a choice. The choice is to let go of your sense of control and let something else, perhaps something wiser than your ego self, take control.

While the pressures of life can exacerbate difficulties, as illustrated by Stephanie's story, the root of the uncontrolled mind—a mind that is restless, easily distracted, obsessive, and confused—is the anxious, fear-based mind, one centered on ego-based rumination. When this mind dwells on problems through this lens, past and future viewpoints become dominant. It can then more easily get snagged in problem-solving mode and behave as the "monkey mind." This is a metaphor for the feral, wild, obsessive, and uncontrollable aspect of our nature. It's important to emphasize that an uncontrolled mind's motivations are self-centered actions, motives, and thoughts. It causes confusion and helplessness when unmanaged. The solution, however, is not to get rid of this mind, but to bring its operation into the proper context, for this uncontrolled mind is also the creative mind. Training and guiding this monkey mind back to its more natural and original impulses, those associated with Original Mind, ignites creativity and allows us to deal with the challenges of living in-the-moment.

Flies in the Ointment

But how does the uncontrolled mind come to be? In her book *Big Magic: Creative Living Beyond Fear,* Elizabeth Gilbert writes that living creatively is "living a life that is driven more strongly by curiosity than by fear."[1] She acknowledges a certain reality about life, and that is, that curiosity and fear coexist. Despite the normal and unencumbered unfoldment of the exceptional mind at birth, the interaction with the world sometimes creates hindrances, allowing fear and anxiety to creep in. If such negativity continues unimpeded, they reach a threshold in which the active, adaptable, energetic, curious, and creative or AAECC impulse associated with the mind at birth turns into a more negative force disrupting creative living.

The reasons producing this change differ, but fear and anxiety, as Gilbert implies, are prominent variables and common flies in the ointment of our interaction with life. Fear of failure or success, or fear of being judged by others, are also common reasons. Other hindrances might be the belief you have not accomplished enough relative to your peers, or that you are not good enough. The reasons may even be based on uncertainty about your relationships. Whatever the reason, the result of these many psychic snags is a blockage of the creative flow of energy and the transfiguration of the AAECC impulse from a positive to a negative force. As this transfiguration increases, Original Mind recedes, obscured by a bourgeoning, uncontrolled, and problematic mind. As life goes off the rails, you experience the birth of the monkey mind. To understand the development of this uncontrolled mind, it is necessary to understand what creates this change from a life lived from curiosity and creativity to a life lived from fear and anxiety.

The Conflicted Brain

Based on my studies of the mind-brain and personal experiences with meditation, I describe normal waking consciousness as having at least two aspects or impulses associated with the type of mind we exhibit. The active, adaptable, energetic, curious, and creative or AAECC impulse exhibits a playful character and an urge to engage the world of ideas and forms. This open, positive, and outwardly oriented energy provides the motivating force for the mind at birth. You cannot extinguish, only block, the innate, playful, and calm AAECC impulse. In contrast, the opposing shadow aspect is what I describe as the avoidant, fearful, resistant, arrogant, inflexible, and distrustful or AFRAID impulse. I link this impulse to awareness, rational deliberation, the ego, and interpreter (as will soon become clear), and is under conscious control. The AAECC and AFRAID impulses represent two sides of the same coin (see Table 2.1).

As Daniel Smith describes in his book *Monkey Mind: A Memoir of Anxiety*, ego-based processing is thinking that is "solipsistic, self-eviscerating, unremitting, vicious, destroys unity and produces a mind capable of scattered deliberation. Such thinking is also restless, whimsical, fanciful, inconstant, confused, indecisive, and uncontrollable."[2] This reflects the AFRAID, or ego-based impulse, operating in the past and future modes. While the AAECC impulse is similar in vitality, it differs in its other-, present-moment-centered nature, and selfless attachment. Comparable to conjoined twins, the AAECC and AFRAID impulses share commonalities, yet show distinct qualities and create different opportunities and problems for the individual.

Table 2.1 Comparison between Monkey and Original Mind

Monkey Mind	Original Mind
The frenetic, intellectual chattering, self-obsessed, inner critic, and ego-centric me	The pure and unencumbered mind that you have at birth
Conscious awareness	Nonconscious processing
AFRAID impulse	AAECC impulse
Avoidance	Approach
Introversion	Extraversion
Ego	Self
Left-brain interpreter	Observer
Error correction	Flow
Limited intelligence	Vast intelligence

While both impulses are engaged during the normal course of life, the fears and pressures of modern day-to-day living create an imbalance. Modern pressures include interactions with a greater diversity of people, and involve comparing oneself to impossible standards of beauty, social interactivity, or accomplishments. They reflect increased levels of specializations, increased efficiency of everything, and an increased pace of life. Such modern pressures stimulate the AFRAID energy more than the AAECC impulse—the consequence being that this engenders an uncontrolled mind that slowly obscures Original Mind, delegating it into the background of a harried life.

A typical, generic example of someone living this modern lifestyle is Michael, an alumnus of the Wharton Business School. After graduating from business school, Michael landed a prestigious job with a six-figure starting salary. He found himself in need of a nice car to take clients around town and bought himself the latest BMW 7 Series luxury car model. He then realized that to be truly successful, he needed a sizable house to entertain his clients. To decorate this large house, he found the need to buy expensive furnishings and paintings.

Sadly, all the material objects Michael accumulated to satisfy his life requirements did nothing to improve his quality of life. In fact, the more money he made, the more objects he needed to get and the less happy he felt. Michael's story is an all too familiar one. He was afraid of failing and did whatever it took to maintain appearances. By the end of the second year on the job, Michael began suffering from depression, anxiety, and fatigue. To deal with the bourgeoning psychological problems making him miserable, Michael started therapy with a recommended psychiatrist. Counseling and medication were things that could help him keep up and cope with all the pressure. Like Michael, many individuals turn to health specialists, drugs—legal and illegal—and to even more destructive behavior to deal with the onslaught of life.

AFRAID-based thinking produces suboptimal and irrational behaviors that result in mental and physical fatigue, depression, anxiety, and stress. Similar to an exhausted gymnast, problems arise just from the constant rumination, worrying, and flitting of mind from thought-stream to thought-stream. Jennifer Shannon, in *Don't Feed the Monkey Mind*, describes anxious individuals who go through life as if "hooked up to an IV drip of fear."[3] That describes Michael's case. The overwhelming, chronic, and deleterious challenges from this burden destroy brain cells and their connections. Cells and their dendritic branches dry up, become brittle, and literally die from the lack of nutrients and support. Resisting, avoiding, distracting, and pacifying the AFRAID impulse only encourages and compounds the problem—"what we resist, persists."

For people like Michael, there is only one genuine answer. It is to train the mind to concern itself less with appearances, with pleasing others, with being fearful, and to focus more on what we once were, childlike curiosity and creativity personified. It is a change in perspective and awareness that produces a more positive, creative, and fulfilled life.

Questions to Ponder

What is your basic personality impulse?

Is the urge an active, adaptable, energetic, curious, and creative (or AAECC) impulse?

Is it an avoidant, fearful, resistant, arrogant, inflexible, and distrustful (or AFRAID) impulse?

Is it a combination? Or something else?

Which of the following traits describes you? Introvert/extrovert; social/ antisocial; passionate/uncaring; passive/active; talker/listener; artist/scientist; skeptic/believer.

What other aspects of your personality reflect your basic impulses? If you made a list, which one would be longer? Does the list reflect actual differences or simply more attentiveness to one personality type?

Left-Brain Interpreter

The origins of the uncontrolled mind become clear by detailing the conditions that give birth to this chattering intellect and inner critic.

Rather than the reflective, clear mirror that is pure and unencumbered Original Mind, a unique and problematic aspect of the mind comes into being. The relevant question is: just what gives rise to it? Certainly, the development and expression of language, something that occurs between three months and eight years of age in children, plays a key role. But language itself is not the source; its actions only aggravate the problem. More relevant to the origin of this problematic mind is the appearance during early development of what neuroscientists call the inner narrator, or "left-brain interpreter."

The interpreter is an insightful concept that the neuroscientists Michael S. Gazzaniga and Joseph E. LeDoux conceived in the late 1960s and early 1970s.[4] The notion helped explain how we rationalize, reason, and generalize current information to maintain logical consistency with past and future experiences. They assumed this function to be a component of the rational or verbal (and therefore left-hemisphere-based) brain that produces after-the-fact explanations about behavior.

Some scholars have described this after-the-fact behavior as "gut reaction first, think up the reasons later." Its function is to integrate the information encountered in the moment, which is vast and typically below conscious awareness, with stored memories and future actions in response to the information. The interpreter normally works smoothly and is paid little to no attention until psychological glitches and deviations occur. Thus, the interpreter is a fundamental player, if not the source, of the uncontrolled monkey mind.

Pertinent examples of left-brain interpreter in action are quite common, but for now let us consider Juan, who as an undergraduate student is typical of the many applying to graduate programs in biology after completing a bachelor's degree at a four-year university. Juan excelled as a student, doing well in all his courses. Because of a good academic track record, family, teachers, and friends encouraged him to pursue graduate training. To maximize his chances, Juan volunteered as a research assistant in a biology lab for a semester and found the experience enjoyable, showing the potential to do well in research. During his senior year, he took the chance and began filling out graduate school applications to top-tier universities.

The results, however, were disappointing and Juan did not get accepted to any of the top programs to which he had applied. He became frustrated, disappointed, and then depressed at what appeared to be the end of his academic career. During the months following his last rejection, he learned that many of his friends had received acceptances. Juan grew suspicious. Irrationally, he concluded his rejections were because of his ethnic background and assumed that the admissions committees at these universities comprised individuals with implied biases against people of color. Juan's explanation was an emotional gut reaction based on little rational thinking.

While emotions reflected his experience, they reflected more of his frustrated and disappointed self at that moment. With time, Juan's initial reaction gave way to a more reasoned explanation. He recognized that his GRE and GPA scores did not meet the required thresholds for acceptance at these top-tier schools. When he applied to other institutions whose requirements he could meet, they readily admitted him.

Explanations about uncertain situations like these, whether verbal or nonverbal, account for actions and sensations in a way that makes logical sense of the world (sometimes by denying other information). This inner narration, like the rationale of racial bias conceived by Juan, stretches the truth and creates confabulations about reality to keep the inner logic consistent.

Another relevant example of this interpreter function has stayed with me since adolescence, based on an incident that occurred to me during eighth grade. I recall one afternoon walking out of the elementary school I attended and heading home. At an intersection, I saw a tall boy along with two other eighth-grade classmates hanging out by a stop sign. The tall boy towered over most other eighth graders, but his height didn't trigger any concerns until I felt him push me from behind. "What are you doing?" I shouted, turning to face my classmates. "Why don't you go back where you came from?" came the reply. This bullying behavior happened more than once. But for me, the insults they used didn't produce the expected response since they seemed more like compliments. Some names, however, were more hurtful. I reasoned they were acting out of jealousy, and rather than sensing a threat, I felt pity for them. That assessment reflected my firm sense of self and positive self-esteem. As an adult, I reflected on my actions and saw them as self-deception or confabulation that helped me deal with the problem facing me. This old recollection shows the efficiency of my interpreter in taking an unexpected event and assessing, interpreting, and integrating the events seamlessly into my personality. The outcome, had I chosen a different interpretation, could have been vastly different.

A confabulation is a lie, but in these situations, they are explanations of an event based on incomplete information that turns out to be false. Scientists give the brain the benefit of the doubt by suggesting that sometimes the left-brain interpreter must infer causality with very little information. This lack of data makes confabulations more likely. The interpreter must explain how a cause gives rise to an effect. With little or no information, the need to maintain a coherent story of its behavior drives the interpreter to make extraordinary leaps of logic to create a *rational*-sounding story.

Actual experiments during the early 1970s on split-brain patients led Gazzaniga and his colleagues to this fascinating neuropsychological conclusion. Split-brain patients are individuals who suffer from intractable epilepsy. In these patients, their seizures do not respond to drug treatment. To diminish the effects of the epilepsy, surgeons, beginning in the 1940s, isolated the two cerebral hemispheres by deliberately cutting the fiber connections, called the corpus callosum, the bundle of 200+ million axons that connect left and right hemispheres. This radical surgery separated the cerebral hemispheres to keep the seizure confined to the hemisphere where the problem originated.

This isolation of the hemispheres helped to contain the seizures, a kind of wildfire, from spreading to both sides of the brain. The surgery isolated the speech center of the brain, which in most individuals is in the left hemisphere. Studies on these patients show that to maintain consistency in their worldview, split-brain individuals create and make up stories using their verbal left hemisphere. The following story from Gazzaniga's original studies illustrates the unique nature of this situation and the role of the interpreter:

> We showed a split-brain patient two pictures: A chicken claw was shown to his right visual field, so the left hemisphere only saw the claw picture, and a snow scene was shown to the left visual field, so

the right hemisphere saw only that. He was then asked to choose a picture from an array of pictures placed in full view in front of him, which both hemispheres could see. The left hand pointed to a shovel (which was the most appropriate answer for the snow scene) and the right hand pointed to a chicken (the most appropriate answer for the chicken claw). Then we asked why he chose those items. His left hemisphere speech center replied, "Oh, that's simple. The chicken claw goes with the chicken," easily explaining what it knew. It had seen the chicken claw.

Then, looking down at his left hand pointing to the shovel, without missing a beat, he said, "And you need a shovel to clean out the chicken shed." Immediately, the left brain, observing the left hand's response without the knowledge of why it had picked that item, put it into a context that would explain it. It interpreted the response in a context consistent with what it knew, and all it knew was: Chicken claw. It knew nothing about the snow scene, but it had to explain the shovel in his left hand. Well, chickens do make a mess, and you have to clean it up. Ah, that's it! Makes sense.

That the left hemisphere did not say, "I don't know," is interesting, since this was the correct answer. It made up a post hoc answer that fit the situation. It confabulated, taking cues from what it knew and putting them together in an answer that made sense.

Split-brain patients offer a basis for understanding, from a neuroscience perspective, why all of us, including those considered normal, confabulate, exaggerate, and make up stories to account for events. The left hemisphere appears to have evolved the ability to create and maintain an ongoing narration and explanation of events to make sense of the world. We know this ongoing effort as the chattering intellect, the inner critic, the inner voice, or the inner dialog.

To explain confabulation in split-brain patients, Gazzaniga and colleagues concluded that "The interpreter is only as good as the information it gets." To them, this equivalency between information and interpretation meant that brains do not have a rational central command station—and are at the mercy of the information they receive. Garbage in, garbage out.[5] This explanation, however, turns out not to be quite right. In a widely cited study on how normal individuals make judgments about uncertain events, other scientists clarified the error of this conclusion.

Tversky and Kahneman, Israeli psychologists, beginning in the 1970s and over the next thirty years, showed people evolve strategies to deal with uncertain events, called heuristics.[6] These strategies are economical and work well under most circumstances at predicting events. Heuristics are used to form judgments, decide, and find solutions to complex problems quickly. They are the best guesses made under the circumstances. And distinct strategies are used to arrive at various guesses, including focusing on the most relevant aspects of a problem, or basing responses on similar experiences. Heuristics are imperfect ways to solve problems or make predictions, but good enough to reach a solution or decision quickly. These convenient and evolved strategies lead to severe and systematic biases and errors because the methods have a built-in trade-off between accuracy and effort. Nature designed them to maximize the speed of decision making with the least amount of effort, but they suffer in terms of accuracy.

Gazzaniga's interpreter uses these heuristics. The mind continually receives a flood of information at every moment of the day and makes the best interpretation of the information quickly in order to respond appropriately. Individuals "confabulate" as a convenient shortcut to make logical sense of the world and of the flood of information received each moment. Many times, when you are in a hurry or stressed out, the flood of information is overwhelming and the guesses turn out to be wrong and problematic.

Imagine the following scenario: You are at a favorite local movie theater enjoying the latest Disney movie with your son. You hear a loud sound, turn around, and observe people running away from the sound. Others are screaming around you. Your brain cries "terrorist attack" and you grab your son and start running with the crowd toward the exit, fear and panic growing with each step you take. Your brain is running at a million miles an hour. Are they shooting people? Which is the safest way out? How do you protect your son? You reach the exit and are outside with a sense of relief, but vigilant. From the corner of your eye, you notice an armed person running toward you. You freeze, unsure of which way to go, and fall helpless to the ground, sure that you and your son will soon be dead. "It's okay," you hear the armed man shout and realize he is a police officer. An overwhelming sense of relief replaces the thoughts of dying. "It looks like a boiler at the movie house exploded," you hear him exclaim and realize that the whole scenario your mind created isn't real. Your mind confabulated and created a scenario based on incomplete data that turned out to be wrong.

What your brain did is what the brain does. Out of necessity, the brain maximizes the speed of decision making with the information at hand to get you and others to safety, with the least amount of effort. In doing so, it created a false narrative out of necessity. When dealing with many life situations, whether at work, school, synagogue, or the ball field, the brain's interpreter responds the same way. It does its best based on prior experience, memories, and the information available at the moment. But wrong judgments and decisions creep in. If repeated often enough, they increase stress and the likelihood of error of interpretation. The process easily turns into a vicious cycle that gives birth to an obsessive mind in which the rational interpreter becomes irrational. Consider, for example, how individuals in a war zone or in the streets of an urban city where crime is rampant become paranoid, suspicious, and even violent toward innocent strangers.

Questions to Ponder

Consider conditions at home, work, or any other location where you previously made a quick decision and later realized this decision was wrong. Why did you make such a quick decision?

Could you have waited and gathered more information? What made you realize it was wrong?

Consider these scenarios: the situation, the decision, and what precipitated the decision. Why did it turn out to be the wrong decision to make? As you recognize and accumulate these events, do you notice a pattern in your behavior?

A Growing Sense of Self

The existence of the interpreter means the preexistence of a sense of self, since developing a sense of individuality must come before the birth of the interpreter. A sense of self is the discernment of having an individual existence, with judgments about that existence, including self-esteem and confidence about those thoughts. Studies by Gazzaniga's group on their split-brain patients provided insights into this development of our sense of individuality. The results show normal individuals typically experience the conscious mind as a single entity with the sense of being a single person. Split-brain patients, however, experience two distinct minds, one mind for each of the disconnected hemispheres. This separateness leads to serious and debilitating behavior.[7]

Not long after her surgery and while shopping at a grocery store, Vicki had difficulties deciding what to put into her shopping cart. As she describes it, "I'd reach with my right [hand] for the thing I wanted, but the left [hand] would come in and they'd kind of fight. Almost like repelling magnets." Putting on a dress every morning produced the same competition and challenge. This ongoing struggle between the two hemispheres, each controlling the opposite side of the body, extended Vicki's simple act of dressing or shopping for groceries from a few minutes to several hours. The outcome shows that, contrary to the popular saying, two minds in one head are *not* necessarily better than a single mind. Instead, the experience when two minds cannot coordinate is inefficiency in carrying out the simplest of actions.

Gazzaniga and colleagues speculated about how the experience of being a single self comes to be in a normal brain when distinct "selves" exist in each hemisphere. They proposed that a unified self emerges from the thousands of low-level actions that occur in a phenomenon they called "emergence." The two separate streams become integrated into a unified entity when the hemispheres connect via the corpus callosum.

The evidence from split-brain patients raises the possibility of similar experiences in childhood when the connections between hemispheres are first developing. Reaching a balanced and unified sense of self in a normal, adult brain means that the two hemispheres must connect to communicate. This complex wiring and organization take time to complete. The corpus callosum takes a while to develop and mature. This is true given that myelination, the insulation of axons to allow neural signals to travel faster and without loss of signal, begins four to six months after birth. It then proceeds slowly through the first two to three decades of life. During that time, the brain is prone to making errors of interpretation and miscommunication. In fact, studies reflecting this lack of full control estimate that close to 96 percent of adolescents, for example, lie to their parents. In one study, 82 percent of high school and college students admitted to lying to their parents the previous year. Peak dishonesty, or confabulation, occurs in adolescence, and every parent knows these classic lines from their adolescent children:

- "I wasn't speeding—I never speed!"
- "I will clean my room tomorrow, I promise."
- "Oh, yeah, Sarah's parents will be there."
- "No, I didn't break that glass!"
- "I already finished my homework!"

Psychologists agree that the unified sense of self emerges between two to five years of age, a time that overlaps with the appearance of language and Gazzaniga's interpreter. It then takes several decades to reach maturity. The interesting fact is that until the emergence of a sense of self, life is mainly a nonconscious, automatic affair. Then, in this early period and with the sense of self developing, you begin to interrupt nonconscious processing more often, either voluntarily or spontaneously, by switching to conscious processing. There are many reasons driving this change, including the ability to capture and maintain memories, which becomes operational around two years of age. The memory system requires many more years to become totally wired up, allowing for smooth reflective awareness.

The sense of self; the expression of language; the birth of the interpreter; the ability to use abstraction, memories, and other remarkable functions reflect this newfound ability of conscious processing.

The changes are so remarkable that the bright spotlight of science has focused on this capacity to the exclusion of everything else. Rene Descartes is the seventeenth-century French philosopher, mathematician, and scientist who wrote, "I think, therefore I am." In doing so, he established conscious awareness as the supreme mode of knowing in Western thought.

The way the interpreter and awareness work in relation to nonconscious processing resembles the Global Positioning System (GPS) on our smartphones. The GPS is a sophisticated navigational system that uses at least twenty-four satellites, a receiver, and algorithms to provide location, velocity, and time synchronization for air, sea, and land travel. In this metaphor, the GPS is the nonconscious mind. Most of the time, GPS provides what you need to navigate the environment. The GPS works well to get you around to the places you need to visit, in particular the unfamiliar ones.

Occasionally, a glitch or error occurs and leads you to take an unexpected wrong turn. The GPS comes online to warn you to adjust the route. The system shows you how to get back to the "predicted" route (the analog of conscious awareness). With the new directions, you return to the planned trajectory and everything resumes its normal course. There are moments, however, when your ego interferes and judges that it knows better than the GPS and exercises its own plan to correct the error. This self-centered behavior can lead to complications, getting turned around and lost. In the middle of this confusion, monkey mind shows up and you complain and rant—perhaps to your friend or partner sitting next to you. Persistence on following your ego and not the GPS might make you get lost, frustrated, and disoriented. Indeed, more severe conditions may develop, including arguing with your friend or spouse while trying to justify your behavior.

Many scientists agree that both conscious and nonconscious processing streams interweave and integrate, bringing reality into existence. Contemporary ideas, however, are slowly changing about how we view this relationship. This reevaluation is giving nonconscious processing a big public relations boost.[8]

Nisbett and Wilson, social psychologists, started the reevaluation trend in 1977.[9] They reviewed published experimental work providing the first substantive set of evidence that we "never really know why [we] do the things [we] do, why [we] choose the things [we] choose, or why [we] prefer the things [we] prefer." These researchers, and many others who followed, showed that most of what we are and what we do occurs below conscious awareness. There are physiological processes, such as regulating body temperature, or controlling levels of neurotransmitters released by cells, that never reach awareness. There are cognitive processes that also occur below awareness, including how we string words together during speech. Certain processes become nonconscious following intense awareness, including the movement of muscles to drive, ride a bike, or play the piano.

How to Cultivate an Unencumbered Mind: Practice Present Moment Centering

Mindfulness is the first step in cultivating an intuitive, unencumbered mind. The technique involves learning to be still and in the present moment. Stop Monkey Mind (SMM) is the suggested approach. This style of mindfulness helps reduce the self-centered activity of the uncontrolled mind. Practicing SMM helps to still obsessive rumination, and when that happens, you have access to intuition and creative cognition.

- *Pick a moment to practice.*
- *You need not be sitting since practice can occur anywhere and anytime.*
- *Anchor situational awareness to the present moment.*
- *Be present by focusing and centering on your actions.*
- *Attend to the sensory experience reaching your brain (sights, sounds, smells, etc.).*
- *Attend to the mental activity.*
- *Identify dominant, intrusive thoughts.*
- *Take authority and confidently command these intrusive thoughts to "SLOW DOWN."*
- *Later, you will command them to "STOP."*
- *Direct the mind first through verbal command. Later, reflect on this command silently. And much later, drop the command altogether—the intent will be enough.*

As scientists learn more about the mind, they recognize that non-conscious processing is not only a positive aspect of life and personality, but perhaps *the most important part*. Nonconscious processing is a major aspect of Original Mind, active at every waking moment of life, exhibiting a level of intelligence that is vast yet unfamiliar.

Questions to Ponder

If the nonconscious mind is a major aspect of Original Mind and an important component of adult life, does it make you want to connect with this aspect of your mind more? What do you do in daily life now to access this vast intelligence?

If you remain unconvinced about the role of nonconscious processing in your life, what questions do you still have concerning it?

Awareness and Error Correction

Modern theories of brain and mind function consider nonconscious activity important in the prediction of future events and in the ability to plan for the future.[10] The growing consensus is that thoughts and actions result from the interaction between automatic, nonconscious, looking ahead processes and more controlled conscious activity.

A "predictive brain" model maintains that the switch from non-conscious to conscious processing occurs if and only if the brain's nonconscious predictions fail. This model implies that engaging conscious awareness occurs to correct an error, a deviation, or an unusual and unpredictable event. This viewpoint has led scientists to propose that a biological function of awareness is to respond when automatic actions fail.

To that extent, such a viewpoint narrows the intelligence of conscious awareness to problem-solving. Undoubtedly, there may be other functions. For example, awareness connects experience with emotions and actions and, therefore, may have an aesthetic function. You appreciate, delight in, and respond emotionally in conscious awareness. In that light, art becomes a nonconceptual, reimaged consciousness in action. However, an aesthetic role in conscious awareness is beyond this book.

The perspective here is that nonconscious activity reflects the contingencies of the moment and the processing of the enormous amount of inner and outer experiences occurring every single moment. This broad domain contrasts with the narrower domain of conscious awareness, which reflects internal, preconfigured plans and memories to smooth out interruptions.

To describe it another way, you activate the rational interpreter to narrate and logically integrate information during interruptions of nonconscious activity because of unexpected, unusual, or erroneous occurrences. This error-correcting function assumes an important principle: that the interpreter is engaged when dealing with glitches and is, therefore, a potential source of the uncontrolled mind.

Error correction activity may occur in the following way: Something unexpected or threatening occurs. You realize this and must respond. You act to resolve the issue and then rationalize the event, trying to explain while incorporating the change into your narrative, the ongoing story of you. For this error correction function to occur, several sources of information must feed into the brain area that determines the response and creates the narration. That neural focus is assumed to be in the left hemisphere, the specialized language functions of the brain.

The language-based interpreter executes well in awareness. Its narrations are necessary to keep the logic of life consistent by accounting for all the unexpected things that occur to us. The interpreter attempts to explain unusual and out-of-the-ordinary occurrences that bombard our senses every moment of life. The narration works without a hitch, using the heuristics described before, and alongside the vaster, nonconscious activity. But sometimes a problem arises. Problems can happen in the actual switching between nonconscious and conscious processing. Conscious awareness cannot easily handle the amount of information that is unexpectedly "in mind" during the switch. The difficulty gets worse when the obsession with rational deliberation becomes part of the mix. Because of the rewarding nature of rational deliberation, the assumption that rationality is the only way to get answers makes the mind spin even more.

Questions to Ponder

Do you agree that you never know, or are aware of, why you do the things you do? If not, why not? Do you know why you choose the things you choose? Or why you prefer the things you prefer? If you don't know, then who is it that decides? Does the thought of not having control concern you? Consider the reasons why this lack of control concerns you.

Key Takeaways

- The change from Original Mind to uncontrolled mind is rooted in anxious, fear-based thinking, centered on ego-based rumination, and focused on past and future.
- Two impulses are in conflict in this uncontrolled state: an active, adaptable, energetic, curious, and creative (AAECC) impulse that has a present-moment-centered focus and an avoidant, fearful, resistant, arrogant, inflexible, and distrustful (AFRAID) impulse that operates in the past and future modes.
- The uncontrolled mind depends on a sense of self, discernment of being an individual, of having an existence, and judgments about that existence. It uses language, and the "left brain interpreter," to rationalize, reason, and generalize current information and maintain logical consistency with past and future experiences.
- The interpreter uses heuristics to maximize the speed of decision making with the least amount of effort, but these suffer in terms of accuracy, sometimes reflected in confabulations.
- Conscious awareness is engaged to correct errors, deviations, or unusual and unpredictable events. Getting snagged in that mode produces the uncontrolled and often chaotic mind.

Next chapter: How do you rediscover and regain your Original Mind?

3

Finding Your Way Back

*Change requires an inward and outward
commitment to be more open and flexible.*

A New Kind of Freedom

*In her attempts to deal with the obsessive, self-destructive persona that had
taken over and imprisoned her, Stephanie sought help and explored different
alternatives. Psychotherapy improved, but it did not eliminate the negativity. Her best friend introduced her to meditation and spiritual practices,
and while progress was slow, Stephanie persisted until something finally
gave way. She realized that the "problem" she wrestled with daily and the
answers she searched for were, in fact, intertwined. She recognized herself in
her surrounding life and understood she could not escape the world she had
created and inhabited, so she accepted it. As if an unveiling, this new recognition gave her a freedom she had once known but forgotten. Having studied
to be an architect, she had convinced herself that "achieving" was a necessary
part of her work. Public works, accolades, developing new designs, and other
aspects had defined the importance of who and what she was. Now, with
this new realization, the script flipped. She saw planning and designing
as having its own unique aesthetic without the need to make anything. The
making became secondary. Along with this experience, Stephanie regained
her inner confidence and a sensitivity to the "sacredness" inherent in things.
She learned to appreciate the beauty and uniqueness of every moment, while
conscious of the larger unity of which she was part. The driving energy that*

had made the adolescent Stephanie active and curious came roaring back, still motivating her to learn and explore, draw and design, but without the anxieties and fears that accompanied her adult mind. Stephanie recognized that her new identity represented a return to the original, unencumbered state she experienced as a child. And as normal as it gets.

For Stephanie, as for many of us, the existence of an uncontrolled and often chaotic mind, along with its obsessive thought-spinning inner critic, is an existential predicament. When the effects of life experiences persist and affect mood, rational deliberation, and behavior, they disrupt the normal flow, joy, and unity of life. The disruptions obscure life's natural wonder and the remarkable mind we had at birth. If unmanageable, the psychological snags become the basis for disorders, both autoimmune and emotional; heart problems; addictive behaviors; and suicidal ideation. If these negative ideations become a recurring issue, psychopathology is an inevitable consequence.

While many factors contribute to an uncontrolled mind, the root of the problem is fearful and chaotic thinking, especially one centered on ego-based rumination. One step in the solution is to transform negative incessant and obsessive chatter into a more positive form of creative thinking, one that is complex, multifaceted, multilayered, intricate, elaborate, embellished, flexible, and fluent. These are, in fact, two sides of the same coin. Switching from one type of thinking to the other can be as easy as breathing or as difficult as changing your mind. In this book, I describe one path with two parts to achieve this. The first part is self-parenting the mind. Self-parenting is necessary to increase the likelihood of a true transformation. The second part is present-moment centering using mindfulness, or learning to be in the moment. Both parts provide the means for a return to the extraordinary Original Mind, the mind at birth, the one associated with a joyful and creative life.

Knowledge of how to control mental chaos and transform the uncontrolled mind into Original Mind springs from wisdom accumulated over centuries coupled with a modern understanding of the neuroscience behind these changes. For many reasons, not everyone is aware of or privy to this knowledge, nor has the time to search for it.

My professional experience as a cognitive neuroscientist by itself did not give me the expertise needed to propose solutions to this singular psychological problem affecting humanity. What closed the circle was a spiritual crisis experienced during middle age. The outcome of the crisis made me come to grips with the thought that intellectual activity is only one of many ways to uncover the truth. And I set out to explore those other avenues.

Science is an honorable, challenging, and enjoyable profession, but I saw limits in the intellectual information gained from this perspective. Blaise Pascal, the French mathematician and philosopher, said that "The last function of reason is to recognize that there is an infinity of things which are beyond it." The major question I faced during my personal crisis was whether the probing of science leads to truth, or only an approximation of the truth. If so, partial truth was a very unsatisfying thing. The question consumed me, and dissatisfaction with science became magnified by what appeared to be limits to my rational understanding of things. I sensed the need to do more and a responsibility to pursue a larger perspective. That impetus led me to the practice of mindfulness meditation. I was confident that this new perspective would give me a larger viewpoint about being in relation to life, while reducing the worrying, anxiety, and other mind problems I faced.

Because of my stubbornness, these efforts did not provide immediate answers and required fortunate encounters with remarkable people who provided needed guidance.[1] Only after nearly twenty years of practice and toward the end of my academic career did I come to understand what I considered a critical insight—that I am more than ego-based thoughts. This understanding, that "I am not my thoughts," proved liberating and uncovered a mind I always had, but that ego-based rumination had obscured and I'd forgotten. What Buddhists call Original Mind burst forth in an unprecedented and unexpected way, bringing extra curiosity, freshness, and creativity I did not know I could experience. The realization also brought forth a bountiful source of energy that has produced a healthier and joyful life.

The life accomplishments of talented and creative individuals like Leonardo da Vinci, Jennifer Doudna, Jean-Dominique Bauby, Barbara Lipska, Grandma Moses, Rumi, and many others described in this book mirror this Original Mind and my personal journal of discovery. The obstacles sometimes seem immense, but this calm and joyful mind is present in the most ordinary of extraordinary lives. For many, this path is not the normal road since we remain prisoners of ego and uncontrolled chaos.

Self-Parenting: Flexibility

An often-stated truism is that children need to live in a predictable rather than a chaotic environment for optimal development. Predictability need not mean rigidity and control. Thus, self-parenting flexibility, being open to new things and possibilities, is just as important as long as you express it in a caring, loving way. Flexibility does not mean giving in to the mind's every whim and desire.

The following will help you build flexibility of mind:

- *Avoid making impulsive decisions. Thoughtful decisions require the rational mind.*
- *Try to decide based on present circumstances.*
- *Avoid relying too much on prior choices or old rules.*
- *Trust intuition and let the nonconscious mind guide your behavior.*
- *Reward special moments (e.g., when the mind is calm, attentive, and creative).*
- *Respond to impulses, feelings, and crazy thoughts with curiosity instead of shutting them down.*
- *Appreciate your mind; show it loving care, kindness, and compassion.*

What Is the Controlled Mind?

Original Mind in synchrony with nature is another description of a controlled mind, and it defines Jalāl ad-Dīn Muhammad Balkhī. This thirteenth century poet and scholar is one of the greatest mystical poets of all time.[2] He was born on the Eastern shores of the Persian Empire in 1207, in the city of Balkh in what is now Afghanistan. He is an example of someone who lived a natural state of creative living most of his life. A powerful, independent spirit, he shattered the status quo, the dated social norms, the primitive cultural taboos, the dusty dogmatic thinking, and the slave mentality of his time. In recent years, he became one of the most widely read poets in America, and talent-wise is on par with Beethoven, Shakespeare, and Mozart. But Jalāl ad-Dīn was also a messenger of truth. He grounded his philosophy in love and a clear vision that allowed him to carry out his life journey free of ego, guilt, fear, and shame.

More popularly known as Rumi, Jalāl ad-Dīn came into wealth, power, and the world of politics early on, becoming a member of high society. He was a charming, wealthy nobleman; a genius theologian; a law professor; and a brilliant scholar. Rumi met a wandering and wild holy man by the name of Shams-e Tabrizi in his late thirties. Shams was a blunt, antisocial, and powerful spiritual wanderer whose nickname, "the Bird," suggested he could not stay in one place for too long. But meeting Shams transformed Rumi from a bookish, sober scholar into an impassioned seeker of universal truth and love. In a twist of fate, Rumi's youngest son killed Shams as part of an honor killing. After that grim episode, Rumi fell into a deep depression. Out of this pain, Rumi's Original Mind bloomed. And from this experience flowed verses of poetry, of an extraordinary quality, that talk of love and individuals not bound by cultural limitations. Rumi represents someone who, out of a state of pain and depression, found his natural state of creative living and natural spirituality.

My Personal Freedom

From a personal perspective, my freedom from a similar mental prison became a unique and gratifying experience, as told in my autobiography, *Piercing the Cloud: Encountering the Real Me*.[3] It is the primary reason why I felt motivated to write this book. My story is both different and similar to those described throughout and to most other stories of human existence. While the variety of experience is unlimited, there is a common thread when the integration of ego and the self occurs and the uncontrolled mind gives way to the creativity that has always been there. In that moment, I felt and encountered a sense of freedom I did not think possible, which was and continues to be a transformative experience.

I was fortunate that, through consistent questioning and practicing of mindfulness meditation, I recognized and saw through my created ego identity and saw it as a belief more than a reality. In the process of that discovery, I understood that ego-centered thoughts do not define me, that beyond the uncontrolled and chaotic mind was a bigger, calmer, and loving presence. This realization led to a lessening of my need to search for what I always felt was missing. Once the make-believe cloud of ego dissipated, what I encountered was self-evident, and intellectual rationalization was unnecessary. It was as if the stormy clouds parted and the sun, which had always been there, shone through brightly. The experience was both rational and intuitive.

What became obvious was that setting aside my ruminating mind uncovered my authentic sense of self. And this experience stared at me as if it had always been staring at me in the face, but had been unrecognizable. This realization, as anyone who experiences it will tell you, is both comically funny (since a common response is, "Is this a joke?") and infinitely "enlightening." For me, the experience produced a lessening in my need to achieve in terms of my professional goals. The self-evident purpose of my life became not to achieve anything, *per se,* but to enjoy the simple act of being present. Having studied to be a scientist, I always felt that doing and achieving were necessary for my career. Now, that discernment was reversed. I saw scientific knowledge for the sake of knowledge and as having its own unique beauty without the need to make anything out of it. Accolades, grants, publications, and other aspects of my research work became secondary and much less important.

Along with this new motivation, I gained a growing confidence that this realization is not a temporary state or another creation of the mind that is soon forgotten. The change is a permanent awakening to and appreciation of life—to what is, with less of the distortion of ego-based thinking. This new reality has brought forth a sensitivity to the sacredness of things, in the sense of appreciating the beauty and uniqueness of the objects in the world in the present moment, while appreciating their role in the larger context of life. Unexpectedly, prayer and mindfulness have become my natural engagement and appreciation of this new sensibility.

The world of my senses did not vanish, nor did choirs of angels appear following this experience. There were interesting new experiences. I had a sense of rediscovering my childhood sense of curiosity. I saw things for what seemed like the first time and gained an appreciation of the wonder of the world in the smallest things: the dew on the grass in the morning and how each blade reflected light; the intricate details of the leaves and colors of flowers and the light on objects drew me to them. A hyperattentiveness and focused curiosity accompanied this sensitivity. But the sensitivity was not a negative, schizophrenic-like experience, in which my brain could not filter out irrelevant things and thus felt overwhelmed. Instead, there was a calmness and a joy to it, a genuine delight in the experience.

Another interesting change I experienced that connected me more with life was a natural increase in my social behavior. As an introvert most of my life, I found the unfoldment of an increase in empathy and concern for others quite remarkable. These changes in perspective and awareness do not mean I am no longer interested in doing my job, attending baseball games, making friends, or making love. Rather, the motivation for doing things has changed. The doing to achieve and get an outcome is no longer important, because the joy of being and doing is enough. Thus, an intrinsic joy in being able to do normal things, to see, feel, talk, walk, eat, etc., has come to the forefront. The experience is a natural flow, without the anxiety I felt formerly, and that I previously associated with doing life.

There is a wonderful paradox in all of this, since the desire to know the unknown motivated my paths in both science and spirituality. But the more I understood the nature of my being, the self-centered motivation to know and to do faded and disappeared. In its stead, I discovered an intense desire to let whatever exists unfold without interference, and to be content, without having to do anything to garner such contentment. Since childhood, I have felt an inner, energetic drive giving me the energy to excel, while parents, teachers, and others have channeled this energy in order for me to outdo others. This drive motivated my desire to learn and explore science, but it simultaneously facilitated my dissatisfaction, anxieties, discontentment, and fears.

In my old skin, I felt guilty about not being productive. Now, the driving energy still exists, but the sense of needing to do, and especially to achieve, does not. I am calm yet motivated to learn and explore, and do not experience the anxieties and fears that accompanied and drove my earlier life. For one, I am not guilty while resting. Instead, I am energized by rest and relaxation, by not-doing. As I write this, I recognize how "normal" all these descriptions sound, which is the whole point. This normal state exists if you do not live from the perspective of the obsessive, uncontrolled, and chaotic mind.

How these extraordinary changes came to me flowed from the simple idea and assumption that from birth there has existed an amazing mind that ego-based thinking had obscured. My efforts to remove this cloud involved reducing and eventually undoing, as much as I have been able to, ego-based thinking. A controlled mind can respond to the environment and interacting with life in remarkable, exquisite, and creative ways. As a newborn, you enter the world with exceptional talents and skills, and this mind takes you to heights of creativity in all areas of human performance. The accomplishment of the infant dazzles with beauty, emotion, and insight. You grow a brain, learn to crawl, walk, talk, deliberate, and understand the world. All these are amazing feats of physiology, psychology, and bioengineering. The complexity in how this mind adapts, recovers, and survives the most challenging of circumstances that life presents is remarkable. The paradox of how this exquisite mind becomes the obsessed and negative uncontrolled mind of the adult makes little sense. Until now.

Stop Monkey Mind: Practice Awareness of No-Thought

"No-thought" comes from a Zen expression that literally means "the mind without the mind." This refers to a mind that is calm, balanced, and unoccupied by self-centered thoughts or emotion and therefore open to everything.

As you relax, attend to the racing thoughts your mind is producing in the moment. Is there a physical sensation to this movement? Focus on that sensation instead of the content of the thoughts. Link your breathing to the movement sensation. Can you slow this movement by slowing your breathing rate? As your breathing slows, your racing thoughts should slow. With practice, the sensation of movement will stop completely.

Stop Monkey Mind exercises, practiced anywhere, can lead to this experience, whereby the uncontrolled mind is no longer chaotically moving from one thought stream to the next and the chattering has muted or stopped. The mind is calm and silent. The container is infinite, and problems no longer feel like problems but as opportunities.

Original Mind and Natural Spirituality

Understanding how to control your chaotic mind and seeing that it is a reality you can create allows you to build a path to live without fear, obsessive thoughts, and anxiety. This understanding helps guide you back to that Original Mind with which you were born and is your birthright—and in doing so, returns you to a natural state of creative living. Regaining this mind is a return to an amazing journey—the journey on which you started but somehow got off track. When you make this reconnection, the drudgery and negativity of life, controlled by obsessive and self-centered rumination, take on a fresh perspective. It may even bring forth an expression of spirituality of unlimited potential. All these changes happen if you understand the problem and practice self-parenting and present-moment centering to transform the mind from ego-based or self-centered thinking to one focused on creative living.

The Infinitely "Enlightening" Experience

Many individuals experience creative living with a mind free from ego, and in that experience find a sense of being that I call *natural spirituality*. For many, this freedom happens effortlessly; for others, such realization requires a sustained practice to overcome the negative habits of the uncontrolled mind. This Original Mind is available to anyone at any age and in any culture. When awakened to that reality, the realization becomes the foundational step for a natural spirituality. This term is an off-putting expression because it elicits thoughts of religion. But natural spirituality is best understood as the creative urge to search for the sacred from different perspectives.[4] In its purest essence, natural spirituality is being in synchrony with nature. Or, as Emily Dickinson so eloquently described in her 1863 poem "Nature Is What We See": it is what we see, what we hear, what we know, but have no art to say, she continues, since our wisdom is impotent to Nature's simplicity.

In 1953, K. Y., a Japanese executive, visited a monastery in Japan headed by Nakagawa-roshi to practice a day of meditation. Philip Kapleau, in his book *The Three Pillars of Zen*, retells K. Y.'s own account of his experience after returning home:[5] "At midnight, I abruptly awakened. At first my mind was foggy, then suddenly that quotation flashed into my consciousness, 'I came to realize clearly that Mind is no other than mountains and rivers and the great wide earth, the sun and the moon and the stars.' And I repeated it. Then all at once I was struck as though by lightning, and the next instant heaven and earth crumbled and disappeared. Instantaneously, like surging waves, a tremendous delight welled up in me, a veritable hurricane of delight, as I laughed loudly and wildly."

In another story told by Kapleau, A.M., an American schoolteacher, attended a week-long sesshin. A sesshin is a period of intense meditation, in this case in a Zen monastery. In 1962, A.M. attended a sesshin with Yasutani-roshi in Hawaii, prior to his visit to the U.S. mainland. At the end of the week of intense effort, the schoolteacher reported, "A lifetime has been compressed into one week. A thousand new sensations are bombarding my senses, a thousand new paths are opening before me. I live my life minute by minute, but only now does a warm love pervade my whole being, because I know I am not just my little self but a great big miraculous Self. My constant thought is to have everybody share this deep satisfaction."

These types of realization or enlightenment experiences are still unusual stories for a Western audience. Exotic and distant echoes surround them and they are not relatable to most people. Yet these are all stories of freedom. Of a mind suddenly freed from the mental cage of ego-based rumination. They are, in fact, descriptions of the transformative experience when the chaotic mind is controlled and returns to being Original Mind; a mind that exhibits creativity, wisdom, and joy. As many of these stories tell over and over, Original Mind knows what to do and how to do it. Its wisdom lies in being able to perceive significant challenges, whether simple or complex, and knowing how to address them. It will call forth the innate skills needed to resolve those challenges. It will know how well you are doing and will respond this way, whether free from distractions or inundated by them. But to reach this mindset, you need first to undo the ego that obscures it.

Craig Hamilton, a modern-day spiritual teacher, describes awakening not as a state of consciousness, nor a thought, but the realization of what you are, your true nature. We come to recognize that who we are is not this limited, separate ego-self or any of the thoughts and feelings with which we identified earlier. Awakening is the extinguishing of this ego-thinking. It occurs when we realize that who we are at the deepest level is something much bigger and more profound than who we thought we were. We sense a kind of awareness, intelligence, love, being, and presence that is the foundation of reality itself. This presence is already free, whole, and perfect. Who we are is an aspect of this sacred dimension of reality. One that is beyond intellectual comprehension, yet somehow, we "know" it and know it is missing nothing, lacking nothing, and overflows with love, wisdom, power, and clarity.

Hamilton claims, as have many others, that awakening is not just the realization that God, or whatever we want to call this ultimate experience, exists, but the realization that *That* essence is what we are.[6] The thing we were always seeking and putting outside ourselves is actually our true nature. This understanding shatters every conscious or nonconscious belief we've had in our own limitation. It destroys every sense of lack, of not being enough, of feeling there is somewhere else we need to get to. You realize that the whole thing is already here. I already am *That*. Awakening is when you sense the essence of everything as sacred, beyond measure and glorious, beyond comprehension. Such an experience can be as brief as a thought or as lasting as a lifetime. The difference is how complete the extinguishment of the ego-self is. Which is why, for most of us, the practice must continue throughout our entire life.

There are remarkable stories of individuals who, like those in the enlightenment stories of Philip Kapleau, suddenly or not so suddenly uncover their Original Mind. They find their way to freedom in a variety of ways, even in old age. Anna Mary Robertson was one such person. Born on September 7, 1860, in Greenwich, New York, she grew up one of ten children on her parents' farm. Anna left home when she turned twelve and worked at a nearby farm. Then, at age twenty-seven, Anna married Thomas Moses and settled in Virginia's Shenandoah Valley to raise a family. There, the couple ran a farm, and Anna gave birth to five surviving children after having lost five others. For forty years, Anna lived a normal family life. In 1927, at sixty-seven years of age, she lost her husband. Devastated and trying to keep busy in her grief, she painted. And in doing so, she found her Original Mind.

Anna painted occasionally and did not devote herself totally to her craft until much later, in her late seventies. Although not academically trained, Anna followed her muse faithfully, and in 1938, when she was seventy-eight, she experienced her first big break. She displayed her works at a local store where a New York city art collector named Louis J. Caldor saw them and bought them all. "I will make you famous," he told her.

The following year, Anna exhibited paintings at the Museum of Modern Art in New York in a show of unknown artists. She then had her first one-woman show in New York, displaying her paintings at Gimbels, a well-known department store. Her peers referred to Anna as an American primitive artist, and she developed a huge, devoted following who loved her artwork. In the mid-1940s, Hallmark greeting cards reproduced her images, which introduced her to a wider audience. She won the Women's National Press Club Award for her artistic achievements in 1949. Anna went to Washington, D.C., to collect this honor and met with President Harry Truman during her visit. In 1952, she wrote her memoir *My Life's History* and, nine years later, passed away on November 13, 1961.[7]

During her career, Anna created about 1,500 works of art. Her paintings provide a glimpse into an idealized version of country life and America's pastoral past, and remain extremely popular today. Best known by her nickname of Grandma Moses, Anna is an example of how even in old age, you can find your way to a state of Original Mind and creative living.

Stop Monkey Mind: Practice Your ABCs

Practicing with A Bigger Container (ABC) means using imagination and creative mindfulness to reduce the magnitude and saliency of obsessive thoughts.

As you relax and still your mind, identify the thought that is dominant. Visualize this thought (e.g., "I am afraid") stuffed into a small container with room for only that one thought. That is your common experience, and in that context, the thought commands ALL your attention.

Now, imagine moving the contents of the small container into a much larger container (the larger you imagine the container, the better; imagine, for example, it being the size of the universe). In this larger container, the bothersome thought represents a very tiny aspect of the contents, an almost invisible part you can easily ignore, allowing you to attend to other things.

Stay visualizing this larger box and the emptiness of feeling you sense. Let the experience of that refreshing emptiness flood your entire being.

Key Takeaways

- The solution to the uncontrolled mind is to transform negative, incessant, and obsessive chatter into creative thinking.
- I recommend two ways for switching from obsessive to creative thinking: self-parenting the mind and present-moment centering using mindfulness.
- The keys to the transformation involve: (a) knowing that you are more than your ego-based thoughts; (b) acknowledging that the essence of who you are is something larger and much more interesting; (c) recognizing your ego; and (d) integrating this ego with your true self.

- Characteristics of the controlled mind:
  - Unique and gratifying feeling.
  - Lessening the need to achieve.
  - Purpose of life becomes "to be and enjoy the simple act of being present."
  - Confidence and increased appreciation of the sacredness and uniqueness of life.
  - Joy in being able to do normal activities.
  - Rediscovery of your childhood sense of curiosity.
  - Increase in empathy and concern for others.

Next chapter: What steps can you take to find such freedom?

4

Steps to a Practical Solution

Take the first step to know yourself.

Stepping Out of Delusion

It took a sense of urgency and a feeling that her life was coming apart to overcome the inertia, and for Stephanie to step out from the delusion her mind had created. It also required sustained work. The first and most important step recognized the problem. Working with her therapist gave her a structure to deal with her obsessively ruminating and chaotic mind. This helped Stephanie identify unhelpful habits and techniques for handling them. Clarity occurred when she understood that the energy motivating her "bad" behaviors could equally motivate "good" behaviors. The effort required switching from trying to eliminate deeply ingrained patterns to changing the perception of her behavior. Such reappraisal, cognitive reevaluation, or seeing things from a new perspective proved helpful. Stephanie had taken the second most important step on her way to recovery: she now knew that a solution was possible and how to address it. She still remembers the day she let go of her fear. Until then, fear had felt like something deeply embedded in her body. Yet, with her psychological and spiritual practices, she learned to label those feelings, to consider labels as simply that, and finally to see that fear was a jumble of thoughts coupled to a bodily sense. The understanding that thoughts were creations of her own mind and could just as easily be "let go" as "created" was a revolutionary insight. It empowered and improved Stephanie's confidence. It also brought back a calmness and a sense of joy in the life she had only experienced as a child. Stephanie knows it is almost like alcoholism or addiction—the work continues indefinitely, for new challenges can resurrect many deeply ingrained habits, at least until the habits are no longer. The last step in recovery is finding a balance between competing drives so that the practice becomes a joyful and natural part of living.

I have learned the hard way that changing habitual behavior requires one to reach a high level of emotional urgency. There is urgency and necessity in knowing that if you don't learn how to control your chaotic mind, you might lose years of life to excessive rumination and recrimination, thus severely compromising your career, your relationships, and your health. How the brain creates the uncontrolled mind and how you can transform it into a more positive and creative force should give you confidence to become a fearless and resourceful individual.

In searching for practical solutions to the monkey mind problem, it took me a while to realize that potential solutions existed embedded in the problem itself. The recognition that I was part of the problem, and the solution, came into better focus when I recognized that an uncontrolled mind exhibits two distinct impulses: the negative AFRAID and the positive AAECC impulses. These energetic urges typically work in complementary fashion. The more the uncontrolled mind and the AFRAID impulse grow in strength, the more the AAECC and Original Mind recede into the background. The opposite, of course, is true. Optimally, there is a dynamic balance.[1]

AFRAID energetic impulses provide the nourishment and basis for the incessant, frenetic, intellectual chattering; the self-obsessed, inner critic; and the ego that uses the left-brain interpreter to rationalize everything. In contrast, AAECC is the creative, energetic, yet calm impulse, as if observing the obsessed mind from a distance and without judgment.

I recognized that this observer mind, with its detached perspective and calm demeanor, was equally basic and real. This insight became a most liberating and empowering discovery. The mental distancing from the storm it provided gave me a way to solve the chaotic mind conundrum. It highlighted the choice I had, to let go of the total identification with the AFRAID and obsessive mind and to identify more with the AAECC and calm mindset. This undoing of an old relationship and identification with the controlled mind required marginalizing my ego-centered, rational mind and accepting nonconscious processing as a better way to be. Allowing the intelligence of nonconscious processing to express itself brought Original Mind from background to foreground.

I conceptualized this radical change in perspective as the recognition that the mind and its chattering intellect behave like an attention deficit hyperactive child. This child has attention flitting from thought stream to thought stream in a never-ending attempt to find the needed psychic balance and bridge the ego-self separation. One of the first questions this child-mind confronts is whether its environment is a safe place and whether those surrounding it are loving and helpful. If they are not, then the mind deploys protective resources and psychological defenses that start a change with enormous consequences. The deployed psychological defenses induce and enhance AFRAID thinking, while dimming the energetic, curious, and creative AAECC mind. Fortunately, the two parts to solving this problem detailed in earlier chapters, self-parenting and present-moment centering using mindfulness, incorporate the solutions described here.

Psychologist, clinical therapists, mindfulness teachers, and others have proposed multistep practices for shifting the focus and emotions of the uncontrolled mind to a track that helps you calm it and move forward. Most of these practices can be effective if followed, but they all have at least four things in common: **R**ecognizing the problem; **U**nderstanding the solution; Finding **B**alance; and **I**mplementing the answers. The acronym **RUBI** describes the core of any practical solution and is the basis for what I am recommending in this book. This is a proven pathway to progress and recovery.

Recognizing the Problem

Whether political, physical, psychological, ego-based, or uncontrolled mind, *the basis for solving any problem requires acknowledging it.* The HBO television series *The Newsroom* ran from 2012 to 2014, starred Jeff Daniels, and was written by Aaron Sorkin. The very first episode of this political drama, which chronicles events at the fictional Atlantis Cable News (ACN), dramatically argues that solving problems begins by recognizing them. There's a scene at a university campus in which news anchor Will McAvoy, played by Daniels, is sitting between a liberal and a conservative. He is responding to the question, "What makes the United States the greatest country in the world?" In the middle of his long response, McAvoy exclaims, "The first step in solving any problem is recognizing there is one."

The truism that you must first acknowledge a problem is fundamental and plays an important role in many recovery systems, including Twelve-Step programs for alcohol and drug addiction. In these various approaches, the goal is first to accept psychological and behavioral problems and then recognize that you may be powerless to resolve them on your own. Thus, the first step in the road to recovery is first to accept that a problem exists. Denial is an ego-based defense that operates to help stay off solutions, sometimes by inhibiting unpleasant, unwanted, and negative experiences.

The ego-based mind becomes an addiction caused and maintained by aberrant learning and pleasurable experiences. And as you well know, addiction is a tough thing to overcome. It presents a formidable challenge because its nature becomes ingrained and apparently necessary. Trying to address such an addiction creates unpleasant, unwanted, and negative side effects that further prevent its solution.

Trying to deal with the uncontrolled and chaotic mind as a type of addiction provides insight into the psychological problems that arise. Although having such an insight is unnecessary to implementing the proposed solution of present-moment centering, such an intuition provides greater motivation to empower change. The prefrontal cortex of your brain is where this battlefield occurs, an area involved with emotion regulation, impulse control, and having a sense of perspective.[2] Recognizing the problem and finding balance in our prefrontal cortex allows us to step into that space where choice, possibility, and growth lie.

Questions to Ponder

Do you prefer a slow (self-parenting) or fast (mindfulness) resolution to the uncontrolled mind? Do certain situations lend themselves better to one solution versus the other?

Take a moment to examine why you choose one over the other.
What do you think are the benefits of the path you choose?
What will you be missing if you only try one path?
What questions do you have that remain unanswered?

Understanding the Solution

To reach a level of understanding that allows for resolution of the problem of the mind and moves you in the right direction, you need to understand and then resolve the problem of ego-self separation. This requires recognizing that the dual nature of personality, the existence of Original Mind and of an uncontrolled mind, and of the AAECC and AFRAID impulses motivating those minds, reflect an even deeper duality. This deeper issue is the relationship between ego and the real self. While these are rudimentary constructs, they are useful labels to help set the stage for the discussion that can provide such understanding.

Ego refers to the impulses, biases, conceptual thoughts, and actions that are most responsible for producing and perpetuating the uncontrolled mind and the psychological mess it creates. This ego plays an outsized role in the loss, reduction, and obscuring of Original Mind. *Understanding the solution means recognizing that the ego is the problem and its dissolution is necessary.* Your real self is Original Mind, a concept meant to point to what you inherit at birth, and the larger context from which the ego emerges.

The relationship between these two constructs—ego and real self—may not be familiar to most people. I provide more detailed exploration and explanation in later chapters, but for now, it is important to emphasize that the ego motivates the uncontrolled mind, interpreter, AFRAID impulse, and the error-correcting nature of conscious awareness. In contrast, the real self reflects nonconscious processing and the AAECC impulse.

Finding Balance

Learning to control the chaotic mind means recognizing you never lost your Original Mind and what has kept it hidden are the machinations of your ego. You must bring those machinations into balance. Sigmund Freud provided the earliest insights into the ego's role relevant to the solutions presented in this book. He saw the ego as that aspect of the mind that referees between other natural drives.[3]

According to Freud, the ego is necessary for reality testing and a sense of personal identity. He noted that "Normally, there is nothing of which we are more certain than the feeling of our self, of our own ego. This ego appears autonomous and unitary, marked off distinctly from everything else. That such an appearance is deceptive, and that on the contrary the ego is continued inwards without any sharp delimitation, into an unconscious mental entity which we designate as the id and for which it serves as a kind of facade."[4] This quote makes clear that Freud saw the ego as more than an impartial referee. He saw it as part and parcel of the components creating the personality, which included both conscious and nonconscious processes.

Many contemporary and modern skeptics view Freudian psychoanalysis from the perspective of its methodological rigidity, lack of theoretical rigor, emphasis on childhood, and dependence on free association. Modern research, for instance, shows that conscious and nonconscious processes are not competing centers of brain activity. Nor are they subdivided into subcategories of ego, id, or superego. Instead, they reflect streams of processing that interweave into a unified sense of self. Despite the preponderance of this criticism and whether Freudian ideas are not as sophisticated as current ideas, they serve as a good starting point. They help us draw a simple, two-dimensional, rudimentary, but easy-to-understand sketch of these complex relationships. We can then turn to a more sophisticated and realistic description. A few psychologists argue that "Psychoanalysis is a valuable theory despite its weaknesses because it is comprehensive, serendipitous, innovative, and has withstood the test of time." Freudian ideas still resonate with the public. They are familiar, and therefore useful concepts to help draw a preliminary description that can later develop into a more complex explanation.

Psychoanalytic theory views the ego in terms of function. Its job is to find a balance between the competing drives of the id and superego. The ego ensures that meeting your needs conforms to the demands of the surrounding reality. This perspective assumes a normal, organic equilibrium between various aspects of the personality. Yet many events or circumstances, including aging, growing debt, rebellious children, or a leering boss, affect this balance. Freud described the id as a drive that urges fulfillment of the most primitive biological needs. The superego, in contrast, is the internalized ideals gained from parents and society at large. The dynamics of their interaction play out in every action we take.

Judy is thirsty while having lunch with a group of friends. Rather than waiting for the server to refill her glass of water, she reaches across the table and drinks from Kathy's water glass. This surprises Kathy. Whether Judy's action is conscious matters little in terms of what she discerns about her actions after the fact. What Judy did was to meet her immediate need. Thirst and hunger are necessities that provide a motivating force to get us to act to meet those needs. Freud emphasized the link between this considerable energy and the libido, a more sexualized outlet influencing mental processes and structures that generate erotic attachments.

The superego, as opposed to the id, refers to the internalized ideals gained from social upbringing. This aspect of the personality forms later in childhood because of developing parental and other social influences. For Tom, the final exam was difficult, even though he studied all night. Yet he could not recall the answers to the multiple-choice questions. Tom sat next to Susan, who seemed to breeze through the exam. Tom could glance at her answers if he leaned forward in the chair. As the professor turned to a student asking a question, Tom knew this was his chance to sneak a look at Susan's test. But his conscience stopped him. He felt this action was wrong and decided against it. It was better to make educated guesses than to cheat. Tom's superego exercised its dominance over his other rising emotions.

Delayed gratification is another example of these dynamics and of top-down control. While in the buffet line, Miguel, a shrimp lover, wanted to grab a handful of the fried shrimp and stuff them into his mouth. Because his friends were there, and he knew this behavior was not good etiquette, he waited the minute or two until he sat down to eat. The biological impulse to satisfy his hunger and the social etiquette to eat at the table created a situation that Miguel resolved through his decision to delay gratification. From a Freudian perspective, his ego balanced the need of the superego to follow social convention and overcome the strong id's desire to satisfy his hunger.

Another Freudian aspect of the ego's function is to protect the personality from injury. Failure to do this triggers anxiety. When the demands of life become too much and threaten the personality, causing anxious, guilty, or overwhelmed feelings, defense mechanisms are engaged to protect it. Ego defenses like repression, denial, projection, displacement, regression, and sublimation refer to regulatory processes that evolved to maintain a homeostatic balance. While these defense and protection mechanisms are natural and normal, when they get out of control or are insufficient or ineffective, they can produce neuroses, anxiety, phobias, obsessions, and hysteria. When they do, the storm gates open, giving rise to an uncontrolled mind. The bottom line is we all recognize these competing drives and must keep them in balance to live successfully with others.

Self-Parenting: Designing Rituals

When designing a ritual (a series of actions performed according to a prescribed order, with a specific purpose, and performed regularly), there should be a beginning, middle, and end. There should also be flexibility. Create a ritual to fit your schedule.

Suggestions for establishing a ritual:

- *Designate a day/time at least weekly for a formal sit-down mindfulness session.*
- *Take a weekly walk with the express purpose of being creative, emptying your mind, relaxing, praying, exercising, or any other activity you want to do on that walk.*
- *Take a car drive with a focus similar to the walk: relax, empty your mind, turn over an idea in your creative imagination, etc.*
- *Gather with loved ones to play a game, talk, share a meal.*

Implementing the Answers

The first step in resolving the problem of the uncontrolled mind is to address the self-focus, attachment, and emphasis on AFRAID rumination. Because the AFRAID impulse recalls the behavior of an unruly child, one way to address the problem is to strengthen self-parenting skills. This approach is slow and effortful, but effective.

Setting the goal as the elimination of AFRAID thinking is tempting but not viable because AFRAID and AAECC impulses are aspects of a common energetic source. Removing one affects the other. A better strategy is to minimize and transform AFRAID rumination and promote AAECC thinking. Using self-parenting in this way sets the stage and enhances the likelihood of transformation when addressing the temporal nature of thought through mindfulness practice. This is the transformational step and requires examining the thinking and expectations that individuals have based on their life experiences. The tactic of changing the temporal nature of thought is something that produces rapid and transformative results compared to self-parenting the mind. In fact, it may only be necessary to practice this feature to achieve excellent results, but only if the ground has been properly prepared.

To live in the present moment is a way of life, and you have a total choice over it. In fact, you can change the temporal nature of thought and activate the experience of the present moment at will. Try it now. Attend to whatever is happening at this moment, whether it's the sounds you hear, objects you see, or feelings you have. Place your total attention on one of these and you experience that the change is as immediate as that. At that moment, whether you can hold that total focus for one second or longer, problems disappear from your mind. Maintain this situational awareness consistently and you will reach a point where staying in the present occurs for longer and longer periods with less and less effort. This practice is the key to learning to control the chaos that was previously present. As you fine-tune your new skill, the fearless and creative person you are appears, where problems become opportunities for growth.

The temporal nature of thought means that some thoughts occurred in the past and are captured as memories, others are occurring in the present moment, and the mind can equally project thoughts into the future as plans. Focusing the mind on the present eliminates AFRAID rumination, since this style of thinking occurs only when focusing on the past and future. The solution is as simple and immediate as it sounds. Conceptual understanding of why this works is really unnecessary for implementing the solution, although it is helpful. Being in the present moment is enough. Whether you choose self-parenting and mindfulness practice, or only one of these, the choice is yours and therefore the willingness to change must come from you.

Key Takeaways

- AFRAID impulses provide the nourishment and basis for the incessant, frenetic, chattering, self-obsessed inner critic that uses the left-brain interpreter to rationalize everything.
- AAECC is the creative, energetic, yet calm impulse that observes the obsessed mind nonjudgmentally. It reflects the real self.
- The more the uncontrolled mind and the AFRAID impulse grow in strength, the more AAECC and Original Mind recede into the background, and vice versa.
- Four steps are necessary to let go of identification with the AFRAID impulse and engaging with the AAECC one:
  - **R**ecognize the problem (*solving any mental problem requires acknowledging it first; this battlefield occurs in the frontal lobes of your brain*).
  - **U**nderstand the solution (*What is ego? What role does it play? How does it relate to your real self?*).
  - find **B**alance (*recognize the multiple competing drives you must keep in balance to live successfully*).
  - **I**mplement the answer (*self-parenting the mind and present-moment centering through mindfulness*).

Next chapter: What does self-parenting the mind mean?

Setting the Stage through Self-Parenting the Mind

Use the strength inherent in your own resistance.

Exceptional Parenting Is a Protective Factor

Even before giving birth, Stephanie's mom, Danielle, knew the child she bore would be special. There was a unique quality to her pregnancy that seemed at variance with those of her friends. Her child would be exceptional—not so much like a human computer or with a mental disability, but stand out in difficult to describe ways. She knew her own personality would have to change as well. Her love would be unconditional. More precisely, she would nurture and celebrate her child's gifts with careful and loving understanding. As much as her child would differ from others, she understood that the child's extraordinary nature might irritate and make it hard for others to accept, but she would do her utmost to help her navigate the uncertainties of this world. It likely would require a unique set of communication skills and an equally extraordinary willingness to listen to and accept changes to her developing personality without trying to force unnecessary disciplinary measures on her.

The best way to find your way back to Original Mind is to reduce and undo ego-based rumination, of which the uncontrolled mind is a reflection. Ego-based rumination is comparable to a storm cloud obscuring the light from the sun. When the cloud dissolves, you experience the sun. From a psychological perspective, the undoing of this mental cloud requires resolving the ego-self differentiation and separation that arises during development. The two solutions proposed in this book for achieving this outcome are self-parenting the mind and learning to be present-moment centered, which means changing the relationship between thought and time.

We are all born dependent on parents or other caregivers. Not only our physical but our social, emotional, and cognitive development depend on a loving relationship with our primary caregiver. There is increasing evidence that neglect, parental inconsistency, and most important, lack of love, can lead to long-term mental health problems and reduce overall curiosity, creativity, and happiness. When parental and caretaker love is missing or insufficient, it is difficult to make up completely, although as we grow older, we learn to depend more on our own self-parenting. Self-parenting the mind to resolve the problem of an uncontrolled and chaotic mind helps set the stage for a true transformation to occur. Self-parenting the mind is the more methodical, step-wise, and slower approach compared to present-moment centering, but both are necessary for a good outcome.

The solutions to a problematic mind, including self-parenting, are variations on insights known for thousands of years. When applied, they lead to what others have experienced: freedom of mind and an encounter with something once thought lost. Self-parenting means recognizing the problem of the uncontrolled mind as comparable to that of an unruly, disobedient, and undisciplined child. We address the behavior by implementing a steady diet of reasonableness and loving care. These insights come from the successful parenting of actual children.

Everyone can learn and practice self-parenting, but these techniques are most useful for anyone who received insufficient loving parenting during their early years. Throughout this chapter, I provide self-parenting exercises to help improve a set of behavioral qualities: flexibility, setting boundaries, learning good self-talk, designing a ritual, and knowing your life's purpose. While other activities are possible, these exercises provide easy to follow routines and a set of exercises to get you started. The overarching goal is to learn to love your mind.

Extraordinary Parenting

Louis Martin and Zelie Guerin met, fell in love, and married on July 13, 1858, in the beautiful Basilica of Notre-Dame d'Alencon. The Basilica is a Gothic parish church in Alençon, a commune in Normandy, France, capital of the Orne department, and 107 miles west of Paris. The couple met in April of that year and were engaged to marry three months later. Louis was thirty-four years old, tall, with the appearance of a military officer, handsome, with a high, wide forehead, fair complexion, chestnut hair, and hazel eyes. Zelie, at twenty-six, was an anxious, hypersensitive woman lacking self-confidence but filled with a strong religious conviction.[1]

In fact, her faith convinced Zelie that God had called her into a religious life. While living like brother and sister because of her religious conviction, the couple lived an ordinary married life. They worked hard, each owning a small business. Louis was a watchmaker and Zelie made Pont d'Alencon lace. At some point, their relationship changed, and they became parents to nine children. Five daughters survived, all of them becoming nuns. Indeed, one daughter became the most popular saint in recent history. Devotees know her as St. Therese of Lisieux—"The Little Flower of Jesus," or "The Little Flower."

The Catholic Church recognized the extraordinary parenting of Louis and Zelie in raising their five surviving daughters. Because of this, they became the first set of parents of a saint to become saints themselves after they died. In the nineteenth century in which they lived, this two-career couple faced challenges similar to those faced by many in our own century. They were constantly busy; worked while raising children; needed and found good childcare; achieved professional excellence; operated profitable businesses; cared for aging parents; educated a special-needs child; raised their children in the faith; and finally died of familiar illnesses, breast cancer for Zelie and arteriosclerosis for Louis.

For Louis and Zelie, a religious sensibility guided their parenting style, including the desire to be holy and saintly. This attitude meant a trusting and loving response in daily life to what they felt was something greater than themselves. Their faith was something at once anchored in the real and the ordinary and involved a self-sacrificing attitude lived to the fullest, which they transmitted to their children, around whose lives their own lives revolved. For Zelie, "they were all our joy, and we never found our joy except in them. Nothing was too costly for us to do for them." Both Louis and Zelie felt a desire for holiness in marriage and in parenthood. They responded to the religious call to have many children and to raise them for a heavenly purpose.

Unruly Child with a Spoiled Mind

The parenting style of Louis and Zelie in the mid-nineteenth century seems quaint, unreachable, and of a different era. Yet, for many, they set an enduring example of what parenting could be in any century. Their example allows us to extract principles and lessons from their relationship to their children, and apply these lessons to a most loved child—our own mind.

The defining characteristic of the problematic mind is its uncontrolled leaps of attention and emotion from one thought-stream to another, and the accompanying inner chatter that follows. This behavior recalls that of an unruly and spoiled child throwing a tantrum. Comparable to such a spoiled child, the uncontrolled mind is rude to others. It does not respond to questions, ignores instructions, and does not share with others. Instead, it is domineering and demanding. An uncontrolled mind will figuratively throw a tantrum of crying, howling, and fist pounding the floor when it does not receive its wishes. These are the signature qualities of a chaotic mind controlled by ego-based rumination.

In extreme cases, clinicians have defined this behavior in children as *spoiled children syndrome*.[2] This syndrome is an appropriate term to apply to the mind since it fits so well, although rarely used in pediatrics. I describe the uncontrolled mind as spoiled *mind* syndrome. What spoiled mind syndrome reflects is another name for problematic dynamics showing excessive, self-centered, and immature qualities. I assume the uncontrolled mind will worsen from inappropriate or inadequate self-parenting.

Try to remember a time when you engaged in behavior that was wrong but were too tired, unmotivated, or in less-than-full control to rein in or discipline yourself. Recall a time when you became sensitive to your own self-esteem ("I just don't want to consider this") and tried to avoid causing work for yourself. Recall that sometimes you experience pleasure from an emotional outburst ("Man, letting him have it felt good!"). Or, you feel fear at how you would react ("I fear how I will respond"). Or, you knew you would not enjoy self-imposed boundaries ("I'm just going to drink when you leave"). All these behaviors are expressions of spoiled mind syndrome. Dan Kindlon, author of *Too Much of a Good Thing: Raising Children of Character in an Indulgent Age*, states that spoiled children are more prone to excessive self-absorption, lack of self-control, anxiety, and depression. We can say the same about a spoiled mind.[3]

Good parenting allows responsible adults to raise model offspring while providing them with protection and care to ensure their healthy development. Healthy development means rearing successful adults and transmitting appropriate sociocultural values. A similar benefit accrues when self-parenting the mind. The undisciplined mind exhibits inappropriate behaviors. Therefore, the use of time-tested parenting techniques can help transform this mind, redirect its energy to more useful behaviors, and bring back what it was at the beginning. By doing so, the individual can more successfully navigate the world.

Stop Monkey Mind: Fading Thoughts

- *Relax and still your mind.*
- *Identify and label the thought dominating your mind.*
- *Identify and label the emotion associated with the thought.*
- *Visualize the thought/emotion in terms of white writing against a blue sky.*
- *Watch the writing slowly dissipate and fade.*
- *Feel the emotions attached to the thought/emotion dissipating and fading.*
- *Experience the remaining empty, blue sky for as long as possible.*

What Is Self-Parenting?

The idea of self-parenting arises from the common experience most of us have that there is an ongoing conversation in our mind between two or more voices. Many assume the origin of those voices relates to different regions of the brain, perhaps the two hemispheres. Psychologists typically characterize one voice as the "inner parent" and related to the left hemisphere, Gazzaniga's interpreter, and its specialized language functions. The other voice is associated with the "inner child," and related to the right hemisphere and its less developed language functions. Self-parenting is the manner and quality of the inner conversation that takes place between these two voices.

There may be other sources of this internal dialog, but regardless of the origin, learning and guiding, the self-parenting mind is important for the sake of calming and undoing the uncontrolled mind. This is true even if you received the type of nurturing care that Louis and Zelie Martin provided their daughters. Feeling loved, protected, nourished, and supported are the key ingredients for self-parenting and necessary to transform the chaotic mind into the controlled mind and the freedom from fear and more creativity that it brings. The lack of good self-parenting makes it more likely that the AFRAID impulse will overcome the more curious and creative AAECC one.

In my own life, positive learning gained through experience occurred because of good parenting and self-parenting. Treating my mind respectfully, lovingly, and without judgment helped calm its scattered nature. I accepted its attention deficit, hyperactive nature instead of fighting it because the more I resisted and tried to change it, the worse the behavior got. Acceptance, therefore, was one of the first lessons learned. Observing and cataloging the mind's jumping around to understand just what was so interesting to it, followed naturally. The unexpected experience was that once the situation resolved, and I settled into this practice, the uncontrolled mind began cooperating and slowing down, until I could calmly converse with it.

Successful self-parenting, like successfully raising a challenging child, depends on several factors. It means recognizing and accepting limitations: for one, the limits of genetics, the effects of the environment, the influence of peers, how schooling molds rational deliberation, and the effects of parental and moral training. To argue that self-parenting the mind solves all the problems is unconvincing and untrue. While self-parenting has many positive effects, it may not affect some deviant behavior. Thus, additional factors need consideration.

One factor is to be constantly on-guard for ego-based thinking and its immediate gratification. A gentle vigilance is necessary to prevent a return or buildup of ego-based thinking. Nourishing a social life, seeking and maintaining friends, looking after your physical health, and seeking help when life becomes overwhelming are all enormously important. Equally valuable is not to ignore motivational factors, which maintain engagement with this work. These motivational factors become self-fulfilling prophesies. When you reach greater intimacy with the controlled mind and experience the freedom from fear and creativity it engenders, a calming takes place, work becomes more fulfilling, and the more motivated your attitude to keep at it becomes. The cycle is virtuous.

How to Raise a Good Mind

Social scientists have identified unique styles of parenting, from authoritarian, authoritative, permissive, to uninvolved. Many of these same scientists advocate that the best approach and key in any style of parenting is flexibility. And that means adjusting the characteristics and expectations of the parents and the child to work together. In a study with 1,600 parents, researchers found that a direct connection exists between firm parenting styles and success with college performance.[4] Academically successful and well-adjusted children often have parents with an authoritative bent. How parents go about producing excellent overall outcomes is important to determine; as is whether these principles apply to self-parenting, especially of the AFRAID mind, and if they help resolve spoiled mind syndrome.

Studies show that authoritative parenting emphasizes flexibility and balances clear, high parental expectations with emotional sensitivity and responsiveness. These parents recognize a child needs to learn self-sufficiency and autonomy. Setting clear rules and boundaries and explaining the logic and reasoning behind the rules is important.

Often, parents will listen to the children's feedback, questions, and objections to the established rules. They have discovered that including children in creating the rules is important. Even more important, they try to focus on positive reinforcement when the child meets expectations, rather than punitive reinforcement when they do not. As a result, children of authoritative parents do well in school, develop good social skills, and avoid problem behaviors.

You can extract principles for self-parenting from these examples of good parenting. The first is to recognize that a problem exists and there is a need for self-care. Next is to establish a flexible attitude and a safe zone for the mind to explore its environment. This flexibility becomes of the highest priority. Louis and Zelie Martin showered their children with unconditional love. Such openness allows the child's mind to be itself, to make mistakes, to have different thoughts, and to do so in a nonjudgmental, loving, compassionate, and empathetic context. Unconditional love nourishes while protecting. It helps create a safety zone in which the mind expresses its out-of-the-box deliberations, carries out novel experimentation, and learns about life without the fear of negative repercussions.

The mind, like children, needs to learn self-control, and parents promote this by boosting self-esteem through praising and not belittling. The mind craves attention and if not given, will act out. Hence, you must spend time with it, as strange as that sounds. There is a need to be sensitive and pay attention to its needs. This attentiveness can take place during quiet moments of relaxation or meditation. It occurs while talking with your mind, like an adult talking to a child, or sitting and doing nothing while watching a sunset or listening to music. Setting boundaries with standards and goals within a safe zone is equally important. This way, the mind learns what is right and wrong. Not setting expectations and boundaries exacerbates spoiled mind syndrome and creates a mind incapable of controlling its impulses.

Self-Parenting: Setting Boundaries

A good psychological boundary for the mind is the mental space between your thoughts and those of others; a clear delineation where your mind begins and the other person's ends. The purpose of setting boundaries is for psychological protection, making better decisions, and establishing identity.

- *Establish values by determining what is important: for example, deciding to tell the truth is something you want to do, so establish that as a goal.*
- *Understand how to set boundaries. Tell yourself the importance of being truthful by deciding that being honest is more reflective of the real you and your desire to experience that aspect of your personality.*
- *Make expectations clear: tell yourself that you expect to be as truthful under all circumstances.*
- *Determine the consequences: if you catch yourself not meeting expectations, say "no" or "stop," without the need to explain. But, if commanding the mind fails, try to understand why the failure occurred; make note of such reactions and try not to repeat them. Try not to respond angrily to failures; instead, imagine a loving kindness engulfing your mind.*

While it might be easier to develop accountability and responsibility for actual children who defy expectations and exceed boundaries, the best corrective measures are not always physical. Instead, they are more psychological and, hence, applicable to an unruly mind. Setting boundaries includes redirecting the behavioral pattern of a mind by teaching it to understand that if a behavior is wrong in one context, it is wrong in others. Boundary setting requires removing privileges by taking away rewards when the mind misbehaves. Other measures involve time-in and time-out periods. During these times, you ask your mind about a difficult emotional time, and to express its feelings until it cools or calms down. Or, tell your mind to sit facing a metaphorical wall, alone, for a determined number of minutes. As the parent, you need to be clear and consistent with these consequences. Similar to training children, empty threats will only help to maintain the mind's irreverent and destructive behavior.

Communicating with your mind through self-talk seems redundant, at first. Yet self-talk is most important in considering how to self-parent. Self-talk is the internal dialog that is both negative and positive and distresses or validates the mind's uniqueness, allowing it to work through emotional and cognitive issues on its own. True self-talk reflects love and compassion. Mature and loving self-talk becomes a model for the mind's own relationship with others. Both the conscious mind, as reflected by the interpreter, and the nonconscious mind, as reflected by your intuition, are important in self-talk. They reflect the thoughts, beliefs, questions, and ideas of your true self.

Self-parenting the mind means treating the mind uniquely in moments of crisis or rebellion. Modeling healthy ways to get through these periods, including showing respect, friendliness, honesty, kindness, tolerance, and unselfish behavior, is important. You must not understate the importance of your parental self in modeling healthy behaviors. Likewise, trust comes from treating the mind with dignity and respect and including it in decisions. Again, this behavior may sound strange, but for self-parenting to be effective, you need to approach your mind like a child you are teaching to behave appropriately. Love and care of the mind must not extend to rescuing or overprotection because, similar to children, the mind learns by experiencing the consequences of its actions.

Successful self-parenting of the mind involves creating a culture to promote healthy living. This intention means establishing consistent rituals, routines, goals, rules, and expectations. Habits provide stability and are necessary for establishing good values. The goal is for the mind to be productive, responsible, and independent. It should enjoy a meaningful relationship with others, be caring and compassionate, and have a happy, healthy, and fulfilling attitude. Successful self-parenting provides the AFRAID mind a positive sense of self and the ability to cope with stressful situations. This attitude engenders self-control, and doing so will temper emotional arousal, overcome fears, and accept disappointments and frustrations.

Self-Parenting: Self-Talk

Inner dialog can be negative, positive, or neutral. At the start, the goal is to reduce negative self-talk. The eventual goal is to eliminate self-talk altogether and only allow functional self-talk, which is mood neutral. Functional self-talk refers to an inner dialog that helps resolve daily life problems.

Pay attention to any recurring messages that occur. What does your self-talk concern most of the time? Is this self-talk positive or negative? Does it focus on a specific element of your life?

Try the following exercise, first as a writing exercise and then as a mental one.

Use the triple column technique developed by psychiatrist David Burns:

- *Make or imagine three columns and label the columns: "Automatic Thoughts," "Cognitive Distortion," and "Rational Response."*
- *In the first column under "Automatic Thoughts," jot down the negative thought from your inner dialog. For example: "My girlfriend dislikes me. She will break up with me."*
- *In the second column, pick the "cognitive distortion" category into which your negative thought best fits. If the thought fits into multiple categories, then write them all. You will need to become familiar with cognitive distortions. These include: all-or-nothing thinking, overgeneralization, mental filter, disqualifying the positive, jumping to conclusions, magnification or minimization, emotional reasoning, "should" statements, labeling or mislabeling, and personalization. The above girlfriend example fits best into the "jumping to conclusions" category, which you would write in the second column.*
- *In the third column, develop a more reasoned response by making the description more rational and positive. For example, you might say, "What I did last night was wrong. My girlfriend is right about being angry. I will apologize and try to make up for my awful behavior."*

Feeding Curiosity and Wanderlust

Misbehaving and undisciplined children produce angry parents. In the same way, you can fall prey to anger and resentment when your mind acts up. Studies show that failure to discipline children often results in unhappy, angry, and restive kids. Similar consequences occur when the uncontrolled mind is undisciplined. The results are unhappy, angry, and fidgety thoughts. The key is how to carry out this disciplining. Many approaches have attempted to deal with the problem by assuming that you must discipline the mind to keep it from wandering and acting up. Suppression of this behavior, however, is a mistake, since curiosity and wandering are inherent and necessary aspects of the mind.

The AAECC impulse, which is the mind's essential energetic curiosity, forms the foundation for creative living. Severe discipline can affect and scar this impulse and blunt curiosity and wonderment. It is, therefore, important to recognize that the core problem is not the wandering mind, but more what the mind attaches to, which provokes a perseverative and obsessive AFRAID mindset. Comparable to a child, pushing the mind away or punishing it into submission is not appropriate. You need to live in harmony with it and understand its function. You must channel the mind's energy along more positive lines. Anger is not an effective long-term method to accomplish this, although such a strategy might work in the short term. Rather, love and kindness serve better in the long-term. This compassionate approach is a core principle of successful self-parenting.[5]

Key Takeaways

- Comparable to a spoiled child, the uncontrolled mind involves chaotic leaps of attention; it is rude; does not respond to questions and ignores instructions; does not share and instead is domineering and demanding. It will figuratively throw a tantrum of crying, howling, and fist pounding the floor when it does not get its wishes.
- Self-parenting can help calm this mind, redirect its energy into more useful behaviors, and bring back what it was at the beginning. By doing so, it can successfully help the mind:
  - Create a culture to promote healthy living by establishing consistent rituals, routines, goals, rules, and expectations.
  - Create an environment of love, protection, nourishment, acceptance, and support.
  - Set expectations that are flexible, with clear rules and boundaries, while explaining the logic and reasoning behind the rules.
  - Nourish a social life, encourage friendships, look after physical health, and when life becomes overwhelming, seek help.

- ○ Provide positive reinforcement when misbehavior occurs.
- ○ Promote motivational factors that maintain engagement with the practice.
- ○ Recognize and accept limitations.
- ○ Be vigilant to prevent a return or buildup of ego-based thinking.
- Severe discipline and suppression of behavior can affect the curiosity and wandering that are inherent and necessary aspects of a healthy mind. A compassionate approach is a better way of conducting self-parenting.

Next chapter: What is the path of present-moment centering?

6

Transcending the Problem

*The struggle with resistance, expressed as fear,
is part of the creative process.*

Living the Present Moment

Stephanie's life settled quickly into the normal rhythms of life, work, and relationships. It was her old life, but with a difference following her breakthrough and realization. Her past, while precious, and her future, while necessary, no longer created unwelcomed interruptions and unnecessary distractions to this life flow. Her awareness of the moment made her more consciously aware and intentional about when and whether to reminisce and recall or expect and plan for the future. This ability to be in the present moment grew stronger with her mindfulness practice and felt like a wonderful, precious, and joyful gift. Stephanie's mental and physical wellness improved considerably. She felt more energy to be active, to explore, and to indulge her curiosity about matters besides architecture. Her stress levels were manageable. She no longer worried, or needed medication to lower her blood pressure or boost her immune system. Stephanie could not recall the last time she had experienced a cold or a headache. Everyone around her seemed to comment on her smile and bright face, and everyone, it seemed, wanted her at their parties. Her mom had always told her she was special, but that feeling had been missing for a long time. Now, she was feeling a special connection to others, nature, and something deeper. She did not want to get ahead of herself and tried to maintain a humble attitude, being kind to others, helping those who needed help. An overwhelming sense of gratitude followed her everywhere.

Self-parenting of the mind is a methodical, slow, yet effective way of transforming the AFRAID mind and learning to love what grows out of that discipline. From your own parenting experience, either with children or as a child yourself, you know it works when done well. Yet the twelfth century proverb "You can lead a horse to water, but you can't make it drink" summarizes a key problem. The implication is that while you can provide an AFRAID mind with a loving and nurturing environment, it may not be enough to eliminate the impulse. The uncontrolled mind returns. In fact, the key problem is that *it is impossible for the rational mind to fix the problem from which it suffers.* Self-parenting the mind helps but is not a complete solution given the stubbornness of a chaotic and unruly mind, its incessant chattering, and AFRAID impulse. What it does, though, is create the opportunity for true transformation to occur. I and many others know that a questioning mind, grounded in the stillness of meditation, can transform the heart and mind.

Training and Mastering the Mind

Previous sections have clarified that the extraordinary Original Mind reflects the uncontrolled mind's freedom from fear. When that occurs, it engenders a natural creativity in which the mind explores its environment and handles enormous amounts of information in a joyful and creative way. Yet we know that something happens during development to blunt this curious and creative energy. One factor is that multiple glitches, snags, and malfunctions occur to move the mind away from the present moment toward avoidance and a life focused on the past and future. Slipping out of its natural element of functioning in the present moment changes the mind's motivating drive from curiosity and creativity to fear and anxiety. The long-term and definitive solution to this requires eliminating expectations about being present-moment centered and the efficacy of the approach. Changing expectations cannot occur through conceptual thinking or rational deliberation. Having a sense of what approach works can motivate your actions toward using it.

Present-moment centering is not a novel idea, although there are now science-based explanations for why it works.[1] The approach suggested in this book involves the use of mindfulness, which is bringing one's attention to the immediacy of the moment, whether it involves thoughts of the past, contemplation of the future, or the immediate sensory experience. It is holding these thoughts in awareness nonjudgmentally. There are, of course, many other methods and approaches that could be just as effective, including talk therapy, such as Cognitive-Behavioral Therapy. The key is changing the expectations concerning the mind's rumination by focusing on the awareness of present circumstances.

Mindfulness, when done correctly, stops anxious, unmanageable thoughts in their tracks. The effect is immediate and, with practice, long lasting. That turning point, a long-lasting experience of the present moment, marks the return of Original Mind. Controlling mental chaos restores the mind with which you were born, whose actions are free from ego-based rumination. This mind never left, but the shenanigans of the uncontrolled mind and its ego-based ruminations obscured it.

Like joining a gym and doing exercises to train and master your body, mindfulness is an approach to train and master the mind. With this as the foundation, you build greater control reflected in the choices available to you. There are many mindfulness techniques requiring unique skills, making it difficult to know which approach is best. Concentration, for example, involves focusing on a single event, either the breath, repeating a single word or mantra, or listening to a repetitive gong. In this approach, you focus and refocus awareness on the chosen object of attention, each time noticing the scattered mind. Through constant repetition of focusing and refocusing attention, the ability to concentrate improves.

Mindfulness differs from the concentration approach in that instead of redirecting attention away from the scattered thoughts and bringing the mind to a single focus, it encourages attention and observation of thoughts as they drift through the mind. This openness

encourages observation o/
volved with the thoughts
mental dustup that arises
tion you must implemen⸱
ness develop, and the ene
ally stops. The key to this
the natural flow of thou⸱
particular.

The specific mindfu
Monkey Mind, or SMN
ma, SMM emphasizes
also means having the co
are confronting. With this understanding in your background, ⸱
teaches you to anchor to the present while being attentive to the flow
of sensory experience. Another term for this situational awareness is
what Gerald Edelman, the Nobel Prize–winning physiologist, called
the "remembered present."[2] As he described it, it is reflecting the fact
that all your experience is engaged in forming your integrated awareness of this single moment. I would change that slightly and also call it
"remembering presence."

I base SMM on the understanding that you always have a choice
about this integrated awareness—your thoughts—and the approach
teaches you to take control over unwelcomed thoughts by confidently
directing them to slow down and stop. You do this verbally first, later
by reflecting on the command, and much later by dropping the command altogether and simply experiencing the *intention* to stop. SMM
is something to practice anywhere and anytime. You need not set aside
time in a quiet place, although isolation and quietness may help at first
to learn the mechanics and basics of doing it. The critical aspect is to
practice, practice, practice. I have sprinkled the following SMM exercises throughout the book, some of which you have already encountered, to help guide your practice:

- Practice Awareness of No-Thought (*Chapter 3*).
- Practice Your ABCs (*Chapter 3*).
- Fading Thoughts (*Chapter 5*).

- A Real-World Example (*Chapter 6*).
- Write Upsetting Thoughts (*Chapter 6*).
- Kim's Game: Increase Your Observational Skills (*Chapter 7*).
- Notice Recurring Thoughts (*Chapter 10*).
- Direct Monkey Mind to "STOP" (*Chapter 10*).

Mindfulness and Creative Living

Science has convincingly shown the benefits of practicing mindfulness. One study conducted to compare concentration with mindfulness approaches determined the best style for stimulating creativity. Lorenza Colzato, a Dutch cognitive psychologist, conducted the studies in 2012 and 2013.[3] She and her collaborators examined a group of novice meditators while they practiced concentration or mindfulness. After each session, subjects underwent tests to determine their ability to perform a range of cognitive skills. The results showed that mindfulness was more effective in stimulating divergent thinking. Divergent thinking is flexible, iterative, and web-like, focusing on the connections between ideas and more associated with fluid intelligence. In contrast, they found concentration to be related to convergent thinking—a more linear, targeted, and systematic approach, narrowing down multiple ideas into a single solution. Researchers associate concentration with crystallized intelligence, the use of knowledge gained through learning and experience. Since both fluid and crystallized intelligence are necessary for creativity, then both types of approaches provided benefits. The difference centered on the strategy of creativity each of these methods emphasized, either divergent or convergent thinking. I explore these ideas more fully in later chapters.

Stop Monkey Mind: A Real-World Example

It might seem difficult to control thoughts when the uncontrolled mind has a grip and is acting obsessively. But the experience of many who have practiced mindfulness has shown that with time, you reach a point of being able to direct this mind to slow down and even stop. With practice, you don't even need the command. The wish becomes the direction, as if by magic.

One way to get started is to use the principles of self-parenting to condition the mind. Then, do SMM exercises in a calm, loving, and nonjudgmental way to get the best long-term results.

Example: *You worry about the presentation your supervisor has asked you to give during the weekly meeting. You have worked on it, polished it, and know the presentation backwards and forwards. Everything seems ready. But then the thought starts, the one that always comes to you during these presentations, the one about which you cannot stop worrying.*

You imagine that someone will ask a question for which you will not know the answer. You will look foolish and feel like a deer in headlights. What do you do?

Be present, center your mind, and label the thought by saying, "Here I go with the deer in headlights thought." Then say authoritatively, "Stop." The thought will stop momentarily, but might return quickly. Repeat the command and do it a few times. Do not obsess if the thought persists. To make the mind obey will take practice. Remember that a stubborn child will learn with loving but forceful repetition.

To learn to meditate mindfully requires specific skills. One of those skills is the ability to observe internal phenomena, including bodily sensations, thoughts, and emotions. Likewise, the observation of external stimuli is important, including sights, sounds, and smells. Improving these observational skills is a major benefit of practicing mindfulness. This type of technique involves engaging in activities with undivided attention; being able to describe phenomena without analyzing conceptually; and being nonjudgmental about experiencing the present moment.

Matthijs Baas, a Dutch psychologist, expanded on Colzato's study a few years later, and explored which skills were most relevant to the creative process.[4] A major finding of his work was that observational skills, such as improved observation, are the only reliable predictors of creativity. Improved observation promotes working memory, increases cognitive flexibility, and reduces cognitive rigidity. These critical skills are all relevant to the creative process.

Baas's findings show that mindfulness skills, including description and accepting without judgment, were unrelated to creativity. Acting with focused awareness, a skill enhanced by concentration-style approaches, actually had a negative impact on cognitive processes related to creativity. Overall, the results suggested to Baas that "A state of conscious awareness resulting from living in-the-moment is not sufficient for creativity to come about. To be creative, you need to have or train in the ability to observe, notice, and attend to phenomena that pass your mind's eye." It is the difference between passively and actively attending. Consistent mindfulness practice and prior experience are the benefits of doing Stop Monkey Mind training anytime and in any place. The benefits of this active attention training accumulate and, at a critical junction, the more positive AAECC mind bursts through the negative AFRAID mind.

Stop Monkey Mind: Write Upsetting Thoughts

The simple act of writing stressful thoughts, from the least stressful to the most stressful, helps in several ways:

- *Strengthens acceptance so that doing SMM becomes easier.*
- *Consistent practice helps to shape feelings.*
- *Reduces the emotional rawness of the feeling.*
- *Makes the feeling more malleable so you can work with it.*
- *Strengthens agency and control.*
- *May allow you to conceive of the situation in a unique light.*

Realization

Many scholars of the mind describe individuals as having an original sense of wholeness, called the self. Out of this original unity, a separate ego crystallizes during development. While this individuation and ego-self differentiation is a normal aspect of development, the schism between what is real and what is not creates problems when not understood properly. Realization refers to a psychological resolution or understanding of this ego-self differentiation that produces an integration of these aspects of personality. From other perspectives, such as a spiritual viewpoint, realization means understanding your true nature, the unity of life, and your role in this greater sense of connection. Whether psychological or spiritual, the understanding means realizing that ego and self are two sides of the same coin. With this comes trust in the interdependency of these systems, and confidence that you can orient them toward avoiding harm. Helping others then comes naturally.

In many Eastern approaches, the best way to achieve realization is through meditation. Aside from concentration and mindfulness approaches, there are other methods, including moving techniques, like tai chi, qigong, and walking contemplation. Interestingly, in the West, these approaches have gained a secular, health-promoting purpose. This focus on health is understandable, since relaxation and improvements in brain and immune function often result from their practice.[5] The most important outcome of a mindfulness practice is an awakening experience in which you realize at a deep level that thoughts, namely self-centered ones, are not the basis of what is real and of who you are. When these self-centered thoughts fade, something else fills the mind. The benefits of awakening or realization include regaining and maintaining a focused, curious, vigilant, and inquisitive mind, an AAECC-driven mind. This mindset carries over to an attitude of speech and actions that spring from an external orientation to helping others. The kindness and compassion are nonjudgmental, accepting, trusting, and patient. Finally, and most relevant to this realization, is the undoing of AFRAID thinking and rediscovering of Original Mind.

An important claim is that transforming the uncontrolled mind means its negative energy lessens while becoming more positive, original, controlled, free from fear, and creative.[6] Through mindfulness, you can bring this change about by altering the expectations you have, based on experience in rational deliberation. Of greater importance is that this change allows for the transition to occur quickly. Like the Dutch psychologist Matthijs Baas concluded, being creative requires training in the ability to observe, notice, and attend to phenomena. Observing, noticing, and attending mean not getting caught up, avoiding the stickiness of thoughts in the drama of the events. This awareness helps to relieve the sting of emotions associated with the experience. When that happens, the chaotic mind switches to optimal functioning. In the present moment, and in this mindset, AFRAID rumination evaporates and what remains is the AAECC impulse, an integral aspect of Original Mind. The mind finds its natural home, where it sustains attention to the innumerable things that call upon it; and where you notice commonalities and new associations much more readily. The process is no longer passive but an active, creative activity.

While present-moment centering can occur quickly and place you in an optimal state of mind, it is necessary to understand the context to gain greater benefit. There is the need to trust the process. It is through trust that the intelligence of the body and mind begins more clearly to guide development.

Key Takeaways

- Slipping out of the present moment can change the mind's motivating drive from curiosity and creativity to fear and anxiety. It is sometimes difficult for the rational mind to fix the problem and return to functioning in the present moment.
- Mindfulness, an approach to train and master the mind, stops anxious, unmanageable thoughts in their tracks and returns you to the present moment.
- Mindfulness encourages you to attend and observe thoughts as they drift through the mind without attaching to any, while encouraging observation of the scattered mind without getting involved with thinking and the emotions it stirs. With practice, an inner balance and calmness develop, and the energetic, uncontrolled mind slows down and eventually stops.
- Mindfulness stimulates divergent thinking, flexible, iterative, and web-like thinking, focusing on the connections between ideas. This promotes creativity.

Next chapter: What are the specifics of the **RUBI** *solution?*

PART II

The RUBI Program

7

Recognizing the Biggest Obstacle

Ask, what is it you're resisting?

Recognizing the Problem

During her dark night of the soul, Stephanie believed her shyness, insecurity, low self-esteem, fear of failing, lack of a social network offering support, and lack of trust in others caused her problems. It was a litany of weaknesses she knew well by heart, as her inner critic constantly reminded her. It came as a significant surprise when Stephanie made the connection that perhaps the problem lay not in her own weak self, but in the storyteller's truthfulness. Questioning that assumption led her to realize that most of the problems she faced had that inner voice as the single source. Why should she believe it? Stephanie tried telling herself more positive stories, but the energy of that original voice kept coming back and overwhelming her. Then, Stephanie re-alized that her inner critic seemed rather like a wounded child, immature, and fixated on events that happened to her as a teenager. It was then she understood that this inner narration represented a real aspect of her life, and rather than trying to cover it up, she accepted it lovingly. It was the begin-ning of healing her ego-self separation.

The second half of this book describes in greater detail the four stages necessary for a deeper dive into the transformation from uncontrolled, chaotic mind to Original Mind, the one free from fear and innately creative. These stages involve (a) **R**ecognizing the problem; (b) **U**nderstanding the solution; (c) finding **B**alance; and (d) **I**mplementing answers. I describe each of these four specific steps in individual chapters that will take you through systematically from beginning to end: Chapter 7: Recognizing the biggest obstacle; Chapter 8: Understanding why we have experiences; Chapter 9: Balancing the varieties of thoughts in a restless mind; and Chapter 10: Implementing the solutions.

The Root of the Ego-Self Separation

Recognizing the problem of an uncontrolled mind means first acknowledging there is a problem. And the fundamental issue is the apparent separation between ego and true self. This was the major lesson I learned on my journey of discovery. I was responding to life with a distorted sense of self. And this made me volatile, irresponsible, uncaring, and depressed. Yet, slowly, I noticed another perspective that seemed more genuine, calm, and caring. Once I began identifying with this truer self, I knew I was on the way to recovery and to a more genuine and joyful life.

Any solution to the uncontrolled mind conundrum begins by undoing this fabricated separation. Many consider this an illusion in the sense that circumstances have hypnotized the mind to believe it is true. The illusion begins when something goes awry, creating glitches, errors, or unpredictable events that trigger engagement of the interpreter and conscious awareness. These are aspects of normal error-correcting brain function, especially if the error gets corrected and you continue normal functioning. However, prolonging the glitches (recall the GPS example in Chapter 2 and the feeble attempts to outsmart it) and especially when the corrective mechanisms are ineffective, normal functioning suffers. Inability to deal effectively with glitches increases stress, anxiety, and the ability to respond well to circumstances. The normal, rational behavior of the interpreter becomes obsessive and problematic, producing a range of abnormal responses. These range from mild to severe, perhaps even irrational, which is the point at which the interpreter transforms into the chaotic, monkey mind. As these problems become more unmanageable, they foster severe psychopathology and a full-blown, pathological mind.

Individuals are apt to exhibit mental dysfunction and psychopathology regardless of their genetics and environment. In the nature versus nurture controversy, it is the *interaction* between the two that is critical. In ancient civilizations like Egypt, China, and Greece, as well as in parts of the modern world, like Haiti, people attribute mind struggles to the actions of "spirits" and "demonic possession." Possession is a convenient way to explain symptoms that accompany intense trauma given a lack of scientific understanding. Nowadays, demonic possession has given way to more scientific explanations. "If only I could shut my mind off" is something you may exclaim when work and personal circumstances overwhelm your capacity to handle problems and preoccupations. The obsessive worrying and rumination of the left-brain interpreter makes shutting off the mind more difficult, preventing you from dealing with issues in a calm, clear, and rational way.

The interpreter is a wonderful adaptation that evolved to explain causality in the world, how circumstances give rise to feelings and thoughts. The existence of the interpreter has led most of us to understand and explain the world to great advantage. But when there are no solid facts; or facts are at a premium; or you have little time to decide, while stress is building, there are potential misinterpretations. Misinterpretations throw a "monkey" wrench into the smooth functioning of the brain, and responses become maladaptive. These maladaptive behaviors are indicators of a problematic mind.

The survival of personality, of your sense of self, even when ego defenses and protection mechanisms get overwhelmed and out of control, is key. Imagine living when a pandemic has caused everyone to shelter in place. There is fear all around; you lose your job; the rent is due and you cannot pay it; the children have to eat and food is scarce; and you see no help and no way out. Anxiety and panic grip and paralyze you. Yet, in the middle of all this turmoil, you acknowledge that without an out-of-control mind, circumstances would be different ("If only I could shut off my mind").

Most of us have experienced those moments when the mind seems lost. And yet, somewhere deep in the background of the fears and anxieties, the expression "If only I could shut off this whirlwind of a mind" reflects another aspect of the same mind. This other mind, which many have called the *observer mind*, sees things in a different, calmer way. Its ability to recognize anxieties suggests there are centers of mind that remain serene and experience things for what they are and not what you have imagined. This ability to dissociate from the problems and anxieties suggests this other aspect of yourself remains outside the mental storm, waiting for it to subside. When this idea finally became concrete for me, and I could identify with this calmer presence, I knew the solution to my uncontrolled mind problem was near.

Stop Monkey Mind: Kim's Game— Increase Your Observational Skills

This exercise increases your ability to observe, pay attention, remember objects, events, or people. The name comes from Rudyard Kipling's 1901 novel Kim, *in which the hero plays a similar game during his training as a spy. A variation of Kim's game is to walk into a room (at home, school, work, or mall), observe what is there for a minute, and then walk out. Recollect as many things as you can.*

Have a friend place several objects on a table (start with six; then move to twelve, twenty-four, or more). Study them for one minute and then cover them. Recollect as many of the objects as you can.

Insight into the Illusion

If you experience the continuous existence of a calm mind in the middle of repeated mental storms, does it not suggest that your mind storms, like actual storms, are temporary and self-created? Indeed, after my many years of practicing mindfulness meditation, I am convinced that emotional storms are experiences we create and, therefore, can choose not to elaborate and make real. This level of control does not mean you become numb to life. In fact, the opposite is true. I became more emotionally sensitive, although not wildly reactive. To understand this conceptually, it may help to take a simplified view of personality and understand the dynamics of the mind in relation to the proposed components of our personality.

The idea of a nonconscious aspect of being had its origin with Galen (ca. A.D. 130–200), a Greek physician and founder of experimental physiology who recognized that one makes nonconscious inferences from perceptions. At the start of the twentieth century, Sigmund Freud (1856–1939), an Austrian neurologist considered the father of psychoanalysis, saw the nonconscious—or unconscious, as he called it—as more negative than positive. Freud's popularized ideas became key contributions to the field of psychology.[1] For Freud, the nonconscious is the product of one's personal experience. He suggested we fill this psychological space with unacceptable or unpleasant content, including feelings of pain, anxiety, and especially sexual conflict, describing personality as the interaction between competing drives, such as the ego, id, and superego.

Not everyone agreed with Freud's perspective. Carl Jung (1875–1961), for example, a young contemporary of Freud's, promoted a more positive view of personality dynamics.[2] Jung, a Swiss psychiatrist and psychoanalyst, founded the analytical psychology movement. He came to Freud's attention early in his own career, and the two carried on a lengthy correspondence on a joint vision of human psychology. Freud saw the younger Jung in the role of someone who could promote his new science of psychoanalysis, and eventually considered him as his adopted eldest son, his crown prince, and successor. Yet disagreements cropped up, namely about Freud's emphasis on sexuality and the role of the libido. Jung deemphasized sexual development and criticized Freud's theory of the Oedipus complex. All these disagreements developed into an unbreachable schism.

Unlike Freud, Jung thought of the nonconscious as the product of both personal and collective experiences, which he called the "collective unconscious."[3] In the collective unconscious, Jung conceptualized the accumulation of knowledge available to individuals because of their familial experience, and something passed on in their genes. Jung described two systems of mind. The first, associated with nonconscious processing, relies on perception, intuition, and emotion, and is governed by habit. The second, associated with conscious processing, is a guided, controlled approach that is effortful and involves reasoning.

Jung also advanced a more elaborate view of the ego, as that aspect of personality that occupies the *center of consciousness*. He envisioned the self as the *center of our personality*. From birth, he argued, there is a sense of wholeness in the self. Then, the ego crystallizes and separates out of this original unity in a process of differentiation, or individuation. Individuation is something we undergo to become individualized entities and successfully meet the onslaught of challenges that life provides. In most cases, individuation leads to the creation of a protective shell identified with the ego that evolves from the set of mechanisms that shield the openness and sensitivity of the developing mind.

This developing shell, which I call the *virtual me*, is the constellation of thoughts, expectations, and perspectives that coalesce and harden out of the rational, emotional, and action-based responses to the earliest and ongoing concerns we face following birth. Many of those concerns involve our safety. As this virtual me grows in its protective strength and hardens into our ego, it overshadows and obscures the true self. In modern parlance, it is as if we create an avatar of ourselves to deal with the world, while our actual personality hides behind it in fear. For this reason, philosophies, therapies, and metaphysical paths have targeted this illusory or virtual creation and the undoing of it as the answer to the singular psychological basis for human suffering—including the uncontrolled mind. When the solutions succeed, they allow an understanding of the true nature of our ego-self relationship, making possible the rediscovery and recovery of Original Mind.

Psychologist Mihaly Csikszentmihalyi describes what occurs when life encounters Original Mind, an experience he associates with a concept called "Flow."[4] Csikszentmihalyi concludes that this "optimal state of consciousness where we feel our best and perform our best" correlates with outstanding creativity and performance. He also found that people find genuine satisfaction during this state of consciousness. Flow absorbs an individual in an activity involving creative skills. In this state, individuals are "strong, alert, in effortless control, unselfconscious, and at the peak of their abilities."[5]

Some psychologists argue it is impossible to experience flow when other distractions disrupt the experience, and therefore suggest one must stay away from distractions in this modern, fast-paced life.

There is some truth to that advice, but is it really possible to stay away from distractions? My experience suggests once you have seen through and set aside ego-based rumination and the virtual me, what remains is Original Mind and the free flow of thought *is* the natural state. There are no distractions, as they become "grist for the mill," meaning that this new mind considers everything it experiences as the basis for new learning. The discovery is permanent, with no going back, and flow occurs whether alone on a mountain top or in the middle of Times Square.

A wisp of ego-based rumination may survive and continue to interfere for some time, although never to the extent it did before. Continued practice will extinguish even that. The effort to get to this point consists not of trying to gain creativity and flow, since those are default, inner states. Rather, what we need is to see through the fictitious ego-based rumination and virtual me creation and begin identifying with the real you. The effort is nothing less than a change in perception—the easiest and hardest thing you can do—but it will create a lifelong creative mindset.

Questions to Ponder

Do you have a problem that is driving you to irrational behavior? Identify and write it in your journal. Why can you not resolve it? What are the barriers? And how would its resolution affect you? Write anything related to the problem, barriers, and its resolution that comes to mind.

The Price of a Civilized Society

Understanding the ego-self differentiation at the individual level, as described above, is insufficient by itself since it must be seen within the context of the culture and society in which you live. Western culture, beginning in the Middle Ages and especially during the Renaissance, has emphasized rationality and thinking as the most important aspects of life. The emphasis on humanism, the Scientific Revolution, and the Enlightenment occurred as a reaction to religious dogmatism of previous centuries. Three centuries after Rene Descartes, the seventeenth-century French philosopher, mathematician, and scientist who said, "I think, therefore I am," the importance of rationality predominates over our life.

This bias toward rational and conscious thinking overshadows other modes, namely intuition and nonconscious processing. The study of these alternative modes of thinking has been fraught with problems because of their historical association with mysticism, paranormal, the occult, and other ideas on the fringes of science. In modern times, questioning the existence and validity of instincts and intuition reflects an ingrained and healthy skepticism. Psychologists have learned the lesson, or at least seem more willing to concede that logic and rationality are not enough to overcome the irrational, error-correcting, and judgmental self. Ego-based conscious awareness is not enough to cede or even share control with the powerful, nonconscious mind.

In fits and starts, the supremacy of conscious awareness is being challenged. Recognition is growing that nonconscious activity, driven by the contingencies of the moment, is of similar, if not of greater importance, in how we respond to events and problems.[6] Scientists assume that nonconscious processing comprises a multitude of aspects of mind and brain activity. But it is unnecessary to consider them all because the troublesome, uncontrolled mind is a product of a specific subset—specifically, one that includes the interpreter and its rational and partially conscious attempts to understand and unify our response to the world.

"Who is John Galt?" This question is the intriguing beginning of the 1957 book called a libertarian rant or masterpiece, depending on your point of view. Ayn Rand, the author of *Atlas Shrugged*, described the theme of the book as the role of the mind in humanity's existence.[7] Rand contends that the mind is the root of all knowledge and values—and lack of mind is the root of all evil. In *Atlas Shrugged*, which is a one-sided view of life that nonetheless raises important questions, all the novel's heroes are thinkers, individuals who behave rationally, including John Galt, the dominant character. The villains are those who defy reason and evade facts, acting on feelings instead. Because of this, the villains accomplish nothing, for they are in constant conflict with reality. Thinking, according to the heroes, is the basic virtue life requires.

John Galt goes on strike and retreats to the Colorado mountains. He encourages others like him—intelligent, rich, very good-looking, and, above all, rational individuals—to do the same. When that happens, the civilized world goes into chaos and collapses.

Who, then, is John Galt? He is the hero who represents the epitome of modern civilization—its science, its medical research, its technological progress, and its application of intellect in service to humanity. Galt embodies the principle that only with the mind are individuals able to achieve prosperity on Earth. Although a fictional story, *Atlas Shrugged* is a story of the unique, overblown love affair and attachment humanity has to rational deliberation. It was what Rand perceived as the nature of the intellect. This fictional story summarizes the essence of Rene Descartes' philosophy from the seventeenth century that, at least in Western thought, conscious awareness is the supreme mode of knowing.

The intellect and its rational deliberation, personified by John Galt, do not, however, exist in isolation. They reflect a process of integration and differentiation that occurs when actually confronting problems. Thus, rational behavior falls out of the many interactions with the intellect occurring inside larger systems, like the environment, society, and culture.

Sigmund Freud discusses this more integrative and complex view in one of his most important and widely read books, *Civilization and Its Discontents*.[8] Written in 1930, this classic discussion of the topic preceded Rand's masterpiece by three decades. Freud's book explores the unhappiness that results from the clash between the desire for individuality and the expectations of society. On the one hand, individuals crave a desire for freedom. On the other, civilization has a need for conformity. That is the tension Freud explored. For him, the pleasure principle, rather than pure rationality, motivates the desire for freedom. And because individuals seek pleasure, they enjoy and seek freedom. But this search comes at the expense of the welfare of society. To protect itself, society turns to creating laws that restrict the freedom created by this basic pleasure impulse. Freud's sociocultural struggle recapitulates the psychological struggle that produces the uncontrolled mind, the need for the ego, and the search for an escape from this dynamic.

The social discontentment that Freud described arises out of the sense of helplessness and a longing for protection—a very primitive impulse. For Freud, these emotions and undercurrents represent the failed attempt to return to a psychological state that existed before ego separated from the larger self. Freud extended his argument of discontentment to experiences of dissolution, like when you fall in love and lose the boundary between your ego and your external love object. He further extended the argument to the religious experience, including how some might experience limitlessness and eternity. Discontentment in all these cases reflects the unfulfilled desire to return to a psychic sense of unity that existed before individuation.

We can reach this state of unity when the boundary between ego, the virtual me, and the real self no longer exists. From my personal experience, when my real self came to the foreground, I recognized the utility of the virtual me as a protective impulse and could then reconcile the two. This reconciliation is the larger context in which the relationship between ego-based AFRAID rumination and the real self's AAECC impulse occurs. Comparable to individuals and their culture, an interaction between ego and real self affects their equilibrium. For Freud, a discontented conscience is the price paid by an individual wishing to belong to a civilized society. Likewise, obscuring of Original Mind and the AAECC impulse is the price paid for runaway AFRAID rumination. The end of such discontentment is finding the original unity or balance.

Types of Awareness

Scientists recognize that various categories, groupings, and styles of thinking occur in two dominant modes: nonconscious and conscious awareness.[9] Nonconscious activity determines individual function. This process exists in every moment of life and is the basis for creative living. Imagine that a foreign friend who wants to visit five of the largest cities in the United States asks you for a list. You reply, "New York, Los Angeles, and Chicago. But I don't know the others. I'll get back to you." To give her the immediate reply, you had to access memories of cities you knew, and while you could guess at the others, you weren't sure and needed to check. But you have no awareness of how you derived that answer. Most of the work occurred through nonconscious activity, including accessing memories, realizing you had a partial answer, and arranging a verbal response. This nonconscious processing provided the results to conscious awareness to relay the response. But despite how much we have learned about the brain, we still do not know how you arrived at the answer: it is truly a mystery.

In the vast literature of conscious and nonconscious activity, the general sense is that most mental processing occurs below the level of awareness. The capabilities of nonconscious endeavors, whether because of parallel or other unknown forms of computation, are enormous.[10] Unlimited—or at least having many—resources means you can carry out multiple tasks in a fast, efficient manner. Autopiloting, the neural functions involved in mind wandering, daydreaming, and stimulus-independent and task-unrelated contemplation, is an example of this nonconscious efficiency. These activities underlie the bulk of mental processing and form a major portion of the functions associated with who you are, how you think, and how you respond.

Self-Parenting: Life Purpose Activity

This exercise is for you to do out loud (adapted from Adam Leipzig, 2013). Leipzig has suggested that to discover who you are and what you should do with your life, all you need is to answer a few questions in under five minutes:

- *Say your first name.*
- *What do you love to do? (Answer this question out loud in one word.)*
- *Who do you do this for? (Visualize them and then answer the question out loud.)*
- *What do these people want and need that you have?*
- *How will they change because of what you can give them?*

The outcome of this exercise gives you an intuitive sense of who you are and what your life's purpose is.

In contrast, conscious awareness appears to be a type of brief interruption or switch from the normal flow of nonconscious activity. Researchers associate conscious awareness with different levels, types, or states, including self-awareness, minimal awareness, perceptual, situational, introspective, observant, error correction, etc.[11] One way to simplify this complexity is to categorize the distinct types into two major categories: active and passive. Active awareness refers to actions taken in response to what is perceived. You step outside, observe that it is raining, and recognize the necessity of wearing a raincoat and retrieving your umbrella.

This active response to circumstances includes an error-correcting function. This morning, for example, you feel stressed about the job interview with the prestigious firm you have dreamed about. Your mind imagines numerable circumstances that could go wrong and diminish your chances of getting the job. The normal error-correcting function is to exercise choice and cut off this active barrage of conceptual thinking, calm the mind, and focus on all the preparation you have done and still need to do. Faulty error-correction is to continue the anxiety-provoking mind storm. Another example of error-correction is trying to overcome your implicit biases since your goal is to be a better person, or at least return to the better person you thought you were. The role of active awareness is to respond flexibly when the automatic actions of nonconscious activity require correction, such as turning down the judgmental thoughts concerning your black colleagues. In this way, active awareness helps to smooth things out, dealing with mistakes, disturbances, or glitches in your perceptual experience.

In contrast to active awareness, passive awareness has a more observant, aesthetic, and unmediated quality to it. This awareness observes and enjoys a beautiful sunset or a moving musical performance. In true passive awareness, no action exists beyond the perception. J. F. Martel, a Canadian author, screenwriter, film, and TV director, captured the difference between passive and active consciousness well. He observed that "sensations are the immediate data of consciousness. Before the intellect reorganizes it according to general ideas, reality is a sensuous affair through and through. That's why it isn't wrong to speak of an esthetic experience as unmediated. There is always a moment before the intellect does its thing, during which reality reveals itself to us directly. Something exists before we name it, before we attribute a function to it, before we subordinate it to our ideas, beliefs, and judgments—before 'we' come into play at all as rational subjects. This is what I call the Real. It isn't generic reality but the raw Real that comes to us in works of art."[12] However, when we attach labels to this "raw Real," such as "what a beautiful sunset!" or "that's a wonderful painting!" we move into active awareness.

Both active and passive awareness are systems that connect future-based plans with memories that reflect the past. Hence, the pleasure of a beautiful sunset occurs because of the associated emotions of watching a sunset with a loved one, and the pleasant memories of previous sunsets. It is a reasonable conclusion that conscious processing engages the interpreter. The rational assessment this interpreter makes of the situation, of the contingencies of the moment, is more limited in resources, slow, and susceptible to dysfunction. Switching back and forth from the unlimited capabilities of nonconscious activity to limited conscious awareness is the norm, but this switching process has received very little study in terms of when, how, and why it happens.

Only recently have scientists identified brain areas that play a role in this transfer function. For the first time, researchers have been able to switch off consciousness temporarily by electrically stimulating an area buried deep in the folding cortex. In 2015, a group of researchers at The George Washington University found that stimulation of the left claustrum and the anterior insula (see Figure 7.1) produced a loss of consciousness in a patient.[13] Prior to this work, scientists were unsure about the function of the claustrum since previous work had suggested a role in top-down cognitive control of action. Along with the anterior insula, findings implicated the claustrum in detecting salient changes in the external environment as part of the Salience Network. This network is a collection of regions of the brain that select which stimuli are deserving of our attention. It appears relevant for monitoring both the internal and external streams of consciousness and for highlighting sensations to attend to or ignore.

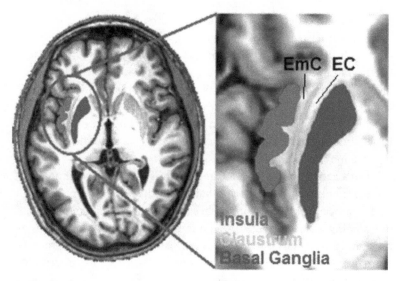

Figure 7.1 The claustrum and insula. *Source:* Bajada, Claude J., Ralph, Matthew A. L., and Cloutman, Lauren L. (2015).

While the George Washington University observations are pre-liminary, they show that the claustrum and anterior insula receive a variety of inputs from other cortical areas. They integrate those sources of brain activity into a cohesive whole. Thus, activity in these regions may indeed be critical for the control of switching from nonconscious to conscious processing and back.

The Bug in the Code

Error correction is thus a normal aspect of active awareness, but the uncontrolled mind shows up when it gets stuck in this mode. This is the bug in the code. It is the mind's version of saying, "If the only tool is a hammer, then every problem looks like a nail"—meaning that if your only tool in your toolbox is this error-correcting function because the mind is stuck in this mode, then every situation looks like a problem that needs correction. Consider, however, what life might be like if you did not perceive everything in terms of problems or errors needing correction—if you weren't stuck in this mode. In that state of mind, you could see the disagreement with your boss as an opportunity to show her how much you care about the company. Or you could view the paper due in class as a chance to learn something new and not as a burden. Imagine the psychological relief this attitude could bring, and how much more smoothly and productively your life might run.

As a group, creative individuals perceive problems as opportunities rather than as burdens. Glitches and unexpected events become opportunities to learn, grow, improve, or change in ways that leave them better off than before these problems occurred. In reality, this change in perspective alters nothing other than how you interpret the information you are processing. It is a choice. This means that the bug in the code occurs in the way we use our mind and, therefore, is imminently correctable. It's a matter of interpretation. Sometimes, unexpectedly, new interpretations come as an intuition or dream. I view intuition in these cases as gaining access to the creative solutions or increased mental flexibility, however briefly, of nonconscious processing.

The story of August Kekule, a German chemist in the mid-1850s obsessed with the structure of carbon-based compounds, is a wonderful illustration of creativity as problem-solving. The concern for Kekule was that no one could figure out how carbon atoms organized themselves to form these molecules. He claimed that one day he dozed off after considerable intellectual work and had a dream. In the dream, he saw atoms whirling and dancing before his eyes. The atoms reassembled themselves into long rows, moving about in snake-like motion. As he watched the snake dance, he observed the snake devour its own tail. After waking up, Kekule saw the vision as an opportunity to resolve the problem of the structure of the carbon molecules. The vision of the snake eating its own tail led Kekule to imagine the structure of the benzene ring, a chain of six carbon atoms organized in a circle, like a ring. The dream provided a crucial insight. Because of this foundational intuition and solution to the problem, science today regards Kekule as a principal founder of the chemistry of carbon-based compounds. However, as Louis Pasteur noted, "chance favors only the prepared mind." By this, Pasteur likely meant that only a mind mentally focused on the task at hand and prepared to be enlightened by the results would properly interpret the intuition. Another interpretation might be that you must wrestle with the problem first in order to intuit a solution.

The uncontrolled and sometimes chaotic mind arises and remains active when every situation is viewed as a problem, when the solutions are unrecognized, and the mind continues to apply ineffective error correction strategies to resolve the issues. When that approach fails, the mind ramps up the frustration, stress, and fear, and this failure further energizes the problem-solving approach. This positive feedback loop gives motivation to the obsessive, inner critic—the unhinged interpreter of the uncontrolled mind.

How the mind gets stuck in problem-solving mode is speculative, but one major clue is an understanding of how the mind processes time. Conscious awareness is memory-based processing and, since memories are time dependent, it reflects this dependency. In contrast, nonconscious activity is not memory based and exists in a different temporal state, one more akin to an atemporal or timeless domain. Accepting those differences is critical for the resolutions proposed as self-parenting the mind and present-moment centering. This is discussed in greater detail later. At the moment, the more relevant interest is whether you can do something about this. The insight to understand is that the solution to these psychological challenges already exists in the mind's own activity—which is to focus on present-moment actions. But because this solution remains unrecognized, unattended, and unimplemented, the madness continues.

Biased Thinking

Other major factors in the mind getting stuck in problem-solving mode are the biases in thinking that develop as we mature. Psychologists have suggested that biased thinking reflects errors in deliberation, affecting the decisions and judgments that individuals make. Biased thinking is like the heuristic functions described previously. Both biases and heuristics need memory and attentional resources. As the GPS example suggested, sometimes you think you know better than the nonconscious mind. The overconfidence may reflect the normal bias toward rational and conscious processing, which may have benefits. But overconfidence also makes life harder, for the bias can make you unable or unwilling to let go of conceptual reflection. This clinging makes change difficult, especially when what you need is to let go and let nonconscious processing resume control.

One bias related to thinking is what psychologists describe as "positivity bias."[14] This bias occurs when adults hold themselves in higher regard than they do their peers. These individuals are of the opinion that their future is rosier than that of others and convince themselves that they are more in control of their future. Also known as the "Pollyanna Principle," it makes conscious processing biased in a positive direction, although the bias in conscious processing itself may produce Pollyanna-ish thoughts. Whichever way it goes, what is fascinating is that adults also exhibit an opposite bias called "negativity dominance."[15] This negative bias occurs when individuals describe spontaneous, nonconscious thoughts or mental chatter negatively. Negativity may be the tendency to react more to undesirable than desirable information.

Freud's pessimistic views of the nonconscious are another potential source of negative biases. His ideas exploded in the popular media and still hold sway for many people. It is unclear whether Freud was an astute observer of "negativity bias" himself or helped fuel the negativity by popularizing it. Still, another explanation for these biases comes from an evolutionary perspective. This view argues that our brain developed to detect threat-associated information and to give greater weight to negative events, objects, and personal traits. Perception of threats and of negative stimuli promotes greater survivability compared to focusing on positive events. Researchers point out that these biases and their tendencies produce ingrained habitual responses that influence the birth and maintenance of the chattering intellect. This explanation has also penetrated the popular media. Thus, whether influenced by Freudian thought, evolutionary theory, or something else, we aggravate the problem when perceptual biases combine with the natural tendency to give more weight to negative thoughts.

Implicit biases describe attitudes toward people, or the stereotypes associated with them, that occur without conscious awareness. A concerning implicit bias happens when Caucasians, even those who claim not to be racist, associate criminality with people of color without re-alizing they are doing it. Studies have shown that racial biases spring from primitive social biases toward strangers who do not look like you, or are unfamiliar. From an evolutionary perspective, caution about unfamiliar people makes sense. One explanation for implicit biases is that most actions occur without conscious awareness to allow smooth functioning in a very complex world. Similar to heuristics, implicit bi-ases often predict how you will behave, often with more accuracy than conscious perceptions, although many times not.

Questions to Ponder

Take a moment to assess whether you show the Pollyanna Principle, negativity bias, or implicit biases. Answer the following questions to help you get started:

Do you hold yourself in higher regard than your peers?
Do you believe your future is rosier than that of others?
Do you react more to negative than positive information?
Do individuals of a different race trigger negative assessments?

Treating the uncontrolled mind with self-parenting means treating it like an undisciplined child that has not yet learned all the clever tools in her toolbox to solve problems. And she needs to learn how to use all her skills, such as grasping problems as opportunities to learn and grow. The problem of mind is even more directly addressed by chang-ing the primary reason for it getting stuck in the past and future. That immediate solution suggests focusing on the perception of the present moment using mindfulness, an effective method for changing this as-pect of thought while largely bypassing conceptual thinking. That is the power of the technique.

Of course, your particular problem can be so emotionally wrench-ing it is impossible to dissociate from it to observe and experience mindfully or even self-parent. In such a situation, a strategy to distance yourself from the problem may be necessary before attempting these solutions. Try the following *How to Cultivate an Unencumbered Mind* exercise before moving on.

How to Cultivate an Unencumbered Mind: Distance Yourself from the Problem

People often have a self-centered view of the world, leading them to imagine all the negative ways a problem could affect them. This might explain why someone becomes a better chess or card player when they are observing a game rather than participating in it. One way to put distance between you and your problem is to pretend that the problem is unrelated to you.

Visualize yourself as an observer and not a participant. Accepting the problem objectively will help temper your emotions so they won't interfere as much. Imagine, for example, that the problem is happening to a friend: "My friend Mary is unemployed. I feel for her, but she needs to stop whining, dust off her résumé, and start submitting it to other companies." This distancing helps you avoid (or minimize) the ego-based emotional reactions that can arise.

Key Takeaways

- Thoughts occur in two dominant modes: nonconscious and conscious awareness.
- Conscious awareness is a type of error-correction interruption from the normal flow of nonconscious activity; it connects future-based plans with memories; is limited in resources, slow, and susceptible to dysfunction.
- When normal error-correcting brain functions are ineffective, they create glitches, errors, or unpredictable events that trigger engagement of the interpreter and conscious awareness, giving birth to the obsessive monkey mind.
- Nonconscious activity is not memory-based. Its capabilities are unlimited. It exists in an atemporal or timeless domain, and it forms a major portion of the functions associated with who you are, how you think, and how you respond.

Next chapter: What gives the ultimate insight into the uncontrolled mind?

8

Understanding Why We
Have Experiences

What can you learn to welcome change?

The Nature of Experiences

Recognizing that she had a problem put Stephanie on the road to recovery. But that initial recognition and her perseverance were not enough until she gained a basic level of understanding regarding the nature of her problem and how to resolve and correct it. For Stephanie, the problem centered on her inner critic, that voice that told her over and over what she lacked. It made her feel less in control of her life, and that made her even more anxious and depressed. Stephanie's brain and mind, like those of other individuals, evolved to perceive and catalog sensory experiences impinging on her sensory receptors. Understanding how those particular experiences come about, especially the role of the brain's executive system in the frontal lobes, provided her with a sense that she could do something about her circumstances. A sense of control came simply from learning to flow with conditions when it was necessary. This flexibility of mind by itself did not provide all the answers, but it was foundational for other strategies to deal with the chaos that was Stephanie's normal life.

It is easy to get caught up in the recriminations about why things happen to us. It might seem that God or Fate is angry and we become recipients of their punishment. The fundamental problem is a feeling of lack of control over our life, along with a sense of helplessness and depression. Understanding why we have experiences is not an antidote to this, but it can provide a measure of confidence and a sense we can do something about our circumstances. That sense of control may come simply from learning to bend with conditions when that is necessary. Flexibility of the mind by itself may not solve every problem, but it is a necessary condition to survive the chaos we encounter.

Scientists have argued that, contrary to our intuitive understanding, conscious awareness does not have an active, executive role in determining behavior. It does, however, have a biological function, especially when awareness is basically information in various forms. Understanding its biological function can tell us why we have experiences, and this may give the ultimate insight into the uncontrolled mind.

A biological function of conscious awareness appears to be dealing with problems, deviations, and errors that interrupt the flow of nonconscious processing. Another way to put this is that conscious awareness contributes to responding flexibly when automatic actions are unsuitable. To engage in such a function means that conscious awareness affects mechanisms that guide behavior.

Scientists argue that conscious awareness reflects a *flexible response mechanism* for decision-making, planning, and responding in nonautomatic ways. This is the source of thoughts, intentional actions, decisions, plans, daydreams, and so on, suggesting that the control mechanisms of the brain most relevant to this are in the frontal lobes. Active, conscious awareness has evolved for this specific purpose and dominates in those situations. When a problem occurs, giving rise to this aspect of the mind, nonconscious processing recedes into the background, giving way to the error correction methods of the now dominant awareness.

The increased attentional focus may affect daily life if additional stress, fear, and anxiety obscure the flexibility of the normal mind. This inflexibility impacts the ability to function well. If the effect on mood, deliberation, and behavior persists, then more severe psychopathology arises. And psychopathology forms the basis for disorders like autoimmune and emotional maladies, depression, anxiety, heart problems, addictive behaviors, suicidal ideation, and even schizophrenia. In a genuine sense, rational, conceptual, logical awareness suffers from the "dis-ease" of its uncontrolled nature.

The New Science of Mind

To more deeply understand this psychological relationship from a fresh perspective, it is helpful to consider what neuroscience research has to say about mind flexibility. While the full story of the human brain is being written, enough is available to conclude that the popular understanding of what the ego and personality are, how they relate to conscious awareness and monkey mind, and how they affect flexibility of mind is rudimentary. Experience and intuition are primary sources of information about the overlap and association between personality, ego, and monkey mind. The word *ego* has become overused and lost most of its significance in daily conversations. As a result, there is only minimal understanding of what the word refers to and the magnitude of its power. In the current context, ego refers to impulses, biases, conceptual thought, and all the actions that produce and perpetuate the inflexible monkey mind.

Neuroscientists assume that the ego, personality, and uncontrolled mind have a neural basis. Francis Crick—who, along with James Watson, discovered the structure of the DNA—wrote a book in 1994 titled *The Astonishing Hypothesis.*[1] In it, Crick opines that "a person's mental activities are entirely due to the behavior of nerve cells, glial cells, and the atoms, ions, and molecules that make them up and influence them." Many neuroscientists have concerns with this extreme view—since it narrowly identifies us with our biology. But the definition captures the essence of a modern neuroscience perspective concerning the relationship between mind and brain. This serves as a good starting assumption.

Questions to Ponder

If personality (your sense of self), ego (the self-esteem or sense of self-importance), and uncontrolled mind (obsessive rumination) have common origins, what aspects of personality do you associate with it? Do you recognize these traits (nervousness, fear, calmness, certainty, inability to act, etc.) as unchangeable, or as something you could alter in yourself?

Where Is Your Personality?

Barbara Lipska lost her mind in 2015. She describes her unusual experience in the book *The Neuroscientist Who Lost Her Mind: My Tale of Madness and Recovery*, published three years later.[2] At the time of her tragedy, Lipska was a neuroscientist and director of the Human Brain Collection Core at the National Institute of Mental Health in Bethesda, Maryland. If anyone should have recognized the changes that her brain and personality were going through, it was Lipska. But she did not. Lipska had been "an energetic, determined, ambitious researcher, devoted to her work, family, and running marathons." But the year 2015 brought her grim news—a diagnosis of brain cancer. As expected, she started taking medications for it.

What was unexpected was that the cancer therapy started her on a downward spiral of change into someone else, and as she describes it, "not someone she liked." Her description of her new personality is heart-wrenching. "She was angry, cranky, demanding, insistent, unreasonable, intolerant, and sometimes a danger to herself and others. She made bad decisions. One day, she tried to walk home alone from a supermarket. She got lost, urinating on herself, eventually hitching a ride home to a house she couldn't recognize or point out to the driver. She was mean to her beloved grandkids, and rude to medical personnel who tried to help her. She saw menace in situations that were nonthreatening and missed the real dangers of insisting on doing the things she'd always done, like driving."

Looking back, Lipska is uncertain whether the cancer, the medications, the stress in her life, or all three produced her personality changes. What she is sure about is that the injury to her brain occurred in her frontal lobes. Malfunctioning of the frontal lobes led to a loss of what she knew as herself. She lost control of this sense of self, and "all the rules about where and when to do certain things, and how to communicate, became irrelevant to her." As she explains, "They were inaccessible, for all practical purposes nonexistent." In a passage in her book, Lipska sums up the uncertainty of her experience and the magnitude of the consequences when the brain no longer works as expected. She explains that "despite all my years of studying brain disorders, for the first time in my life, I realize how profoundly unsettling it is to have a brain that does not function."

When the malfunction occurs in the frontal lobes, the area of the brain just behind the eyeballs, the effects on our personality can be severe. The left part of the frontal lobes is the area involved in producing Gazzaniga's interpreter, the ongoing internal narrator of our life. The frontal lobes are the seat of the personality and, equally important, the seat of the uncontrolled mind. It is an important aspect of why we have experiences.

Lipska's descent into mental illness because of treatment for metastatic cancer is extreme, and yet the journey is also a journey of recovery and a return to sanity. A brain that does not function and has a direct effect on the most intimate aspect of being, on who and what we are, is a poignant story. Lipska's story points to the constraints imposed by our biology. But her determination not to give up and to bring the disorder under control overcame that biology. Her story is one of hope and of the power of Original Mind to overcome extreme difficulties.

Becoming an Individual

Wiring up the brain with its 100+ billion neurons and 10 times the number of support cells takes a long time. Neuroscientists estimate each neuron connects with an average of 10,000 other cells. This means the total number of synaptic connections made between all neurons is astronomical (estimated at 10^{16} total connections). Achieving this level of connectivity makes normal development a miraculously slow process.

The frontal lobes, home to executive functions like flexibility and control in planning, working memory, and impulse control, are some of the last areas to be fully wired. The brain matures in a slow and organized way, starting in the back and moving toward the front. These maturational changes do not stop with puberty. Scientists estimate that full maturity extends well into the second and third decades of life. During this time, the mind is in a state of *reduced* cognitive control, susceptible to impulsiveness due to lack of inhibition. There is a high likelihood, during this period, of developing antisocial behavior, delinquency, spoiled mind syndrome, and other forms of dysfunction. It is the reason why we show reduced cognitive control and exhibit impulsive sex, food, and sleep habits well into our twenties. One likely reason is that for nerve fibers to function well and conduct brain signals properly, an insulation protein called myelin must cover them. This myelination is much like insulating standard wires for the proper conduction of electricity. Myelination is a slow process.[3]

Awareness of the normal activity of the mind, in particular the interaction between conscious and nonconscious mind, manifests early in development. Carl Jung argued that, from birth, every individual has an original sense of wholeness as the real self. With maturation, around two to five years of age, a separate ego crystallizes out of that original unity in a process called ego-self differentiation, or individuation.[4] This psychological process emphasizes the "importance of the individual psyche and the personal quest for wholeness," while developing the sense of a unique personality. For Jung, ego becomes the esteem, or self-importance developed toward the larger sense of unity from which it springs. This attitude could be humble, arrogant, important, unimportant, intelligent, or stupid. All in all, individuation is the primary task of human development and involves the lifelong process of differentiation of the ego out of each individual's conscious and nonconscious elements of self. It is the apparent split in the personality that this individuation process generates, which creates problems.

I had an inkling of this separation when I turned three. I suddenly recognized that when I wished to play, my older sister didn't express the same desire. Prior to this awareness, I lived in a kind of undifferentiated world, as if what I wanted was what everyone else wanted. At three, however, my sister and I became separate beings, with separate thoughts. The awareness caused a sense of disappointment that was earth-shattering.

Much later, I learned that individuation or ego-self separation is a normal process that we all undergo as we age. The process reflects the development of what psychologists call a theory of mind, the ability to distinguish self from others, and to know that others have different thoughts. Theory of mind evolves in childhood, and the process continues for the next twenty plus years. Its sophistication matches that of the brain, especially the frontal lobes, as they become more fully interconnected. This process of individuation marks an unambiguous beginning of a psychological separation from others. It marks an onset of distinctiveness and the awareness of ourselves as unique individuals with distinct experiences.

Questions to Ponder

What memories do you have of individuation and development of your theory of mind? Do you recall a time before you became an individual self (before individuation)? How old were you when these changes occurred? What was the world like before?

Ego as Virtual Me

As my personal theory of mind and personality developed, I had a growing intuition, early in my adolescence, that something was not right. The feeling began with the sense of a growing rift and distinction between the real me and my developing ego. I recall wondering why I acted a certain way around some friends and differently around others, and still in a different way with family members. I felt like a chameleon, adopting the traits of those around me to get along and please them. Slowly, this dense constellation of thoughts, expectations, and perspectives coalesced and hardened, and I experienced this created reality as the actual me. I now associated ego with this "virtual me" (a distorted, phantom-like, and not authentic identity). It provided a misleading view of my experiences. Questions about the real me continued after this recognition.

A virtual me, make-believe self, or psychological avatar, as previously described, develops in all individuals from responses to our earliest experiences following birth. Many of these experiences have to do with questions about safety and the nature of the environment in which we find ourselves. "Is this a safe place?" When the answer is "No," we engage innate defense mechanisms, expectations, and postures to protect our fragile personality. Indeed, for a sizeable portion of infants everywhere, the world is not a very safe place. The World Health Organization reports that every year about 2.5 million babies around the world die within their first month of life. Psychological defensive strategies to survive malnutrition, disease, indifference, abuse, etc., develop early in life. The result of engaging these defense mechanisms and developing a sensitivity for our place in the world is what the virtual me is.

The virtual me evolves as a necessary creation of the mind when it is trying to protect itself from events that could inflict psychological injury. Its function is to deflect harmful energies, including the childish and cruel behavior suffered at the hands of siblings, parents, and strangers. Personally, the virtual me provided a defensive shield protecting me from the taunting behavior of bullies during middle grade school. Later, this shield helped soften the blow from the uncertainties in developing a professional career. For others, this self-protective virtual me safeguards them from truly great harm, like mental and physical abuse. While I was fortunate not to experience such serious injuries, my story shows how necessary this protection is. And because it is necessary, I prefer to call it "virtual" rather than "false" since there is nothing false about the ego.

The moment-to-moment changes I experienced while growing up fed this emerging separation. As my capacity for language and for knowing myself and the world grew, the virtual me grew. The personality reflected by the virtual me became more vocal and more identified with who I was. I learned to rationalize, reason, and generalize information to keep the stories consistent with my past and current experiences. The attempt to keep things logically consistent via my interpreter strengthened the growing virtual me. Events in my environment, especially those that created uncertainty, provided further reinforcement and made it increasingly more real. This development and growth were at the expense of my real self, which receded into the background. Then, beginning in my early forties, awareness of this separation and the unfolding dysfunction created a midlife crisis that later morphed into a spiritual crisis. Things came to a crisis because I no longer believed, trusted, nor recognized the virtual me and I had begun to identify with something more genuine.

Everyone is different and there are many reasons for midlife crises, including the recognition that we are mortal and death becomes more certain as we age. A growing list of questions about life can lead to a reevaluation of the choices made. For me, the crisis was about the absence of meaning in my life and in what I was doing as a career. Questioning my life choices overlapped with my growing concern about the meaning of life, and this conflict manifested as a midlife and spiritual crisis. Psychologists suggest that the ego-self separation crisis we experience in adolescence becomes a conscious rediscovery of the original unity. The eventual outcome for me was a resolution and transformation in that perspective. I experienced a reconciliation of my ego-self differentiation and a recognition that what I now felt was my true self and original nature. Returning to this awareness marked a return to Original Mind.

Questions to Ponder

These are several questions that get to the heart of how well you know yourself and who you are:

Are you experiencing an adolescent, midlife, spiritual, or other crisis?
What is the essence of that crisis?
Do you know your true self?
Do you distinguish between true-self and ego-self?
Do you act differently when in the company of other people? At work? At home?
Do you reflect the mood of those around you?
Are you sensitive to your own needs?
What do you enjoy doing when no one is watching?
If you had no fear or financial concerns, what would you do?
Whom do you love unconditionally?

Frontal Lobes as Controller-in-Chief

A neuroscience-based understanding of why we have these experiences requires that we know something about the role of the brain. We have described the frontal lobes as performing executive functions responsible for flexibility and control in the planning, initiation, sequencing, and monitoring of complex goal–directed behavior. Therefore, it plays an outsize role in birthing the experiencing mind and in the solutions to its dysfunction and recovery. The frontal lobes are the brain's territory where the major battlefield occurs: a battlefield that involves emotion regulation, impulse control, and having a sense of past, present, and future. It is also the readily available doorway to the space where choice, possibility, and growth lie.

A war typically has two sides. The two fundamental aspects of mind involved in this battle for control and flexibility include the energetic and controlled aspect and the compulsive and uncontrolled counterpart. In 1892, William James, the founder of American Psychology, described the compulsive and incessant activity of the mind as a "stream of consciousness."[5] Since that time, this compulsive and uncontrolled brain activity has been the most intriguing yet least understood aspect of the brain.

A major insight concerning this stream of consciousness occurred when two neuroscientists in 1934 proposed that "thought processes must be pictured as based upon a constantly circulating stream of neural impulse from cortex to thalamus and from thalamus to cortex." The book, *The Neural Basis of Thoughts*, published by Campion and Elliot-Smith, presented this provoking description of the flow of neural impulses as the instantiation of thought itself.[6] Their intuition that thoughts arise from cyclical streams of information flowing from brain area to brain area foresaw a significant amount of future research. Today, most researchers agree with their hunch. Imagine that what appears as chaotic, compulsive, and uncontrolled brain activity is simply the random activation of these "thought" streams.

How to Cultivate an Unencumbered Mind: Discriminate between Intuition and Mind Chatter

If you are unsure of whether you are listening to your anxious/fearful mind or your intuition, consider whether you can differentiate between the two based on these characteristics:

Intuition is not loud or demanding; it is subtle, gentle, and communicates distinctly in different people. Intuition is more a feeling and sensation than a thought.

Mind chatter is self-talk, creating an internal monologue that can turn into arguing with oneself, like a disturbed person. Pay close attention to which region of your body relates to deliberate reflection versus intuition.

Scientists estimate that the brain receives millions—perhaps trillions—of bits of information every second. The vast amount of data arises from external and internal bodily senses. This flood of sensory information results in thousands, if not millions, of different cyclical streams of information flowing around in our skull. If these streams of neural activation reflect thoughts, rapidly attending to different ones would resemble a highly energetic child switching between different objects of interest. This would be normal until it isn't.

The Buddha's concept of *kapicitta*, or monkey mind, is not too far off from what science has learned in the intervening 2,500 years. It is not surprising that when we investigate the awake mind, we see a large part of the brain activated by this onslaught of information. This contradicts the notion that we only use 10 percent of our brain. To handle the workload and vast amount of information, it was necessary to evolve multiple ways to handle and regulate the parallel, continuous shifts in attention. What separates the controlled mind from the uncontrolled mind is a problem in this regulation, or what William James called "the filmiest of screens." The conversion from one to the other occurs in the blink of a thought. Fortunately, science is slowly gaining an understanding of what causes and regulates such a change.

Campion and Elliot-Smith identified the thalamus, which we know as the bedroom of the brain, as a critical region in managing the cyclical "thought" streams of information. This almond-shaped area sits on top of the brainstem, at the base of the cortex, and is the main receiving information station for the sensory deluge. There are two almond-shaped areas, side by side, involved in relaying sensory information to the cortex for additional processing. Neuroscientists use the "relay" metaphor to describe thalamic function because this region is in a strategic location for controlling the flow of information into the cortex, including the frontal lobes. Like trains at a train station, sensory information arrives in physically segregated lines for individual processing.

Critical to the control of information at the thalamus is the role that attention plays in opening and closing the "metaphorical" gates that exist in this area. When you are alert and eager for information, attention opens these gates. An open gate means the relay of information flows unimpeded from your senses, through the thalamus, and into your cortex. What this means is that while you are alert and watching television, you are engaged by the information, perhaps generating questions, or simply enjoying it. Fifteen minutes into the television show, your alertness wanes and you doze off. Suddenly, the information is no longer flowing unimpeded. The thalamic gates close, either partially or totally, reducing the flow of information to the cortex to a trickle. As you fall asleep, the gates are completely closed.

This attentional control, allowing or preventing information from flowing to the cortex, is crucial for how the brain selects the amount and type of information it needs and can process in awareness. Without the ability to select the cyclical "thought" streams of information relevant to solving a specific problem, the brain becomes overwhelmed and uncontrolled. In fact, studies show that an aspect of the problem in schizophrenia is a lack of control of attentional thalamic gates causing a flood of information arriving at the cortex. These studies show the thalamus as smaller in schizophrenics, suggesting abnormal circuitry and the primary reason for the lack of control. Cortical regions that have the most extensive connections to the thalamus, and exercise the greatest control on these attentional gates, are the frontal lobes. Because this region communicates with most other regions, modern views of brain function consider the frontal lobes as the "Controller-in-Chief."

Since the early 1800s, neuroscientists have known of the frontal lobes' involvement in higher cognitive functions. The unfortunate case of Phineas Gage, an American railroad construction supervisor who lived between 1823–1860, provided evidence of their roles.[7] On September 13, 1848, the twenty-five-year-old Gage was preparing a railroad bed using an iron tamping rod to pack explosive powder into a hole. When he hit the powder with the rod to pack it in, the powder detonated, sending the long tamping rod hurtling upward. The rod penetrated Gage's left cheek, tore through his brain, and exited the top of his skull. Somehow, Gage not only survived the horrific accident but could still speak immediately after it. He walked to a nearby cart so he could be taken to a doctor.

Gage's injury destroyed much of his left frontal lobe, or what we now consider part of the central executive region of the brain. The injury completely changed Gage's personality for the remaining twelve years of his life. His friends claimed not to recognize him following the accident, for he could no longer perform what we now consider are common skills, responsible for the planning, initiation, sequencing, and monitoring of complex goal–directed behavior. Gage could do none of that. Since this famous incident, clinicians have associated frontal lobe injuries with the loss of regulation of this central executive part of brain activity. The story of Barbara Lipska, who lost her sense of self following an injury to her frontal lobes, recounts similar themes with a more modern context.

As one would expect, the Controller-in-Chief, or central executive region, has extensive connections not only with the thalamus but with most areas of the brain. These connections help form the millions of interactive or cyclical streams of information that produce the variety of thoughts we experience. The medical and scientific literature has provided support for frontal lobe deficits resulting from lesions and metabolic deficits in these streams, deficits that result in changes to the personality and in who we are.

The above description supports the role of the executive control system in the frontal lobes, producing the thought streams and what gets attended to and selected for additional processing. In essence, it controls what we experience. Researchers speculate that the proper regulation of this region requires the existence of layer upon layer of control to prevent certain thoughts from hijacking the brain. The attentional mechanisms governing the thalamic gates provide one such method of regulation. When these control mechanisms fail, the selection of information becomes disabled, and irrelevant information floods the cortex. This affects the content of the thoughts and the intrusive nature of those thoughts. Studies in schizophrenic patients suggest a loss in thalamic selectivity results in the brain being overwhelmed by irrelevant information.

Patricia Goldman-Rakic (1937–2003) was a lifelong student of the frontal lobes and a longtime professor of neuroscience at Yale University.[8] She studied and advocated for the role of a special part of the frontal lobes called the prefrontal cortex (PFC).[9] Many consider the PFC the pinnacle of processing since it appears to be involved in creating the building blocks necessary for abstract thinking.

Thought abstraction is the unique ability we have to disengage streams of information from environmental stimuli and the contingencies of the moment. Such an uncoupling of thought from sensory experience allows for symbolic or imaginative deliberation, whose frequent and fluent use is a distinguishing characteristic of our ability to think and communicate. Symbols allow us the ability to uncouple from the bounds of our own direct sensory experience in such a way that allows us to learn about the world directly from others. This is how you can enjoy someone else's vacation stories, as if you were actually there. What makes symbolic deliberation possible is the brain's ability to create its own *mental representations*. A representation is the totality of neural changes associated with an external event or the recount of an external event, and considered a memory when the changes persist. The power of symbols is that someone else's memories and experiences can become your own if you "represent" them in your own brain. This ability is what connects us socially to others, including their dysfunctions.

Through her work, Goldman-Rakic showed that an even smaller part of the PFC, the dorsolateral PFC (DLPFC), is essential for the creation of these mental representations. Impairments in the DLPFC contribute to thought disorders, like those observed in many clinical cases. The integration and manipulation of auditory, visual, spatial, and other sensory information by DLPFC as part of its normal function explains its role in mental representation.

A review by Firat in 2019 proposed that the frontal lobes comprise three hierarchical *subsystems* that regulate human behavior and social connectedness.[10] The first manages voluntary, controlled actions—including motor functions underlying action-perception and mirror neurons, thought to be important in social behaviors. A second subsystem controls more abstract motivation and emotional regulation—such as theory of mind and empathy. The last subsystem manages higher-order executive functioning, such as the inhibition of racial bias. This gives a sense for the organizational complexity of the frontal lobes and the many levels of management and control that must exist.

A Compulsive Brain

Goldman-Rakic's work reveals that the frontal lobes are important centers for executive control. She and others suggest that such control comes about because the frontal lobes operate in a top-down manner, with the PFC having a leading and controlling role over many lower-level brain structures. Similar to the control exerted over the thalamus, the frontal lobes exercise control over multiple regions through response inhibition.

This part of the story begins in 1906, when research showed that executive control works in a very unexpected and counterintuitive way. Instead of control signals allowing an action to occur through direct stimulation of the mechanisms controlling that action, the brain instead holds the action under continuous active inhibition. Execution of the behavior occurs when a command inhibits the inhibition, a process called *disinhibition*. Another way to describe this method of control is that the brain must inhibit alternative courses of action to allow the expression of a specific, goal-directed behavior. The observations suggest that response inhibition plays a fundamental role, through disinhibition, in the self-regulation of normal behavior.

Ferrier in 1886 proposed that response inhibition is necessary for the successful occurrence of an incompatible response.[11] This release of function results from the removal of inhibitory control from higher centers, like the frontal lobes, over lower centers of the nervous system. More recently, Bari and Robinson pointed out that the study of response inhibition is also about overriding a planned action or one that has already started.[12] Hence, deficient inhibition in executive control affects everyday life, causing impulsive conduct detrimental to the individual, or the inability to override a behavior once that behavior has started. Recent fMRI and lesion studies show that areas under frontal lobe control are those most responsible for the aberrant behavior of the uncontrolled mind.

Other scientists have linked this problem of inhibition, the impulsivity it produces, and lack of self-control to addiction, attention deficit/hyperactivity disorder, mania, and other, similar psychiatric conditions. An aspect of the neural basis for the compulsive nature of the uncontrolled mind is a problem with inhibition in the executive system, resulting in impulsivity and lack of self-control. Problems in regulating hippocampal activity by the executive control system, for example, underlie the pathological intrusion of memories into thoughts. These intrusions lead to a mind obsessed with past events. The inability of the frontal cortex to exercise control through response inhibition over memory areas like the hippocampus leads to impulsivity, attention deficit, and fear—essential components of AFRAID rumination.

Another level of control that plays a crucial role in executive control function, along with disinhibition, is the role of a special set of cells called interneurons. These are specialized neurons that relay information between cells. They exist in sensory-motor circuits, the pathways that carry information from external sensory receptors to muscles that control motor movement. Interneurons also exist in cortical-cortical circuits, pathways connecting different areas within the cortex itself, such as from the frontal to the parietal lobes.

Scientists have attributed a variety of functions to interneurons, and their inhibitory activity applies to the control of functions within particular brain areas.[13] These specialized neurons play an important role in controlling cell-to-cell communications. They do so through the release of inhibitory neurotransmitters such as gamma-aminobutyric acid, or GABA. If neural activity gets carried away, as in epileptic discharges, interneurons can inhibit the runaway activity by inhibiting it, or what is referred to as *disinhibition*.

They also have a role in creating rhythmic electrical patterns, called biorhythms, that are important for the timing of brain events. Problems with regulating interneurons in the prefrontal cortex-to-hippocampus stream of information, because of abnormal levels of GABA neurotransmitters, can explain the increase and intrusiveness of AFRAID thinking. The evidence concerning frontal lobe control of executive functions, through response inhibition, and the role of interneurons in those networks, makes a strong case for the neural origins and intrusive nature of the uncontrolled mind.

Another important insight of recent origin that furthers our understanding of executive function in the frontal lobes concerns autopiloting.[14] Autopiloting describes neural functions involved in behaviors that are quite common in all of us, such as mind wandering, daydreaming, and stimulus-independent and task-unrelated contemplation. Autopiloting involves both spontaneous and nondirected reflection, and as science tells us, adults spend at least half of their waking time in these states. When they do, attention disengages from the immediate external environment and switches to more internal processing streams. This attentional disengagement from the outside world and engagement of the internal world, also called the *decoupling hypothesis* by some neuroscientists, takes place below conscious awareness. We rarely recognize when our mind tunes out and daydreams, although we can be technically awake. Autopiloting plays a role in the awake experience; thus the question of its role is important. A specific, relevant question is, How does autopiloting relate to nonconscious processing, creativity, and the uncontrolled mind?

Scientists associate autopiloting with both positive and negative outcomes. It promotes self-reflection and interaction with others and increases the likelihood of creativity and planning for the future. In contrast, the negative consequences include the likelihood of mistakes while performing a task, since autopiloting may lead to distraction or absent-mindedness, and an increased likelihood of accidents that might occur while doing another task, such as driving. Studies also show that individuals diagnosed with depression obsess more about their thoughts, problems, and other negative experiences during autopiloting. In fact, psychologists suggest that anxiety and AFRAID rumination represent "mind wandering gone awry." Does this dysfunction mean that the uncontrolled mind occurs when autopiloting goes awry? And how does autopiloting go awry?

One instance of autopiloting going off kilter occurs when regulation in the frontal cortex falters and leads to the Controller-in-Chief becoming the compulsive Controller-in-Chief. In that instance, the uncontrolled mind is the outcome of a compulsive mind. The culprit becomes faulty attentional regulation of inhibition, which produces impulsive behaviors that overwhelm more rational and positive thinking. The product of this aberrant behavior, which is at the same time rewarding since impulsivity is a type of learning, is AFRAID rumination. Indeed, the rewarding aspect of this behavior is one reason why the AFRAID mindset is so resistant to change. Similar to a drug, the self-focused, chattering intellect produces these *addictive*, yet rewarding, impulses.

Addictiveness is all too familiar when we become attached to thinking, feel pleasure exercising it, and then have difficulty ignoring it. Neuroscience research is quite clear showing that dopamine and opioid neurotransmitters are singularly important for producing reward in terms of the hedonic pleasure and the motivational aspects of behavior (see Figure 8.1). Dopamine circuits originate in a small region in the depths of the brain called the midbrain, a constituent of the brainstem known as the ventral tegmental area (VTA).

The VTA connects with other brain regions, including the frontal cortex, to deliver dopamine signals. The role of dopamine includes making us feel the hedonic pleasure of performing an action, feeling rewarded, and engaging the motivational energy to carry out activities. We also need dopamine to regulate learning in the executive control center of the brain. These functions make dopamine important not only for reward and motivation but critical for conditioned learning, an important mechanism in developing bad habits, like addiction.

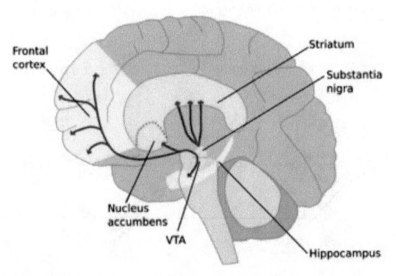

Figure 8.1 The dopamine reward system. *Source:* Bryant, Cameron. (2022). http://sites.bu.edu/bryantlab/dopamine-pathways/.

The uncontrolled mind, in its incessant rumination involving motivation, reward, and conditioned learning, resembles addiction-like behaviors. Indeed, Nora Volkow, director of the National Institute on Drug Abuse, and colleagues reported in 2003 and 2011 that drug addiction results from problems regulating the executive system of the frontal lobes.[15] The model they proposed (see Figure 8.2) suggests that under normal circumstances, the prefrontal cortex (PFC) maintains executive control of circuits involved in conditioned learning, habits, reward, and memory. This control, as described previously, comes principally through response inhibition. Conditioned learning and habits activate areas including the amygdala, which is involved in regulating fear responses. It also affects the hippocampus and memory circuits that regulate short-term memory.

The Volkow model shows that addiction and compulsive behaviors disrupt the downstream control exercised by the PFC. This produces a reduction in inhibition, leading to increased activity in previously inhibited circuits. The disinhibition creates increased fear and stimulus saliency, so certain objects, people, and events gain unnatural importance or prominence. Conditioned learning, reward, drive, and mem-

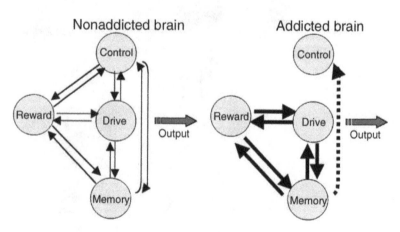

Figure 8.2 Addiction as a model for the uncontrolled mind. *Source:* Volkow, Nora D., Fowler Joanna S., and Wang Gene-Jack. (2003).

ory circuits increase their activity because of disinhibition leading to the intrusion of memories, aberrant learning, and habits. Compulsive activation of these executive circuits becomes the norm, gradually resulting in the loss of self-control. While Volkow proposed this model specifically for addiction, the dynamics that underlie the uncontrolled mind are significantly similar.

Questions to Ponder

Take a moment to examine some of your disrupting habits, recurring thought patterns, and behaviors. Have any of these reached the level of being "addictive"? Can you say no and be free of them? If not, why not? What would life be like if you were free of them?

If you can imagine an alternative reality in which you are free of addictive behaviors, then you are already in touch with part of the mind that can free you from the addiction. It means this "healthier" mind is not an aspect of the chaotic and uncontrolled mind. How can you maintain contact with this healthier you?

Key Takeaways

- Conscious awareness is associated with a *flexible response mechanism* for decision-making, planning, and responding in nonautomatic ways. This is the source of thoughts, intentional actions, decisions, plans, and daydreams, and involves the frontal lobes.
- Malfunctioning of the frontal lobes leads to a loss of what you know as yourself.
- The frontal lobes comprise three *subsystems* that regulate human behavior: One manages voluntary, controlled actions. Another controls more abstract motivation and emotional regulation. The last manages higher-order executive functioning.
- Scientists have linked the problem of inhibition in the frontal lobes, the impulsivity it produces, and lack of self-control to addiction, attention deficit/hyperactivity disorder, mania, and other psychiatric conditions.

- Autopiloting, mind wandering, daydreaming, and stimulus-independent and task-unrelated contemplation go awry when regulation in the frontal cortex falters and leads to impulsive and compulsive behavior, producing an AFRAID mindset.

Next chapter: How do you find balance when your mind is at war with itself?

9

Balancing the Varieties of Thoughts

Change yourself, change the world.

Finding Balance in Chaos

It was the holiday season, with Thanksgiving just completed, Hanukkah starting, and Christmas right around the corner. Stephanie's seven-year-old son, Michael, insisted he wanted to visit his grandparents for Hanukkah. He loved playing dreidel with his cousins and eating special holiday foods like latkes *and* sufganiyot. *He also wanted Santa to bring him the latest Microsoft Xbox Series X video game console for Christmas. "It's probably not happening," Stephanie thought to herself, especially after last year's disaster at the family's Hanukkah celebration, where Michael had thrown a tantrum. She also needed to keep a close eye on their spending after having lost her commission on the new building downtown, which she had counted on to celebrate the season. Instead, her depleted mind turned to her mother, Danielle, who had recently celebrated ninety years of age and was showing signs of dementia. Danielle's memory was playing tricks on her and she insisted on returning to live in her own home instead of the senior residential care facility that Stephanie had found for her. It was a well-run and beautiful facility near the beach. The nursing care was excellent and with easy access to where Stephanie lived, which meant Stephanie could visit Danielle and respond to problems quickly. But Danielle insisted she no longer liked the place and her demands for Stephanie's time were increasing and becoming more adamant. As Stephanie reflected on these and other problems facing her, the walls appeared to be closing in on her. She could sense the stress, anxiety, and unforgiving inner critic readying for an all-out assault on her psyche. Stephanie remembered her mindfulness practice and the advice of her therapist and realized her mind was reverberating over past and future outcomes. She sat down and began breathing slowly and deeply, turning her attention to the present moment. Within minutes a calmness prevailed, the incoming storm averted, and Stephanie could reason more clearly and creatively about what needed to be done. The uncontrolled chaos had transformed into a controlled process.*

Why is it that I, like most well-intentioned humans, cannot keep New Year's resolutions? For much of my life, and following the custom of others around me, I would set unrealistic goals at the beginning of the year, even knowing full well I could not maintain them. After a few months, the gym membership had lapsed, the vegetarian diet had morphed back to unhealthy foods, and my extraverted persona had retreated to my normal, shy self. The reason I sabotaged these hoped-for changes reflected the ongoing struggle in my mind. I characterize these warring sides in dualistic ways (e.g., thinking versus feeling), but most pointedly as the spoiled, demanding child who always wanted what he wanted, whenever he wanted it.

No story of the struggle for mind control between Original Mind and the uncontrolled mind is more pertinent and heartbreaking than that of the eighteenth-century musical prodigy named Johannes Chrysostomus Wolfgangus Theophilus Mozart.[1] Wolfgangus Amadèus Mozart, his preferred name, was born in Salzburg, Austria, in 1756. Of the seven children born to his parents, he was one of only two who survived infancy. Early on, his parents stressed music proficiency and insisted on intensive musical training at home. By the time he was six, Mozart was already composing and performing as a child prodigy across Europe, along with his sister. At eight years of age, he created music already with its own distinct voice and individuality.

Admirers have romanticized Mozart as the ultimate child prodigy. Stories are told how even when his feet could not yet reach the floor, he played the piano with an unnatural facility, blindfolded, improvising at substantial length, on any theme. Perhaps because of all the praise he received as a child, he did not grow up a humble man but "proud as a peacock," as he described himself. Mozart rarely seemed to be entirely present, as if his mind were always somewhere else, dissociated from the immediate environment. He was restless, quick-witted, sociable, flirtatious, and obscene. A man of extremes, his conceited nature progressed into paranoia as he grew older. Inevitably, he experienced extremes of despair, sensual pleasure, and bleak emptiness—all of which found their way into his music. "As touchy as gunpowder," is how a friend described him.

Mozart composed over six hundred works, many of them masterpieces and pinnacles of music in a variety of genres. Although productive, even in his last year, he struggled throughout most of his life. He was ill and exhausted when he started writing his last work, a requiem mass. He finished the first two movements of this masterpiece and sketches for several more. But he did not finish the last three sections before he died in 1791 at the young age of thirty-five. Based on contemporary Viennese custom, he was buried in a common grave.

His personality manifested a mind at war with itself, exhibiting the extraordinary qualities of Original Mind, but also reflecting the feverish confusion of an uncontrolled mind. The struggle created mental problems that grew progressively worse and eventually killed him. Those struggles, however, were not enough to mask his dazzling skills for a portion of his life.

A Generational and Global Sickness

Both the individual, in the case of Mozart, and global levels reflect the struggle between the uncontrolled, chaotic mind and Original Mind. One particular group in our current era that appears to be more affected than most is our millennial generation.[2] The U.S. Census Bureau says there are 83.1 million young people between the ages of eighteen to thirty-four in the United States. They represent this category, and most of them are digital natives, "native speakers of technology, fluent in the digital language of computers, video games and the Internet." Scientists estimate millennials average eighteen hours a day using digital social media. In short, they have an extraordinarily unconventional relationship with technology compared to previous generations.

Unfortunately, millennials suffer from anxiety more than any other demographic group, and are more likely to die from substance abuse, alcohol, or suicide. The causes appear to be manifold, but include the lack of accessible, affordable health care, rising housing costs, and crippling educational debt. When you add the side effects of digital technology and the increased sense of isolation that comes with social media, it puts millennials increasingly at greater health risk.

Because the normal brain takes twenty to thirty years to fully mature, it makes sense that many millennials, still in the process of neural development, are more susceptible to environmental factors. The inherent neuroplasticity of the brain means that it develops based on how one uses it. And since texting and web surfing likely use different parts of the brain than reading or speaking, they emphasize these differences. Thus, the primary concern about millennials is that engagement with technology, especially the constant interaction with smartphones and other social media devices, may make their brains develop differently than those of previous generations.

According to several scientific studies, anxiety coupled with excessive technology use atrophies the frontal lobes, leading to a breakdown in neural connections between the executive system and different parts of the brain.[3] This can lead to impulsive and obsessive behaviors. Excessive use of technology also changes a person's ability to regulate emotions, remember certain events, and pay attention to different stimuli. At a minimum, these changes affect how individuals communicate with people. The worst-case scenario occurs when millennials become clinically addicted to technology.

Although Internet addiction disorder (IAD) is not a disorder according to the World Health Organization, the *Diagnostic and Statistical Manual of Mental Disorders* (DSM-5), or the International Classification of Diseases (ICD-11), it is as dangerous as drug addiction. Psychologists and other clinical professionals describe IAD patients who, like drug addicts, have the same poor social skills, grades, and health because they can't control the urge to be online. Some develop blood clots from sitting in front of their computers for hours on end. Many of these patients experience chronic problems, like attention deficit disorder and obesity. They report being distressed, disinterested, and disengaged, while having trouble reading traditional books because they are used to reading off computer screens.

According to the Pew Research Center, millennials live in a world that to them appears technologically amazing but meaningless psychologically, culturally, and spiritually. Part of the reason for this existential angst is that science, like technology, has slowly demolished many bedrock ideas that gave young people the understanding of the values and nature of who and what they are. This challenge to *fundamental ideas of being* has only sped up in the twenty-first century, leaving individuals adrift without institutional landmarks, like the government, civic organizations, and organized religion, to help them.

To be nothing, immaterial, stand on nothing, and have no guidance on how to proceed can be psychologically disconcerting, paralyzing, and frightening. This is part of the millennials' problem. They search for answers, but traditional explanations offer little guidance to the art of living in such an apparently empty universe. The result is a mind beset by anxiety, fear, stress, and through excessive rumination, at war with itself.[4]

At another level, a rising obsession during the last one hundred years of human history is a purported lack of awareness about global problems, like those dooming the masses to disease and despair. In the 1950s following World War II, overpopulation and nuclear weapons captured the imagination of much of the world. At this moment, the existential crisis is climate change, although other growing global concerns include sexual abuse, alcoholism, drugs, and addiction, domestic abuse, malnutrition, immigration, and pandemics.

The overwhelming belief connecting these concerns is that the principal problem facing humanity is a lack of awareness about these important issues. Thus, the most optimistic solution promoted is the need to become "more aware," to "raise one's consciousness," or "be informed," and from this increased awareness, solutions will follow. As a result, many attempts to engage and inform individuals globally and locally have taken place, including World Famine Day, Earth Day, and World Health Day.

What has followed this desperate urge to get informed, unfortunately, has been a lesson in unintended consequences. Not only have these doom and gloom problems gotten worse, but anxiety, fear, and stress have actually increased in the global population. Rates of depression, obsessive-compulsive behavior, autism, and other mental disorders continue to explode. This experience at a global level resembles what is happening at the individual level. We prioritize active, conscious awareness and problem-solving consciousness over everything else. This short-sighted bias leads to falling into the trap of monkey mind madness. Carrying this insanity to the global level means we may, in fact, be creating a universal, uncontrolled mind. Fortunately, the solutions proposed here for the individual radiate out to improve the presumed global sickness that is the lack of awareness.

Approach and Avoidance

The uncontrolled mind reflects a struggle between two states of mind: conscious and nonconscious processing for the control of actions. Normally, transitions between the two go smoothly and unnoticed as you live your daily life. However, when conscious awareness gets snagged in error correction mode, with its focus on the past and future, a struggle ensues. Whether at the individual, collective group, or world level, accumulating evidence suggests that resolving these issues is best when one cedes control to the nonconscious aspect of the mind, with its greater intelligence. Keep in mind that nonconscious processing is a manifestation of Original Mind. Thus, the intelligence associated with this mind seems a better option than the narrow intelligence of conscious awareness.

A simplistic example of this mind struggle happens when you cannot remember a name or an idea but know that you know it. These tip-of-the-tongue phenomena are frustrating because the conscious mind knows that the memory is there but cannot access it. Far too often, the greater the effort to remember, the stronger the blockage. What you discover is that the best way to retrieve a lost word or idea is to stop the struggle and the search and distract yourself. It helps to drop the effort of trying to retrieve the memory. By doing so, you let the nonconscious mind do its work. In fact, switching to something else to preoccupy the conscious mind will help, and more often than not, you gain access to the desired information.

A more complex example of ceding control over to the nonconscious mind occurred to me many times while teaching. I learned that when I tried too hard to follow my lesson plan, the structure such planning required produced dry and boring lectures. In contrast, when I was open to letting the class take unexpected directions based on nothing more than student questions, there was a much more interactive and responsive outcome. I would even argue that more learning and enjoyment occurred when my conscious awareness ceded control.

Contemporary research shows that the conscious mind is resource limited and overwhelmed by a lot of information. Most researchers agree that conscious deliberation, perceiving, and learning account for only a tiny fraction of total mental activity. In contrast, the efficiency of nonconscious processing lies in its unlimited resources and vast amounts of data processed simultaneously. Nonconscious processing is a realm of existence with an immense yet unfamiliar intelligence.

Modern insights indicate that nonconscious processing plays a positive and important role in defining one's personality.[5] Similar to the GPS example in Chapter 2, there are moments when the rational mind assumes it knows better and loses trust in the nonconscious, controlling principle. The result is confusion and chaos. Learning to listen and trust nonconscious intelligence brings a realignment with Original Mind. And one way to increase such trust is to cultivate an intuitive mind.

How to Cultivate an Unencumbered Mind:
Slow Down and Hear Your Inner Voice

Learn to recognize intuition. Be attentive to your conscience, small inner voice, instincts, insights, and hunches. Before you recognize intuition and can hear/feel this state amid the loudness and distractions of life, it's important first to slow down and listen. Take time away from your normal routine. Spend time outdoors or in an isolated place with few distractions to practice this exercise.

Take a brief walk in a park, forest, or the beach. Practice deep breathing and calm down the ongoing chatter of your interpreter and uncontrolled mind.

Imagine that your mind is like listening to noise produced by multiple radio stations playing simultaneously. You need to turn down the volume to listen to the one station that is relevant—your intuitive channel.

Is it possible to explain the brain-mind dynamics we are discussing from a neurobiological perspective? The traditional approach to studying the mind is to study perception. But many aspects of the complex activity of the mind and the potential chaos created when rational deliberation becomes dysfunctional are easier to study in movement than in perception. Perception and movement are not as dissimilar as imagined. Take, for example, the cerebellum and other brain areas that control movement. They do so by creating sequences of meaningful muscle activations. Likewise, these same brain circuits control how speech creates a sequence of meaningful sounds. At this level of control, movement and perception are strikingly similar. Hence, the study of movement and its control provides a unique window through which to examine the nature of conscious and nonconscious interaction.

Psychologists have conceptualized that there are two impulses reflecting basic drives that power action and movement—an approach and an avoidance urge. These are equivalent to what I have referred to as the AAECC and AFRAID impulses. The approach urge, like the AAECC impulse, compels you toward engaging life by reaching out and exploring the environment. The outward nature of this impulse helps you establish relationships with objects and living things. This urge arouses interest in external things, in changing behavior and seeking what provides a positive benefit. In contrast, the avoidance urge, like the AFRAID impulse, produces movement away from objects. This withdrawal moves you away from individuals and circumstances that elicit negative behaviors, may be injurious, and would not benefit you. Approach and avoidance oppose each other. They reflect biological imperatives that underlie cognitive style and personality. The extent to which life experiences orient you toward one of these behaviors means your basic impulse is your common response to life.

The latest neuroscience reports have not identified where or how these urges and impulses arise. Scientists have looked everywhere for their origin, but the search has not yielded definitive answers. Yet there are hints. Studies associate multiple brain regions with the personality, self, and ego functions. These include areas identified for self-awareness, such as the insula, the anterior and posterior cingulate cortex, the medial prefrontal cortex, and the temporoparietal junction (see Figure 9.1).[6] These areas make up a brain network relevant to mind dynamics, and able to produce the personality impulses that underlie the uncontrolled mind. Impulses and urges, however, typically originate at lower levels of the brain, like the brainstem, which controls cortical arousal and compels individual differences in behavior.

Carl Jung foresaw the importance of approach and avoidance principles and conceptualized them in terms of individualized energetic differences, as extraversion and introversion, which he related to the flow of psychic energy. To Jung, the impulses reflected how an individual in a repetitive and preferential way orients herself in the world. Introversion, which overlaps with the AFRAID and avoidance concepts, represents the move of energy toward the inner or subjective world. Extraversion, which overlaps with AAECC and approach concepts, is energy directed toward the outer, or more objective world.

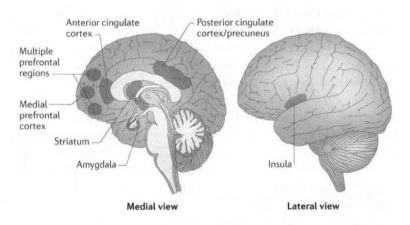

Nature Reviews | Neuroscience

Figure 9.1 Brain areas involved in self-awareness. *Source:* Tang, Yi-Yuan, Hölzel, Britta K., and Posner, Michael I. (2015).

The German-born British psychologist Hans Eysenck (1916–1997) came up with a more refined and biologically based explanation for Jung's energetic flows.[7] Eysenck equated these fluctuations with differences in levels of cortical arousal. Since the 1940s, scientists have attributed control of cortical arousal to the reticular formation, the core region of the brainstem. Control of arousal occurs through neurotransmitters, including norepinephrine, dopamine, and serotonin systems, among others. These systems originate in this central core and maintain the energetic tone throughout the central nervous system. Individual differences in arousal result from differences in the levels of neurotransmitters released onto cortical areas like the frontal lobes. Genetically predetermined differences also result from being born into a specific lineage, defined by race and ethnicity. But they can also vary as a function of socioeconomic status, experience, and other factors. From the combined genetic, biological, psychological, and sociocultural forces emerge differences in energetic tone that create these personality impulses.

The Intuition Interface

It is important to recognize that a normal brain makes use of many functions, whether nonconscious, conscious, instinctive, or logical. Yet mostly, one feels like a spectator to brain and mind dynamics. One can observe outcomes but cannot intervene in the rapid juggling between nonconscious and conscious processing. This push–pull harkens to my story about teaching, where logic tells me to follow the lesson plan. In contrast, instinct tells me it's more interesting to play it by ear and base it on student feedback. An important aspect of this push–pull is whether to trust one set of functions more than the other. There is, in this sense, a personalized aspect of the struggle between instinct and logic that provides a small window during which one can interfere.

Growing evidence shows that such intermediate access exists between conscious and nonconscious processing that is helpful in resolving conflicts. We glimpse this intermediate stage and of the intelligence of nonconscious processing in "intuition," an interface between the two styles of processing.[8] In its broad sense, an interface is someone or something that facilitates the birth of something new during labor, struggle, or conflict. In computing, scientists conceptualize an interface as a shared boundary across which two or more separate components of a larger system exchange information. The icons on your computer screen and the keyboard on which you type are interfaces between what you as the user wants and what the computer itself does. A good interface creates a smooth transition and resolution between two different states, even between two warring sides.

Carl Jung conceived of a mind interface between conscious and nonconscious processing and called this psychological space the under-conscious, or *unterbewusst*—the intermediate region between the two. Others have called this interface the subconscious. Jung argued that an in-between state is of importance because it allows for the perception of the possibilities inherent in the present moment. Jung was an intuitive person, leading him to incorporate this aspect of mind at the core of his psychology.

Intuition is the ability to understand "the possibilities inherent in the present moment" instinctively and immediately, with no conscious mediation or analytic calculation. This type of knowing bridges the gap between conscious and nonconscious aspects of the mind and between instinct and logic. Another definition describes intuition "as an informative conscious feeling without conscious access to the antecedents of the feeling." This definition suggests the existence and perception of emotion-like aspects of intuition. Indeed, studies show an overlap and interactivity between intuition and emotion. Positive moods improve intuitive judgment, while negative moods impair it. Intuition also orients behavior in an appropriate and sensitive manner. Robert Lee Hotz describes sudden insights or intuitions as "the culmination of an intense and complex series of brain states that require more neural resources than methodical reasoning."[9] Such descriptions suggest that intuition exists at the interface between emotion, reasoning, and nonconscious processing and helps to generate potential responses to life demands.

Researchers have proposed that instincts and intuitions are often the only practical ways for assessing and responding to uncertainty, an unavoidable aspect of life. Uncertainty occurs when there is a desire to know the future in order to minimize negative consequences. But our brains did not evolve the computational capabilities or innate methods and understanding to determine real probabilities, so uncertainty arises. Uncertainty is the greatest when predicting complex events like how the stock market will behave, how people will vote in an election, or how a loved one will respond to a medical intervention. We don't spend a lot of time and effort figuring out these outcomes because any attempt would be computationally expensive, if not impossible. Rather, our brains make choices based on innate tendencies and beliefs about the likelihood of uncertain events, and use heuristics to achieve them.

Heuristics are imperfect problem-solving ways that depend on assessments made when we perceive events and communicate with others.[10] These assessments include determining the similarity between two things or attributing how one thing causes another. The brain performs these heuristics computations in the absence of a task, although it often uses them to meet task demands as they arise. Thus, while the interpreter is a rational aspect of the mind, its dependence on heuristics makes it an instinctive and intuitive-based system that accounts for our unique judgment.

Many creative individuals exhibit an ease in combining rationality with intuition.[11] We know Henry Ford as the founder of the Ford Motor Company, and for optimizing the assembly-line technique of mass production to produce automobiles. In 1914, Ford faced a falling demand for his cars and high worker turnover. What he did in response to these challenges astonished the world, including other barons of industry. Ford more than doubled worker pay to $5 per day (equivalent to $130 today). This was a novel, bold, and intuitive move, considered crazy by some, although consistent with Ford's belief in improving the lot of his workers and reducing high turnover in the industry. Within a year, turnover dropped by a factor of over 20 while productivity doubled. Demand for Ford cars boomed because Ford's own workers could now afford the product they were making.

In another similar case, Bill Allen was an American business executive in the aviation industry who served as the president of Boeing from 1945 to 1968. In the 1950s, the Boeing company focused on making planes for the defense industry. Allen had a bold but risky idea. He would build his own commercial jet that would serve what he imagined was soon to be a booming industry—civilian air travel. So Allen bet the future of Boeing on this idea and convinced his board to risk $16 million on a new transcontinental airliner, the Boeing 707. His intuition proved right, and the move built the American commercial jet airliner industry, transforming Boeing into an early industry leader. The stories of Henry Ford and Bill Allen exemplify that instincts and intuition, built on preparedness, can provide a path to negotiate the problems of conscious and nonconscious activity in the face of life demands. Unfortunately, little is known about instincts and intuition, and certainly not enough to trust the process unless you have trained those skills.

Cultivating an Intuitive Mind

To overcome the skepticism toward intuition, it is necessary to reassess what is known. You typically understand instincts as innate, hard-wired behaviors impossible to change. In the book *Rethinking Innateness: A Connectionist Perspective on Development*, Elizabeth Bates, Jeff Elman, and colleagues propose a more dynamic way to think about this type of innateness.[12] Their argument is that genes influence brain development by establishing the physical structure of a system and the learning algorithms or heuristics the system employs. The specific functionality of the system, or how it works, comes about because of the interaction between genetic constraints, learning approaches, and environmental stimulation. These nature–nurture dynamics occur at all levels of the central nervous system to produce emergent behaviors, from the rules of synaptic plasticity to the development of the sense of self. At lower levels of processing, such as in the brainstem, the dynamics may be more constrained than in other areas, yet important for producing critical aspects of behavior, such as cortical arousal. At higher levels, such as in the frontal cortex, they may be less constrained, and responsible for the development of more abstract behaviors, such as a theory of mind.

The conclusion of Elman's book is that instincts are not necessarily inborn, preprogrammed, hardwired, or genetically predetermined, and therefore immune to learning, but emerge during the interaction with the world. A continuum of behavior develops from this interactivity, from rigid instinctive behaviors to experience-dependent flexible ones, but with both ends of the spectrum being highly *adaptive*. Sometimes, some preset rigidity avoids the risks and perils of development by enabling "adult" behaviors from the start. Experience-dependent flexibility over an extended developmental period enables an individual to gain complex skills and intelligent behaviors.

Increased intuition is one outcome of what I describe as my freedom from the uncontrolled mind. Enhanced sensitivity to people, nature, and life improved my anticipation of problems, recognition of others' feelings, and of the mind storms gathering strength. In this way, I could deal with them before they fully formed. Studies have shown that with consistent practice, you can increase and improve instinct and intuitive skills. The intuition interface, which plays a critical role, is available to everyone, and while some individuals may be more adept at accessing it, everyone has the inherent skill to do it. Researchers, psychologists, and clinicians have proposed several ways to increase access to this interface. Throughout the book are exercises on *How to Cultivate an Unencumbered Mind*, some of which you have already encountered, to help develop this practice:

- Encourage Curiosity (*Chapter 1*).
- Nurture Creativity (*Chapter 1*).
- Practice Present-Moment Centering (*Chapter 2*).
- Distance Yourself from the Problem (*Chapter 7*).
- Discriminate between Intuition and Monkey Mind Chatter (*Chapter 8*).
- Slow Down and Hear Your Inner Voice (*Chapter 9*).
- Learn to Trust Your Inner Voice and Practice Empathic Accuracy (*Chapter 9*).
- Promote Associative Thinking (*Chapter 9*).

A particular concern in the normal functioning of the brain is the regulation of the executive system in the frontal lobes. While this mechanistic understanding of frontal lobe regulation, or the ongoing war in the brain, is important, understanding it at a behavioral level is equally so. We need to know the kinds of weapons being used. Gaining an insight into this can help focus the work on therapeutic approaches for minimizing the bad and maximizing good outcomes. Examining the varieties of thought involved is necessary, since, like some weapons, certain styles of thinking are less harmful or more beneficial than others.

How to Cultivate an Unencumbered Mind: Learn to Trust Your Inner Voice and Practice Empathic Accuracy

One reason why some people appear more intuitive than others is they attend to, trust, and act on their inner voice, gut feeling, emotion, or conscience rather than dismissing or doubting it. That does not mean ignoring the analytical mind and critical thinking.

A difference exists between reason as a system of checks and balances (which you want to encourage) and talking yourself out of what intuition knows to be true (which you want to discourage).

Intuitive individuals exhibit empathic accuracy. They base their intuitive awareness of what other people are considering and sensing on cues involving body language, tone of voice, and other nonverbal cues. Empathic accuracy is a powerful form of empathy that helps foster deep connections with others.

- *Choose a relative, a friend, or a stranger whom you encounter every day.*
- *Observe them unobtrusively for at least one minute.*
- *Tune into and identify the mood they are in.*
- *Verify your guess by asking them directly.*
- *Assess what helped you guess correctly.*
- *Assess what you missed if you got your hunch wrong.*

Insightful, Experiential, and Incessant Rumination

Science has suggested several styles or categories of thought: abstract, analytical, creative, concrete, critical, convergent, divergent, and associative. We can group these various styles into at least three outcome-based categories: insightful (used for problem-solving), experiential (focused on the task at hand), and incessant (unknown function). Recent neuroscience evidence shows that these groupings of thought are different in kind and produced by distinct regions of the brain.[13]

Insightful thoughts are those that help resolve problems. Solutions occur when relationships form, or we make novel associations between objects and/or actions that settle difficulties. This judgment provides insights into the motivating forces in nature, ourselves, and others. For a long time, I did not know the amount of water needed by various rose bushes, cacti, and other plants we have at home. The results of my misguided attempts led to the plants' premature deaths. I knew plants needed both water and fertilizer and hence followed a weekly schedule of providing them. It surprised me when leaves turned yellow, dropped off, and plants withered and died. A slow learner, it took me some time to realize that different plants actually have different needs. Specific plants need regular, weekly waterings, and others need a lot less. The same is true of fertilizer. Each plant has individual needs, and my ignorance was killing my houseplants with kindness. When the insight finally dawned on me, I turned around this destructive behavior and learned to grow healthy, beautiful plants.

Insightful thought also helps plan for the future. This kind of thinking allows for the ability to ask, "What am I going to do tomorrow?" This query crops up almost every night for me before I fall asleep. My response is a list of half-dozen tasks I have scheduled or need to do the following day, organized in order of execution: Visit the doctor at 8 am; Get to work by 9; Finish the report by noon; Talk to colleagues at 2 pm; Meet with my partner at 4; Buy groceries on the way home at 6. Without this ability to plan for future actions, the complexity of life becomes unmanageable and paralyzing. This ability reflects the power of insightful thought.

Experiential thought, the second category of thinking, arises from responses to and engagement with the ever-changing current circumstances. The phone rings and you answer it; the water on the stove is boiling over and requires attention; you watch television and get angry about the story of the immigrant child who died while crossing the river with his dad. Hundreds of these mini-events capture your attention every single moment and there is a need to respond: answer the phone, turn the stove down, brush away tears. Thus, experiential thought, like insightful thinking, is a necessary component of living. Both are engaged effortlessly in living creatively. Trouble occurs when facing a multiplicity of demands that the limited conscious mind cannot handle. In a nanosecond, the switch from the original, nonconscious mind to an overwhelmed, aware mind occurs. This change may turn into an obsessed and uncontrolled mind if the behavior persists.

Scientists estimate that incessant thought, the third style of thinking, accounts for 30 to 50 percent of waking life. Compared to insightful and experiential thought, incessant rumination is less understood and less valued. Psychologists describe incessant rumination in negative terms and ignore, deride, and condemn this category of thinking. Negative descriptions include such things as unruly, untrained, undisciplined, restless, capricious, fanciful, confused, indecisive, uncontrollable, judgmental, paranoid, distracted, most connected to the ego, and master rationalizer. Scholars describe the consequences of this type of thinking in terms of fear, guilt, anger, sadness, and envy. Indeed, many have associated incessant rumination with mindlessness and with much of the unnecessary suffering humanity experiences.

The dominant view from academics is that incessant rumination affects behavior negatively, and that this type of thinking is detrimental to functioning in the world. Associating incessant rumination with the uncontrolled mind seems consistent with this view, since this mind appears to have no utility other than a negative one. The perception of a lack of utility has created a natural desire to find solutions to make the problem go away. And yet, incessant rumination is a large aspect of being human. From an alternative perspective, this unwanted and irritating behavior need not control you. And its hijinks need not cause you suffering. Indeed, as we have already alluded to, incessant rumination is more like a lost attention deficit and hyperactive child searching for home—one who needs love and pity more than anger, fear, or condemnation.

Questions to Ponder

Take a moment to recall a day at work, a party, or any other event/gathering where you interacted with others.

What types of thoughts did you have?
What insightful deliberation did you engage in?
What experiential thoughts crossed your mind?
What types of incessant thoughts did you have?

Incessant Thought and Creativity

A biological explanation for incessant rumination is that it reflects a problem with regulating the frontal lobes—even more poignantly, the interpreter. A more psychological explanation is that the processing of information becomes decontextualized. This means that the evaluation of information you are dealing with at the moment is suddenly pulled apart from the circumstances that generated it. It appears at the wrong time and for the wrong reasons.

Imagine, for example, you are at a dinner party, relishing the food and wine, when suddenly thoughts of your impending divorce come to mind. Your mind rehashes the circumstances that led to your breakup and in a flash, you are no longer at the party enjoying it. Your interpreter is now dealing with a problem, but in the wrong context. When mind activity becomes decontextualized or isolated in this way, your Original Mind gives way to the troubled and uncontrolled mind. The decontextualization can happen for several reasons during the switch from an unlimited to a resource-limited process. A voice, a comment, a smell can conjure up the mind storm of divorce thoughts and kick-starts incessant rumination.

Our minds evolved to interrupt nonconscious processing to deal with such glitches, errors, or novel and unexpected events. These interruptions are typically brief, unless things go wrong in the regulatory mechanisms controlling the activity. The idea of divorce, for example, creates a glitch in the regulatory mechanisms of the frontal lobes and takes the interpreter out of context, perhaps because of the greater saliency of those thoughts. Prolonged problems of regulation turn into obsessive rumination and hard-to-manage impulsive behaviors, creating a disruption in the natural flow of creative living.

In its proper context, particularly in terms of its temporal domain, the uncontrolled mind becomes normalized and the chaos controlled. *In this circumstance, negative incessant and obsessive chatter assumes a more positive form of creative thinking, thinking that is complex, multifaceted, multilayered, intricate, elaborate, embellished, flexible, and fluent.* Thoughts about your impending breakup are normal when discussed with your therapist or pastor. In that context, you can bring all your resources to the problem and may even find creative solutions. But this is much more difficult to do at a dinner party.

Several psychological remedies have evolved to address the problems of an obsessive decontextualized mind, including the relationship between incessant rumination, intelligence, and creative living. A few clinicians have built entire psychotherapeutic approaches to reduce or eliminate the negative consequences associated with this type of incessant or decontextualized thinking. Dr. Albert Ellis in the 1950s, for example, conceived of Rational Emotive Behavior Therapy (REBT), a precursor of Cognitive-Behavioral Therapy (CBT), to address this.[14] REBT, like CBT, resolves emotional and behavioral problems to help people lead happier and more fulfilling lives. The therapy grew out of Ellis's understanding that emotional disturbances are *after-the-fact* or post hoc explanations. His ideas predated the work by Gazzaniga and colleagues in the 1970s on the concept of the interpreter.

To Ellis, these post hoc explanations suggested unfortunate circumstances do not disturb as much as the reconstruction of those events. A reconstruction results from language, beliefs, meanings, history, and philosophies about the world. To address this, REBT and its successor, CBT, focus on present-moment thinking to help individuals identify those reconstructions and their self-defeating nature. Clinicians help patients understand how reconstructions create emotional distress, leading to unhealthy actions and behaviors. Finally, therapists challenge the rationality of those beliefs and sensations and help replace them with healthier, more productive ones.

Martin Seligman adapted Ellis's approach and in 1998 created the Positive Psychology movement.[15] His was an effort to study suffering not from the perspective of psychopathology but from a more holistic picture of a healthy human experience. Christopher Peterson described Positive Psychology in 2008 as "the scientific study of what makes life most worth living." By studying life from this perspective, Seligman and colleagues identified factors critical for overcoming the negativity of the uncontrolled mind to move beyond surviving to flourishing. They identified several critical factors in this progression, including positive emotion, engagement, relationships, meaning, purpose, and accomplishment.

Most therapeutic approaches such as these, focusing on the problematic mind, assume negativity as the mind's natural embodiment, and this perspective creates the impetus for fixing by removing this troublesome nature. It reminds me of "if all I have is a hammer, then everything looks like a nail." My perspective is that incessant rumination results from a natural and positive evolutionary process that has gone awry—namely, one occurring in the wrong context. I base this perspective on evolutionary ideas that presuppose the controlled mind reflects the developmental unfoldment of a mind optimized for survival, one free from fear and inherently creative.

The chattering and obsessive monkey mind would seem to contradict this assumption, for such a mind appears to have little or no utility. The alternative conclusion, which I favor, is that this state of mind has positive utility—we just need to figure out what that is. REBT, CBT, and other such psychotherapeutic approaches have been successful at dealing with the uncontrolled mind not by eliminating it, but by refocusing its energy. Many of these approaches still depend on rational deliberation and are lifelong practices that mask but do not permanently resolve the problem. The major drawback is that using the rational mind to resolve a glitch in the rational mind is ultimately impossible and self-defeating. The recurring nature of the symptoms makes this point quite clear.

Other tactics address the problem from a different perspective and with better success. These include mindfulness, yoga, and similar techniques, dating back thousands of years. The methods do not depend on the rational mind to solve mind problems and therefore achieve a better and longer-lasting resolution. They don't mask the problem as much as transform it. Their success is a reason for the growing interest in the West for these approaches. Some therapeutic methods, such as mindfulness-based stress reduction, or MBSR, focus on a deliberative approach while in the storm, while other methods, such as Vipassana meditation, visualize the problem from outside the storm. A hybrid approach combining these two methods is what I am proposing here. Stop Monkey Mind (SMM) involves mindfulness practice to address decontextualized incessant thinking. It rests on the intellectual and rational understanding of the problem. The assumption is that it helps to know the problem when attempting to overcome it. The approach differs from many other methods because it has the potential to provide quick, long-lasting, and transformative change.

In SMM, I assume the basis for the problem to be rumination or incessant thinking or worrying *in the wrong context*. The natural and positive evolutionary aspect of the mind gets off kilter. Rumination refers to the tendency for repetitive processing or obsessive consideration of the causes, situational factors, and consequences of emotional experiences. Rumination reflects self-focused deliberation and undoubtedly engages the left-brain interpreter. We worry about problems because we are natural problem-solvers and planners, and that is normal rumination.

Sometimes, worrying becomes too much about the wrong things and at the wrong time, and never reaches a resolution. Too much worrying produces fear or worse. The mind spins nonstop, increasing the likelihood of severe psychological problems. This ramping-up of the obsessive mind causes the interpreter to go into overdrive, starting a struggle for control between conscious and nonconscious processing. The entire system spins out of control, with AAECC impulses giving way to AFRAID impulses. This is the threshold point at which the uncontrolled mind appears and gains control.

Recent analysis of normal worrying has linked rumination to regions in the brain that together form what scientists have dubbed the default mode network (DMN; see Figure 9.2).[16] The DMN connects areas active during autopiloting, which involves mind wandering, daydreaming, reminiscing, and self-referential thinking. The identified DMN zones include those along the midline portion of the brain, such as the anterior cingulate cortex (ACC), posterior cingulate cortex (PCC), and the ventromedial prefrontal cortex (vmPFC; see Figure 9.2). At least one study has shown that negative worrying emerges when the firing and increased blood flow to the subgenual prefrontal cortex (sgPFC) synchronizes with the rest of the DMN.

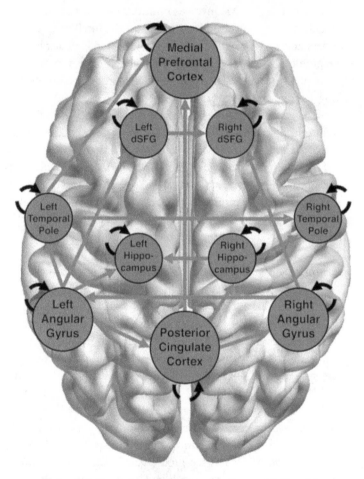

Figure 9.2 The default mode network. *Source:* McCormick, Ethan M., and Telzer, Eva H. (2018). Unchanged from original. https://creativecommons.org/licenses/by/4.0/.

It is noteworthy to pause for a moment to consider that this highly distributed and complex network involved in problem-solving is what triggers the uncontrolled mind. This contradicts the effort to paint this mind as something without utility and only as negative behavior. More likely, scientists have not recognized the positive utility of this condition and have not addressed the actual problem. A need exists to reexamine the functional significance of rumination and incessant chatter and the role they play within the context of intelligent behavior and creative living.

Western culture links intelligence with analytical skills, conceptualization, and conscious awareness. We assume it to involve the ability to reason and understand, instead of doing things effortlessly, automatically, or by instinct. The Western emphasis on conceptualization and awareness has roots in the Greek philosophy of Socrates, his pupil Plato, and Plato's pupil Aristotle. Not until the early 1980s did a serious challenge to this emphasis materialize. In 1983, the psychologist Howard Gardner published work describing nine domains of activity in which individuals exhibit particular skills.[17] These are domains representing different ways of processing information in which individuals learn and perform in a "smart" way. These multiple intelligences include nature, sound, number, life, people, body, word, self, and space. In 1990, Peter Salovey and John Mayer published a paper arguing about the importance of emotional intelligence as another "smart" skill comprising intelligence. Indeed, there may be more skills still undiscovered.

The controversy about whether these various skills are unique and separate versus having a common factor continues even now. The notion that a single construct termed "intelligence," or a generalized intelligence factor, or "g," exists is controversial. In his 1987 book *Intelligence: Its Structure, Growth and Action*, Raymond Cattell pointed out that there are, in fact, at least two independent intelligence factors.[18] He called them fluid or "gf" intelligence and crystallized or "gc" intelligence. Fluid intelligence, for Cattell, is the skill to reason, use logic, and solve problems in a unique and novel situation. Examples of this intelligence involve learning extra information or playing the piano without reference to previous knowledge. Scholars have argued that fluid intelligence is the domain of insightful deliberation and creativity.

In contrast, when you understand material that you are studying, and incorporate that information into short- and long-term memory, the outcome becomes crystallized knowledge. Crystallized intelligence refers to the skills that use knowledge gained through learning and experience and uses experiential reasoning. Crystallized intelligence is maintained and may even increase with age because of its reliance on the accumulation of knowledge.

The brain integrates insightful, experiential, and presumably incessant thinking into both fluid and crystallized intelligence. That integration provides the basis for how you solve problems, generate ideas, and respond to life demands. This integrated approach is the essence of creative living. When I cook spinach lasagna from a family recipe, I use crystallized intelligence to understand and follow the instructions in the recipe. I use fluid intelligence, needed for creative flexibility, when changing the recipe to suit my changing tastes and dietary requirements, or of those for whom I am cooking. Thus, memory-based responses reflect crystallized intelligence, while response flexibility and adaptability reflect fluid intelligence.

An important aspect of creative living is how the mind's flexibility and adaptability, or fluid and crystallized intelligence, express themselves. Researchers use the concepts of divergence and convergence to describe strategies that use fluid and crystallized intelligence to help you solve problems, generate solutions, and respond appropriately. These strategies are two ends of the same continuum (see Table 9.1). Convergent processing describes a linear and systematic process used to narrow down multiple ideas into a single solution. This targeted strategy converges on a solution and finds the single best answer to a problem or a question. Convergent strategies involve crystallized intelligence, and standard IQ tests measure this style of processing. In contrast, divergence is a more flexible, iterative, and web-like strategy, focusing on connections between ideas and associated with fluid intelligence and creative flexibility. Divergent processing settles into an optimal solution from a multiplicity of options, but in a less linear and more open-ended process. Individuals who show curiosity, nonconformity, persistence, and readiness to take risks produce more divergent processing, and engage in activities that trigger such judgment.

Table 9.1 Comparison between Convergent and Divergent Thinking

Convergent Thinking	Divergent Thinking
The strategy for figuring out a concrete solution to any problem. The ability to apply rules to find a solution.	The strategy that explores multiple solutions to generate creative ideas. The activity is more spontaneous and free-flowing.
This process is a straightforward use of analytical and deductive reasoning to figure out the most effective answer to a problem.	This process refers to opening the mind in various directions and trying out multiple solutions for a problem.
Its characteristics include: • Speed • Accuracy • Logic	Its characteristics include being: • Spontaneous • Free-flowing • Nonlinear

Trying to understand the nature of thoughts reflected in this discussion is an example of convergent thinking. I began by putting together the original outline of the topic in an organized, structured, and understandable fashion. The outline started with the idea that the brain uses a variety of styles of thought, from abstract, analytical, creative, concrete, critical, convergent, divergent, and associative. I narrowed this broad characterization to the idea that all these unique styles, categories, or groupings collapse into at least three types: insightful, experiential, and incessant. These occur in two dominant modes: nonconscious and conscious processing. Thus, using this kind of categorization to understand a problem is common in convergent thinking.

My attempts to understand the uncontrolled mind are an example of divergent thinking. The process began by breaking down the topic into biological, psychological, and sociocultural aspects to gain insights into the various dimensions of the topic. While engaged in this process, ideas arose spontaneously and in a free-flowing manner. They appeared random and unorganized. Therefore, to organize the ideas and put the book together, divergent thinking had to intersect with convergent thinking. This meant arranging the ideas and information in a structured way for others to understand.

Many researchers agree it is possible to teach and promote crystallized and fluid intelligence by highlighting and practicing divergent and convergent strategies. Promoting complexity, curiosity, elaboration, flexibility, fluency, imagination, originality, and risk-taking enhances divergent processing. But this may be like a chicken-and-egg paradox, since creative or calm individuals may already show more innate fluid intelligence. What most psychologists agree with is that, after the use of divergent thinking to determine an optimal solution, processing uses convergent thinking to organize the information and ideas. Teaching and emphasizing one strategy will naturally affect the other. Thus, integration of both fluid and crystallized intelligence, and their associated convergent and divergent strategies, reflects normal brain behavior.[19]

Creativity as "Controlled" Chaos

I have argued that the uncontrolled mind and the Original Mind are two sides of the same brain dynamics that is present in all of us. One side is uncontrolled chaos; the other is controlled chaos, the very definition of creativity. These two expressions of mind are like identical twins growing up in different environments yet sharing the same genetics. In fact, *the uncontrolled mind* is *Original Mind*. Original Mind takes care of most everything and is more at home in the present. The troublesome mind emerges when trying to solve specific problems while accessing the past and looking ahead into the future and becomes trapped by the problem. Perseveration in trying to find a solution using the same approach turns into an obsession and soon becomes uncontrolled. The nature of this "chaos" causes a range of negative feelings, from confusion to depression. The solution is not to get rid of such a mind, but to place it in the proper environment and context. *Training and guiding the obsessive, uncontrolled mind back to a more natural, controlled, and original state in which it can deal with the challenges of living in-the-moment is the path to real problem-solving.*

Creative living, or controlled chaos, is the essence of Original Mind. However, most models of intelligence leave incessant rumination unaccounted for in terms of creative living, although some scholars conceive of it as a type of "fluid intelligence." Here, the perspective is that incessant rumination is a necessary ingredient for true creativity. What incessant thinking allows for is consideration, in a free-flowing and spontaneous way, of multiple events to extract many solutions and identify what works. This utility is the essence of fluid intelligence in the solving of day-to-day problems. Unfortunately, insufficient evidence is available regarding incessant rumination to make this argument scientifically convincing. For now, circumstantial evidence must suffice.

A way to approach understanding how intelligence, incessant rumination, and creativity relate to one another is to examine what creativity is and assess how incessant rumination promotes such activity. The relationship is not an easy problem to solve and starts with difficulties in the definition. Creativity is difficult to define, and without a definition, the process is difficult to study. Aristotle in the 4th century B.C. (ca. 384 B.C. to 322 B.C.) considered creativity to be a gift from the gods; as something occurring external to rational thought, or when an individual "lost his senses." From Aristotle's viewpoint, creativity is indescribable and undefinable and therefore not a subject of scientific study.

Others, however, have been more persistent in trying to find a useful definition, including the Hungarian American psychologist Mihaly Csikszentmihalyi.[20] In his 1996 book on *Creativity,* he describes it as resulting "from the interaction of a system composed of three elements: a culture that contains symbolic rules, a person who brings novelty into the symbolic domain, and a field of experts who recognize and validate the innovation." Later in the book, Csikszentmihalyi argues that creativity is "a central source of meaning in our lives . . . most of the things that are interesting, important, and human are the results of creativity . . . [and] when we are involved in it, we feel that we are living more fully than during the rest of life." For Csikszentmihalyi, creativity is an innate ability that expresses itself in a particular medium and others recognize it as something distinctive yet necessary to live well. It reflects our interaction with culture, life experiences, and the demands these make.

Still other researchers define creativity as the capacity to perceive the world in novel ways, find hidden or new patterns, make connections among unrelated phenomena, and generate unique solutions. Most such definitions describe creativity as an interrelated process of perception, cognition, and action. Unfortunately, customary assessments of this behavior focus mainly on what many consider the standard criteria: originality and usefulness. A continuing argument among scientists is whether we should assess traits, knowledge, skills, and ways of reasoning, especially those related to fresh ideas, novelty, curiosity, playfulness, originality, emotional sensitivity, and nonconforming behavior.

An aspect of creativity for which there may be general agreement is how it links objects of awareness and general domains of knowledge. This unique ability was a striking feature of Leonardo da Vinci's personality, and of many creative individuals. Researchers know this feature of personality as the basis for originality. Rather than a linear process, this type of thinking is associative and iterative and helps people with curiosity, energy, and openness notice connections where others do not. The activity requires something like a *controlled* mind or controlled chaos. The very nature of creativity seems to harness the uniqueness of the uncontrolled mind and bring a measure of control to it. This is outright difficult, as well as dangerous, if not done properly or applied in the right way and in the proper context.

Although mental illness is neither necessary nor sufficient for creativity, the question whether a connection exists between the two has been a persistent one.[21] A report in 2011 based on a forty-year study of 1.2 million Swedish individuals tried to answer it.[22] Simon Kyaga and colleagues found that the siblings of patients with autism and first-degree relatives of patients with schizophrenia, bipolar disorder, and anorexia nervosa were overrepresented in creative professions. The correlation suggested that perhaps these individuals inherited a set of traits conducive to creativity, while avoiding the debilitating aspects of the disorder their siblings experienced.

Subsequent investigations revealed that what these individuals had was a high degree of what scientists call "schizotypal personality traits." *Schizotypy* is not schizophrenia. Rather, the term refers to a matrix of personality traits, ranging from normal, dissociative, imaginative states to extreme states of mind related to psychosis. "Positive" schizotypy means individuals are likely to have unusual perceptual experiences,

thin mental boundaries between self and others, impulsive nonconformity, and may display magical beliefs. "Negative" schizotypal traits
include more problematic behaviors, including cognitive disorganization, and physical and social anhedonia, meaning difficulty experiencing pleasure from social interactions and physical activities enjoyable
for most people. Recent findings support the link between a positive
schizotypy personality and originality. This confirms the idea that
overlapping mental processes occur in both creativity and psychosis.
The key to creativity seems to be the ability to open up the floodgates
of sensory information in a *controlled* way, and letting in as much information as possible. A flood of information means the possibility
for the most unexpected and unusual connections that turn into creative ideas. The psychologist Scott Kaufman, in a column for *Scientific
American* titled "Beautiful Minds," argues that "creative cognition
draws on both the executive functioning that is tied to intellect and
the associative divergence that is associated with openness, increasing
the probability that ideas will be *original*. Whether the idea is creative,
however, also depends on the *protective intellectual factors* needed to
steer the chaotic storm."

The presence of protective factors to steer the chaotic storm defines
a "controlled" mind. Such a mind receives exceptional parenting or self-
care. It exhibits enhanced fluid and crystallized intelligence. It displays
unconventional thinking and includes a good working memory and
robust inhibition. These factors allow the experience of treating something as novel no matter how many times you have seen it before or
tagged it as irrelevant. High flexibility and adaptability, openness to experience and exploration, preference for novelty, and hyperconnectivity
in specific brain circuits are additional protective factors. Optimal levels of these factors produce a da Vinci–type mind, whereas nonoptimal
levels make an individual vulnerable to disordered judgment.

Many creative individuals reflect this delicate balance. One example from the past was Wolfgang Amadeus Mozart; another from
our present is Kanye West, an American rapper, singer, songwriter, record producer, businessman, and fashion designer.[23] Kanye is one of
the most critically acclaimed artists of the twenty-first century, earning
praise from music critics, fans, industry peers, and an array of cultural

figures for his musical output. Kanye was born to a photographer and former Black Panther father and a college professor mother. Following his parents' divorce in Atlanta in 1980, when he was three years old, Kanye moved with his mother to Chicago. There, he showed an affinity for the arts at an early age. He wrote poetry at five years old and was singing rap songs in the third grade. By the seventh grade, he was creating musical compositions and eventually selling them to other artists. At twenty, after attending Chicago State University for one year, he dropped out of college to pursue a musical career.

Kanye spent much of the late 1990s producing records for several well-known artists and music groups. He gained recognition as a producer for Roc-A-Fella Records in the early 2000s, producing singles for several popular artists including Jay-Z, Beanie Sigel, Freeway, and Cam'ron. Early in his career, Kanye pioneered a style of hip-hop production dubbed "chipmunk-soul," which included skillful use of sped-up, sample-based beats. Many considered him an extraordinary producer who created a unique signature sound, which he then abandoned to his imitators.

Besides producing hit albums, Kanye also crafted hit songs for Ludacris, Alicia Keys, and Janet Jackson. In 2004, he released his own debut album, *The College Dropout*, to critical and commercial success, despite the perception that his middle-class background denied him credibility as a rapper. The album shot to number two on the Billboard 200 and was voted the top album of the year by two major music publications. It has consistently ranked among the great hip-hop works and debut albums by any artist. The album would eventually be certified triple platinum in the United States, and garner ten Grammy nominations, including Album of the Year and Best Rap Album.

During this same time, Kanye founded the record label GOOD Music. His creativity and intentional diversification of musical styles led him to explore a variety of musical genres in subsequent acclaimed albums. These encompassed soul, baroque-pop, stadium rock, electro, house-music, indie rock, synth-pop, progressive pop, progressive rock, industrial, punk, and gospel. His music is some of the best-selling and most critically acclaimed in the industry, and contemporaries frequently laud him as one of hip hop's greatest artists. Kanye has won twenty-two

Grammy Awards, making him one of the most awarded artists of all time, and second most awarded rapper. *Time* magazine named him one of the 100 most influential people in the world in 2005 and 2015.

Unfortunately, Kanye began experiencing neuropsychological problems, such as suicidal ideation and bipolar disorder, and was committed to the UCLA Medical Center with hallucinations and paranoia in 2016. Later, in an interview, he declared an addiction to opioids prescribed to him following elective surgery, which may have contributed to his offensive behavior and nervous breakdown.

The separation between creativity and mental illness may be transparent for certain types of creativity. Fortunately, experts have broadened the definition of creativity beyond the unique inventiveness of brilliant artists. In 2009, Kaufman and Beghetto distinguished between four levels, and proposed what they called the Four C model of creativity.[24] Their proposed levels reflect the impact of creativity on society, but with a unified underlying physiological process. These researchers suggest that "mini-c" creativity relates to meaningful ideas and insights known only to an individual. "Little-c" creativity involves everyday understanding and problem-solving. This is the style of creativity characterized by fluid intelligence that helps solve everyday problems and allows individuals to adapt to changing environments. "Pro-c" creativity occurs in skilled professionals such as Kanye West. Finally, "big-c" creativity involves transformational ideas that affect the largest portion of society and the world. Kaufman and Beghetto's definition, which acknowledges the multiple, multilayered, and general nature of creativity, comes closest to what I describe in this book as creative living.

How to Cultivate an Unencumbered Mind: Promote Associative Thinking

Associative thinking occurs when you allow your mind to "wander" and "free associate" without providing a direction or a goal. In this mode, the mind will automatically highlight seemingly unrelated ideas, thoughts, observations, sensory input, and memory of existing knowledge in the intuitive interface. Curiosity drives this free association and is the basis for the "controlled" mind. The following is a place to start:

- *Detach yourself from your thoughts and observe them from a distance.*
- *Observe them without constraint and rationale.*
- *Permit and allow your mind to roam without purpose.*
- *Discard nothing that comes up.*
- *Highlight interesting ideas by writing them down.*
- *Avoid judging ideas that crop up.*
- *Increase your tolerance for ambiguity.*

In 2014, Vakhtin and colleagues had participants observe a commonplace object and gave them a few seconds to come up with a creative application for it.[25] Divergent tests like this are the most commonly used tasks to estimate the potential for creative behavior. For instance, if the object shown is a pencil and the participant's response is that "it is an instrument for writing a letter," researchers consider that an expected and noncreative response. A creative answer, in contrast, is that "it is a pointer used during a talk." Therefore, the longer the list of creative answers, the more creative the individual.

The Vakhtin study revealed an association between creativity and increased neural activity in three different brain networks. The three networks included the Executive Attention Network (EAN), the Default Mode Network (DMN), and the Salience Network (SN). These networks comprise interactive regions that act in unison and often fire simultaneously for similar purposes. EAN manages communication between areas of the prefrontal cortex and the parietal lobe. While frontal lobes handle decision-making and complex behavior, the parietal lobes integrate spatial sensory information akin to touch and navigation.

The DMN network is necessary in autopiloting, mind wandering, brainstorming, and social cognition. It underlies the ability to understand what someone else discerns, or how one reacts in a particular social situation. DMN activity mirrors the extensive communication between the prefrontal cortex and the parietal lobe. Because frontal and parietal networks control the performance of mental simulations, they provide a potential origin for creative thinking.[26]

Finally, the SN network is relevant for monitoring internal and external streams of consciousness. As the massive amount of sensory information courses through the brain every single moment, the SN highlights sensations to attend to and to ignore. In short, SN helps select internal or external information that is most apt for solving the problem at hand. The switching or transitioning between various levels of brain processing likely involves the SN. Studies show that the greater the number of connections among EAN, DMN, and SN networks, the smoother and more rapid the transitions are. This correlates with greater activity in these networks and predicts creativity in an individual.

Challenges in understanding what creativity is remain despite decades of research and the accumulation of evidence, the increasing differentiation in creativity, and the understanding of how it comes about. Arne Dietrich, one of the premier researchers of creativity, makes this point clearly.[27] He argues that creativity "has a dubious distinction in the psychological sciences. I can't think of a mental phenomenon so central to the human condition for which we have so little understanding of how the brain does it." Dietrich argues that the evidence concerning divergent thinking, defocused attention, right brain activity, low arousal, prefrontal activation, and alpha enhancement does not support the leading scientific theories about this process.

A big remaining challenge in the study of creativity is the continuing narrow focus on creative individuals isolated from culture and society. The unquestioned assumption is that creativity occurs mainly in isolated individuals, regardless of the environment. But experts in the social sciences have long argued that the proper domain for studying intelligence and creativity is not individual abilities. Instead, attributes of the individual placed and interacting within a particular historical, cultural, and social environment make more sense. Recall Mihaly Csikszentmihalyi's definition of creativity as the interaction between culture, a person who brings originality into play, and a set of experts who recognize and validate the original creation. Thus, a growing movement during the last few years considers creativity not only a psychological but an *interactive* sociocultural phenomenon. In a nutshell, creativity begets the environment, but the environment begets creativity. Explaining the interaction from this perspective takes the study of creativity closer to its natural origins but also makes it an even more complex subject of study.

Aging and Acquired Creativity

There are complications when studying creativity in its natural environment and viewing the process as interactions and emergent phenomena, meaning behavior that is more than the sum of its parts. For one thing, it becomes more difficult to predict outcomes. One complication is that fluid intelligence—the ability to reason—appears to depend on physiological efficiency and how well the body works. Because of this dependency, fluid reasoning declines with age. The older you are, the less flexible and adaptable you become, and the less you use fluid intelligence. Creativity, which involves fluid thinking, should likewise decline with age. But, unexpectedly, it does not. In fact, fluid thinking improves with age, as long as the body remains healthy. Likewise, crystallized intelligence—the skill in using knowledge gained through learning and experience—may also increase with age because it relies on the accumulation of knowledge. These issues illustrate that creativity is a complex interaction, not easily understood, involving fluid reasoning, crystallized intelligence, within the context of the aging process.

The aging brain resembles the creative brain in several ways. For instance, the mind becomes more distractible and disinhibited as you age. Older individuals have an increased store of knowledge generated by a lifetime of learning and experience. They make use of this larger store of knowledge to make novel and original associations. Therefore, older individuals score better on tests of crystallized intelligence. Another similarity relates to demyelination, or loss of the insulation that covers nerve fibers in the brain. Normal myelination means effective transmission of messages between cells, creating precision and focus. But with aging and loss of myelination, less efficient connectivity is the outcome. The positive side effect of demyelination is the loosening of associative links that facilitate divergent thinking and an increase in the flow of ideas. That may help explain the increase in creativity with age.

Recent medical evidence describing healthy individuals who gain remarkable "savant-like" talents in music, art, math, and other fields, either suddenly or following a head injury, is consistent with the uncontrolled mind–creativity relationship.[28] Common occurrence of "savantism" involves individuals who from birth have a neurodevelopmental disability, such as autism, and possess remarkable skills in remembering events, calculating numbers, making art, or playing the piano. The cases of healthy individuals diagnosed with sudden or acquired savant syndrome are rare, although such "accidental geniuses" have been studied by medical and scientific researchers who scan their brains and assess their creativity. Some neuroscientists have expressed skepticism concerning this syndrome. They argue that the behavior relates more to the newly found obsessiveness such individuals display for their field and the lack of assessment on how novel and creative their output really is. The individual cases, however, tell a remarkable and compelling story.

In 2006, thirty-nine-year-old Derek Amato jumped into the shallow end of a pool to catch a football tossed by a friend. While doing so, he hit the left side of his forehead against the concrete side of the pool. The injury sidelined him for approximately a week before he felt better. When he did, he visited a friend whose home had a piano. As if by some magnetic attraction force, the piano drew Derek to it. Derek did not know how to play, and his only dalliance with musical instruments had been with a guitar and drums as a teenager. Derek played complex melodies on this new instrument. According to Derek, he "saw" the music as black and white squares pouring out of him, a condition resembling synesthesia, which can result from highly activated neural connections. Whether Derek's skill resulted from the concussion and this increased activation, his newfound ability and creativity on the piano are still being investigated.

The psychiatrist Darold A. Treffert described several sudden savant cases in a 2018 article for *Scientific American*.[29] In one instance, the participant, S. S., in her mid-forties, noticed changes in how she suddenly saw the physical world of trees, flowers, and other objects. The normal perception of colors, textures, and shadows was different and unlike anything she had experienced previously. It was an entirely new way of seeing, accompanied by a strong need to express this "new vision" on paper. S. S. had no background in painting; in fact, she felt awkward with a paintbrush. To ease her discomfort, she "purchased a set of pastel pencils, found a photograph of a gorilla on the cover of an old *National Geographic* magazine, and sat down to draw it." The result was unexpected, for it comprised a "rich, complex pastel painting with uncanny realism." Given that she had never taken an art class, shown an interest in painting, or thought she had an aptitude for it, the painting astounded her, as well as her friends and relatives.

The emerging data from a dozen similar cases suggest that when the left anterior lobe of the brain becomes *less* responsive, the parts of the brain involved in other sensory processes become *more* responsive. It is as if this prefrontal area inhibits areas of the brain involved in creativity until it becomes unable to maintain such inhibition. The anterior prefrontal region is the neural substrate for the interpreter function and is an important component of the uncontrolled mind. When mindfulness calms this region, inhibition is reduced in other areas of the brain, and the result is a more creative mindset.

Studying what creativity is depends on its definition. To study creativity at the biological or psychological level, we need general agreement on what is being studied and how to assess it. Unfortunately, disagreement and uncertainty still exist, with many inconsistent definitions. What I argue is that creativity is necessary for living and for the everyday expression of Original Mind. This is the ultimate state where the presence of protective factors helps steer the mind storms in a "controlled" manner, making for a calm, beneficial, and productive mind.

Key Takeaways

- Instincts and intuitions exist at the interface between emotion, reasoning, and nonconscious processing, and are often the only practical ways for assessing and responding to uncertainty.
- You can increase and improve instinct and intuitive skills with consistent practice.

- Incessant thinking accounts for 30 to 50 percent of waking life and in the accepted paradigm is associated with mindlessness, the monkey mind, and much of the unnecessary suffering we experience.
- Incessant thinking occurs with problems regulating the frontal lobes.
- In the presence of protective factors, you learn to use incessant thinking as "controlled chaos" and the essence of creativity.
- The controlled brain integrates insightful, experiential, and incessant thinking into both fluid and crystallized intelligence, providing the basis for creative living.

Next chapter: What are effective solutions to the problem of the uncontrolled mind?

Implementing the Solutions

Overcome ego-based thinking by taking action.

Mastering the Mind

Stephanie learned that recognizing problems, understanding what needed to be done, and finding balance in the multiple priorities facing her required inner motivation and initiative to put her aspirations into action. She worked diligently to be more forward-leaning and proactive in facing problems. This meant identifying difficulties and working with them before their impact became too great and overwhelming. She became a master at detecting early warning signs of developing issues. Her emotional radar and intuition acquired a sensitivity to the rising stress, the small burning feeling in the pit of her stomach that something was amiss, the soft buzzing in her ears that revealed her muddled thinking. Above all, she became an expert regarding the sticky nature of her thoughts. She became attentive to these subtle signs because of her steadfast mindfulness practice and slowly but assuredly became a master of her mind.

A major premise of this book is that the temporal nature of thought is key to rapidly and effectively solving the problem of the uncontrolled mind and harnessing this energy for creative living. Temporal nature means having a relationship with time and makes the three types of thought (insightful, experiential, and incessant) distinctive. Insightful and experiential processing are responses centered on the present to solve problems and the task at hand, while incessant rumination focuses on memories and expectations of the future to resolve problems. All three categories of thought are necessary for creative living since they provide an understanding of past-, present-, and future-based information. Conscious awareness is memory-based processing and time-dependent, but this is not true for nonconscious activity, which exists in a different temporal state, more akin to a timeless domain. Accepting these differences is critical for the resolution and transformation proposed.

Transcending the Uncontrolled Mind

The challenge in this effort is first to understand or get a glimpse of how the timeless, nonmemory-based processing of the nonconscious mind interacts with time-dependent, memory-based thinking of conscious awareness. In the back-and-forth between these two domains, creative living flows uninterrupted and smoothly most of the time. Once in a while, however, something triggers an interruption. The interruption may arise because of problems in frontal lobe regulation or the need for the frontal lobe to handle unexpected changes in its expected future. The error correction function that is engaged and the attentional spotlight that characterizes it place a unique emphasis on past memories and future expectations to resolve the problem.

The transition from the timeless domain of nonconscious activity where thoughts exist "all at once," to the time-dependent conscious reality of one or a few thoughts, is like initially looking at a vast set of photographs mindlessly, until one image grabs your attention. Suppose the image is of yourself when you were five years old and celebrating your birthday. In an instant, the spotlight of attention engulfs that photograph, making it the most relevant one in your awareness. Simultaneously, a series of events linked to that image comes to mind. You remember friends that attended the party, the presents you received, the birthday cake your mother baked, the fight you had with your best friend after everyone left, and so on.

These memories appear in a kind of temporary temporal space related to the time of the event in which you are five years old. Yet, simultaneously, you hold other experiences relative to your existence as a thirty- or sixty-year-old looking at the photograph. There is, for example, awareness of your friend or spouse looking over your shoulder as you examine the childhood photos. You faintly hear your children playing outside. You might even worry about your job and the problems you are having with a neighbor. The extent to which all this activity is in your *awareness* is unclear and under dispute in science circles. But they give you a sense of how the mind works in these nonconscious and conscious modes, and what could trigger problems in their relationship.

On the positive side, recognizing the connection helps clarify the role the mind plays in autopiloting, daydreaming, and mind wandering.[1] Scientists suggest, for example, that periods of self-reflection, which occur naturally during autopiloting, yield concerns about the future. Studies have shown that autobiographical thinking permeates mind wandering, which refers in part to the personal ability to simulate the future, allow for prospective thinking, and make predictions.[2] Participants engage more frequently in the future than in past thoughts. This ability depends on lifetime memories to predict future outcomes, in a type of "looking-ahead-by-looking-backwards" type of computation.[3] The normal, controlled mind engages in imagining future possibilities to help you consider the consequences of your actions, and does so below the level of awareness. This ability to consider and predict future outcomes may come about because, on autopilot, it disconnects the interpreter and rational discourse from autobiographical memories. This makes free association possible in considering alternative futures. The downside of a wandering mind is that "people are thinking about what is not happening almost as often as they are thinking about what is," and this makes them unhappy.[4]

From a neurobiological perspective, the evidence of overlapping brain activation when remembering past events and imagining future experiences supports this idea. The relationship between logic, which is self-referential, and the focus of mind wandering is on the future rather than the past. Others argue that engaging this relationship with time, as you become consciously aware, uses a common system regardless of whether pondering past or future. What seems important during autopiloting is the flexibility in using the autobiographical memory system in a time-dependent manner to determine the best course of action. This is creative living.

Sticky Thoughts

As described previously, one significant problem encountered during creative living is that activity gets out of context in relation to time and location—it becomes decontextualized. Instead of dealing with the vast amount of information the brain is encountering in-the-moment, it switches to error-correction, and the normally "controlled" chaos and flow of creative living is interrupted. The switch to conscious awareness and error correction emphasizes past and future actions to resolve the issue. An interpreter appears to narrate the ongoing events and can quickly go into overdrive. These are components of the dynamics that lead to the appearance of an uncontrolled mind.

While the relationship with time is important, the persistence or "stickiness" of thought gets to the heart, or the root of the root (as e. e. cummings expressed it), of what causes decontextualization and produces inappropriate behavior. Stickiness of thought describes how the mind highlights and grabs particular thoughts and has difficulty letting go. This stickiness affects the smooth flow of information. There are at least three relevant aspects to this. One is the desire to reach out and focus attention on an external or internal object of interest, whether people, forms, or thoughts, perhaps motivated by curiosity. The second is the stickiness itself, in which the mind grasps the object of interest, becomes singularly attached to it, and clings to the developing thought stream. Finally, there are the negative outcomes of stickiness, including the obsession, craving, mental pain, and suffering experienced after the fact.

The first aspect, the desire to reach out to explore the world of physical and nonphysical things, is mainly a reflection of the AAECC impulse, approach behavior, and the extraverted personality. This is the active, adaptable, energetic, curious, and creative impulse associated with the mind at birth. This impulse occurs below the level of awareness and beyond control, although there may be biases to this reaching out that support the extraverted aspect of your personality and the urge to approach.

Then there is the critical second aspect, the stickiness itself. From a neuroscience perspective, scientists have identified several key brain regions that may provide a neural correlate of stickiness. In particular is the role of the posterior cingulate cortex (PCC). Judson Brewer and colleagues have suggested that activity in the PCC may be an aspect of self-referential processing associated with "getting caught up in" one's experience.[5] Such changes are time dependent and therefore the basis for memory. Some changes last a few milliseconds, while others last a lifetime. These temporal variations provide the basis for short- and long-term memories, which are the basis for learning and provide substantial benefits for survival and living well. Memories reflect the "stickiness" of experience. But like so many things, while memory functions are important, they also produce learning of the wrong things, producing negative outcomes. Aberrant learning, like the addictive nature of the mind, reflects the stickiness of memories associated with pain and suffering.

One way we have to move experiences from short- to longer-term storage is repetition. This willful action makes experiences stick in memory for longer periods of time, regardless of their validity. Thus, if the question is whether you can reduce and eliminate aberrant learning and stickiness, the answer is yes. All you need to do is avoid repetition of experiences that create a negative outcome. If, for example, you know that watching something inappropriate on the Internet causes you to behave badly toward your girlfriend or boyfriend, then the answer is to avoid watching those things. If watching a news channel causes you to feel jittery and out of control, then the solution is not to watch that news channel. Sometimes it's as simple as avoiding that which causes the problem.

The third and final aspect of sticky thoughts is its negative consequences. Developmental psychologists suggest that with the growth of the ego and virtual me, the mind's reflective surface becomes stickier. More memories create more associations. Stickiness of thoughts potentially results in accumulating mental pain and suffering. Others conceive of the developing stickiness as resulting from ignorance, desires, or karmic payment for past actions. Still others view stickiness as a mental set that, like a spider's web, ensnares other thoughts in a developing tangled mess that distorts reality. Through stickiness and ensnaring of other thoughts, the virtual me and ego gradually come into full bloom.

Original Mind is the opposite of sticky. As described in earlier chapters, this mind is like a mirror reflecting all things. With its focus on the present and not memory-dependent, it is free of the stickiness of associations. Thus, the developing ego and virtual me do not distort this Original Mind, only obscure it. It would seem logical that if you can control, reduce, or entirely undo mind-grasping or mind-stickiness, the uncontrolled mind will give way to this pristine mind—our reflective, original nature. Here again is the root of the root of the problem and its solution. Without the entities you create that make possible the stickiness of thought (ego and virtual me), there are no worries, no depression, just calm mirroring. Only the pure, reflective nature of Original Mind remains.

Stop Monkey Mind: Notice Recurring Thoughts

- *Be in the present moment—in this time and place.*
- *Be aware of thoughts ("I am having thoughts").*
- *Label them when possible ("I will lose my job").*
- *Be aware of emotions associated with the thought ("I am frightened of losing my job").*
- *Do not change the thoughts or emotions; just notice and experience them.*
- *Do this over and over—that is the practice!*

The Normal Experience of Change

The idea of nonconscious processing occurring in a timeless domain where thoughts do not "stick" is undoubtedly difficult to comprehend and accept. First, because we judge time as a fundamental property that is linear, one we can measure, and we experience as flowing in one direction. To measure changes in time, we have invented accurate time-measuring devices, including sundials, watches, clocks, and, most recently, atomic clocks. This has created a mindset of an objective, mathematical description of the experience, perceived in terms of milliseconds that tick on to become seconds, seconds become minutes, minutes become hours, then days, years, and so on. This experience is so powerful, pervasive, and real that you cannot imagine anything else.

It is difficult, even uncomfortable, to know that scientists have to define these time measurements. In the 1940s, they set out to define what 1 second is.[6] With 24 hours in a day, 60 minutes per hour, and 60 seconds per minute, there are 86,400 seconds in 1 day. Thus, these wise men reasoned 1 second was the 1/86,400 of the time that the Earth needed to rotate once on its axis. Unfortunately, they quickly recognized the problem with this definition because the Earth's rotation is not consistent enough to provide a standard unit of measurement. The length of a day changes because of random variations, from the amount of snowfall at the poles to space particles hitting the planet. Other nonrandom variations also affect the measurement, including the rotation of the Earth, which is slowing because of tidal forces from the moon, leading to the lengthening of days. To account for these variations, the International Earth Rotation and Reference Systems Service (IERS) corrects the measurement by adding a leap second during specific times of the year. But this is very uncertain and not very accurate.

The discovery of atomic clocks, and other more accurate measurements of time, provided temporary relief to these uncertainties. In 1967, the Thirteenth General Conference of the International Committee for Weights and Measures redefined time once again. This time it defined a second in a very unusual but specific way: "the duration of 9,192,631,770 periods of the radiation corresponding to the transition between the two hyperfine levels of the ground state of the caesium-133 atom." The definition is easy to understand *if you are a physicist*.

Physicists know that a cesium atom has one electron orbiting the nucleus at the highest energy level, all by itself. The outer electron is "spin up" or "spin down," which refers to a quantum measurement of the electron's angular momentum (derived by the product of mass × velocity × radius). With a device called a maser, scientists can force the outer electron to switch from spin up to spin down, or vice versa, by radiating the electron with electromagnetic radiation. Physicists have determined the specific frequency of radiation that causes that outer electron to transition from one energy level to the other, and that frequency is 9,192,631,770 hertz. So, the most accurate definition of one second is the duration in the transition of one cesium atom from one energy level to another using electromagnetic radiation at 9,192,631,770 hertz. Phew!

Unfortunately, these seemingly precise measurements also change ever so slightly because measurements are different at altitude compared to sea level—something predicted by Albert Einstein's general theory of relativity. Thus, scientists must continuously adjust even the extremely accurate atomic clocks.

Subjective Psychological Time

As science strives to be more and more precise in the mathematical measurement of time, psychologists recognize that our memory systems give us a unique sense of time, of the perception of movement in time, and memories of such things. Psychologists call this knowledge subjective, psychological time, or autobiographical memories. This is the state to which you transition when you regain track of structured time following a vacation. Electronic tools, lights, clocks, and video recorders have changed our subjective experience of time, and made time both malleable and nonlinear.

Imagine, for example, that your favorite television show airs at 7:30 p.m. on Saturday. But because you travel that day, you decide to record the show and watch it at your convenience on any day and time when you return. This ability is nonlinear time-shifting at its best. Interestingly, your memory systems allow for similar nonlinear time-shifting. You recall and replay your fifth birthday celebration from memory while being in this moment years later. Intuitively, the experience of time, whether linear of nonlinear, feels intimate and subjective. And this subjective perception of time, or how long something lasts, changes slightly as you grow older. Earlier in life, time stretched forever in front of you, drifting ever so slowly. As an adult, the runway gets shorter and the speed of events seems faster. Clearly, your subjective time experience differs from structured or mathematical time as you age.

But where does timelessness fit in? Indeed, transcendent time is a concept that may link mathematical and subjective time experiences. None other than Sir Isaac Newton expressed an opinion in his masterpiece *Principia*, in which he outlined the laws of motion that established classical mechanics.[7] Newton noted that, "Absolute, true, mathematical time, of itself, and from its own nature, flows equally without relation to anything external." For Newton, mathematical time was transcendent time, and it "hovered over the rest of nature in blithe autonomy, advancing at a smooth and constant rate from past to future." In defining time this way, Newton separated "absolute" from "relative" time. Timelessness, a subjective experience, approximates the experience of absolute time, while changes characterize relative time. For Newton, these were separate experiences.

Then, in 1905, in what many consider a revolution in thinking and the understanding of time, Einstein reframed all these concepts by showing that our experience of time was itself a fiction. He did so in his theory of relativity, in which he showed that time is not invariant, as Newton had hypothesized, and in fact changes depending on a more fundamental constant, the speed of light. Time expands or contracts as a function of how fast the observer of time is traveling. As this imagined traveler approaches the speed of light (186,000 miles/sec), time slows down. However, the speed of light remains constant in any frame of reference. Time, in contrast, is relative and not absolute.

In the book *When Einstein Walked with Gödel*, Jim Holt describes that what Einstein showed in terms of time was the absence of a universal "now."[8] Instead, "now" becomes individualized, depending on whether two events are simultaneous *relative to the observer*. "And once simultaneity occurs, the very division of moments into past, present, and future becomes meaningless." Holt continues that, "In place of the fleeting present, we are left with a vast frozen timescape—a four-dimensional 'block universe.' Over here, you are being born; over there, you are celebrating the turn of the millennium; and over yonder, you've been dead for a while. Nothing is 'flowing' from one event to another." In this timeless or frozen landscape, events are already whole, timeless, unchanging, and in an unmoving existence.

Other physicists have elaborated this idea and argued that "we are faced with the image of a frozen universe, in which neither time nor space have any meaning, and everything that ever was or ever will be just is." Most physicists now support the idea that time is a timeless, unchanging, unmoving experience. When physicists speak this way, physics bleeds into metaphysics and even mysticism.

The Frozen Universe

Jim Holt's "block" or "frozen universe" is an apt metaphor for the individual mind in the present moment. In this state, time dissolves and you, and only you, have access to whatever is "in mind." John Archibald Wheeler, a preeminent physicist of the twentieth century, quoting from something he read in a men's bathroom, wrote, "Time is nature's way to keep everything from happening all at once." The implication is that if you get rid of the concept of time, everything happens at once.

From Wheeler's perspective, the present-moment experience is just that: containing the unity of the many expressions of form and memories. And these experiences are accessible all at once. If true, this state in which no past, present, or future exists raises many questions, mainly because nonconscious processing reflects such an experience. Conscious awareness disrupts the unity and simultaneity of the present moment. Attention narrows and focuses on a specific object, memory, action, and makes sequential *time* come into existence. The perspective of this book is more in line with what physicists are now saying about the timelessness of time, and that nonconscious processing exists in this timeless domain where creative living unfolds naturally. You cannot sustain this type of processing during conscious awareness, which by definition is a brief period necessary to address unexpected changes or glitches and integrate those changes into normal, nonconscious activity.

By now, it should be obvious that learning to control the mind unmasks Original Mind, a mind centered on nonconscious, present-moment activity. When this Original Mind gets snagged in past and future events trying to resolve problems, the possibility of a dysfunctional monkey mind appears. When no glitches occur, or problems resolve quickly, Original Mind simply resumes encountering the present while dealing with the contingencies the moment creates. Hence, the solution to an uncontrolled mind is not to get rid of it, even if that were possible. Rather, it is best to place its functioning in the right context, especially its correct temporal domain. This solution is like placing a feral tiger in the open wilderness rather than in a small cage. In the open space, the animal will produce more natural and normal behaviors, for this is the context in which it evolved.

Uncontrolled mind focused on past and future events to resolve an error produces dysfunction when this mind becomes obsessed and unable to resolve whatever the issue is at hand. The constraints of such a narrow focus create the metaphorical small cage for the feral tiger. However, centered on the present moment and its limitless and timeless vastness, the dynamics change, and monkey mind becomes the creative mind and the natural expression of being. Hence, grounding the mind in the present or in the "now" changes the relationships to unhealthy thoughts, actions, and behaviors that interfere with current life. Orientation to the present moment resembles the approach taken by Rational and Cognitive-Behavioral therapies.

Stop Monkey Mind: Direct the Mind to "STOP"

- *Anchor your situational awareness to the present moment.*
- *Focus and center on your actions.*
- *Attend to the sensory experiences reaching your brain (sights, sounds, smells, etc.).*
- *Attend to this mental activity and identify the dominant thoughts.*
- *Confidently take authority by commanding these thoughts to "slow down" or "STOP."*
- *Command the mind verbally first, later think it, and much later drop the thought command altogether (the nonconscious intent will be enough).*
- *Avoid addressing your mind angrily. Rather, do it lovingly, as you would a hyperactive child who is acting up.*

Present Moment as the Optimal Solution

Both self-parenting and present-moment centering have the potential for long-lasting change as dual and complementary approaches. Addressing the expectations and relationship with time associated with thought is the more rapid, effective, and transformational approach.

Focusing on the present moment changes the focus on past and future events and directly transforms the uncontrolled mind's maladaptive behavior. Awareness of the moment means being grounded on what is happening now, the contingencies of this moment, and not focused on memories of the past or predictions about the future. Such grounding puts the decontextualized actions of the uncontrolled mind in the proper frame to foster the creative mind.

While focusing on the present or the contingencies of the moment can seem a futile waste of time, understanding what that really means may bolster understanding and motivation. Moving into what many call the "present" means having a situational awareness of your surroundings and the experiences occurring to you at a particular time. Conceptually, awareness of this moment lasts a short time before you are in the next moment and then the next. To our thinking mind, the now is more like a series of events strung together in time. This characterization is the typical way we conceptualize time because of our habit of marking it in terms of days, hours, minutes, seconds, milliseconds, nanoseconds, and so forth. It has conditioned us to think of time as a measurable commodity during which things happen in sequence. This idea seems fundamental, since our own bodies have their own "clocks" and biological rhythms to track physiological changes and synchronize activities across different time domains. Similar to the technological clocks and watches, natural clocks create the sense of change with time. Hence, conceiving measureless time, or timelessness, and comprehending that nothing happens in a timeless present is extremely difficult if not impossible to imagine.

However, a not uncommon experience for you is to lose your sense of chronological time. Typically, this is only a temporary spell, as occurs when leaving the structured environment of work. This loss of the sense of structured time happens most pointedly when on vacation, or when engrossed in reading a book or watching a movie. You look up and for an instant you don't know the time of day or whether five minutes or one hour has passed since the last time you checked. This experience of losing time perception is a powerful sign that something different exists as the default state. For that instant, you encounter the timeless domain.

The notion of a timeless present is counterintuitive and makes you wince skeptically. However, if you can conceive or recall when you experienced such a moment, the changeless nature of things, then that is close to what the present or the now is. Only, this timeless "now" stretches endlessly behind and ahead of you. For those still unable to imagine it, consider the analogy of a video wherein your entire life story exists in digital form.

Assume that someone close to you, say an older sibling, recorded your entire life from birth until your demise using a recording device. The recording itself is a static and unchanging set of patterns on film that comprise every single individual moment of your life captured in a temporal sequence. In another sense, your entire life exists in this video as a timeless, unchanging, and unmoving event. But this recording attains a distinct reality when played on a digital video player. You then perceive not static moments but the flow from one moment to the next and what approximates your own lived experience. However, watching the video, you recognize that this experience of movement is an illusion resulting from how your brain processes the static images in the video. Theoretically, with the right technology, your entire life on that video could occur *all at once*—instantaneously. Or, you could skip through it in a nonlinear fashion, forwarding to specific sections and then going back to prior events, and so forth.

Now, suppose that from the perspective of God, or the universe, your entire life already exists in such a timeless, unchanging, unmoving landscape—it is already "recorded." In this universe, your brain plays the role of the video player, replaying your already prerecorded life. The experience is life unfolding in time, or what you sense as your lived experience. But this know-how could be an illusion of how the brain processes the "static" images that are already prerecorded. The present moment, or the now we are discussing, corresponds to the timeless landscape in which things are already whole and prerecorded, in an unchanging and unmoving existence. If this analogy helps, great. If not, keep reading and maybe the idea will make sense after you have time to ponder it.

This book presents a story based on scientific and personal evidence of the uncontrolled mind and Original Mind as two sides of the same brain dynamics. Comparable to identical twins who grow up in unique environments, they share the same genetics. The uncontrolled mind is, in fact, Original Mind. The former simply focuses on the past and future, while the latter is more at home in the present moment. Dwelling on the past and future occasionally gets the mind snagged in that mode and becomes dysfunctional. This dysfunction causes havoc when unmanaged and chronic. The solution is not to get rid of this monkey mind, but to use self-parenting approaches and present-moment centering to place its functioning in the proper context. Training and guiding the obsessive mind back to its original state is possible—to deal with the challenges of living in-the-moment. To do so, you must lose the obsession with past and future. There are only two aspects of being to cultivate while living in the moment: the first is to develop gentle, nonconceptual vigilance, or mindfulness. Letting go of problems and of past and future happens naturally in this state. Love, compassion, and kindness flow naturally into this openness. The second aspect is the cultivation of trust in the intelligence of body and mind. Don't worry about outcomes. If it comes, it comes, and be grateful, just don't seek it.

It is good to remember that you are already in a place of peace and contentment, but like a thunderstorm around you, you cannot see beyond the threatening clouds. All that is needed is for the dark clouds to dissipate and disappear for you to see that the sunshine was always there. What changes is your perception of the clouds and what they mean. This does not mean ignoring memories and future possibilities, just not letting them control your life. When this obsession recedes, Original Mind comes to the foreground and you experience flowing, present moment, creative living.

My heartfelt hope is that you recognize the wonderful gift your brain-mind is and that what you see as problems in your life are actually opportunities for growth and enjoyment. After my sixty-year odyssey searching for answers, I came to realize that Original Mind never recedes but becomes obscured by the energetic activity of ego, which we can let go easily sometimes, not so easily most of the time. This realization is both funny and disappointing, but most important, liberating. It is a feeling of being both special and yet not so special.

Being special and not at the same time reminds me of what Harold Ramis, a well-known American actor, comedian, director, and writer, said about carrying two notes to remind you of who you are. The first note should read, "The universe was created for my delight." The second note should say, "I am a meaningless speck of dust in the vastness of the universe." His point was that life occurs in the rhythmic oscillation between these two opposite poles. Living happens between meaningfulness and meaninglessness, between creative and mundane living. The rhythmic oscillation of this dance occurs both outside and within conscious awareness, but in either case, you are a participant. Nisargadatta Maharaj, an Indian guru, offered something similar. He said, "Wisdom tells me I am nothing, and love tells me I am everything. Between these two, the river of my life runs."[9] You, me, and everyone else are both nothing and everything.

Key Takeaways

- The temporal nature of thought is key to the riddle of the uncontrolled mind, how it relates to creativity, and to finding solutions that are rapid and effective.
- Recognizing the relationship thought has with time helps clarify the role of the mind in autopiloting, daydreaming, and mind wandering.
- One significant mind-brain problem is that activity gets out of context in relation to time and location—it becomes decontextualized.
- The "stickiness" of thought gets to the heart of what causes decontextualization and produces inappropriate behavior.
- Stickiness refers to the desire to reach out to an external or internal object(s) of interest; attaching, clinging to the object(s), and to the developing stream of thought; which leads to the obsession, craving, mental pain, and suffering experienced after the fact.

GLOSSARY

AAECC impulse: The active, adaptable, energetic, curious, and creative nature of Original Mind, or mind at birth.

AFRAID impulse: The avoidant, fearful, resistant, arrogant, inflexible, and distrustful nature of monkey mind.

Anxiety: An emotion characterized by feelings of fear, dread, uneasiness, and worried thoughts. It can include physical responses such as sweating, feeling restless and tense, and having a rapid heartbeat. It is a normal reaction to stress until these feelings become chronic, overwhelming, and prevent us from doing everyday activities. This makes it a disorder.

Autopiloting: Neural behaviors involved in mind wandering, daydreaming, and stimulus-independent and task-unrelated contemplation.

Conscious awareness: Individual discernment of your subjective thoughts, memories, feelings, sensations, and the surrounding environment.

Convergent thinking: A linear, targeted, and systematic approach that narrows down multiple ideas into a single solution to a problem. We deduce such a solution by applying established rules and logical reasoning.

Creativity: The tendency to view things in new ways or from a different perspective to generate or recognize ideas, alternatives, or possibilities that may be useful in solving problems, communicating with others, and enjoying life. Researchers link it to more fundamental qualities of thinking, such as flexibility, tolerance of ambiguity or unpredictability, and the enjoyment of things.

Creative living: The actions of a mind freed from ego-based thinking. It reflects creative cognition as controlled chaos because it incorporates elements of the creative process.

Crystallized intelligence: The ability to use experiential reasoning resulting from accumulated knowledge, including how to reason, language skills, and an understanding of technology. Tests of general information link it to education, experience, and cultural background.

Disinhibition: A normal and fundamental way in the self-regulation of normal behavior. In particular, the frontal lobe executive system uses disinhibition to inhibit alternative courses of action to allow the expression of a specific, goal-directed behavior. It also refers to the absence of the ability to inhibit inappropriate behavior, resulting in impulsivity, poor risk assessments, and disregard for social conventions, as seen in frontal-temporal degeneration, Alzheimer's disease, and stroke.

Divergent thinking: The ability to generate ideas beyond proscribed expectations and rote thinking. It reflects flexible, iterative, and web-like thinking that focuses on the connections between ideas and associated with fluid intelligence.

Ego-self separation: Many scholars describe individuals as having an original sense of wholeness, called the self. Out of this original unity, a separate ego crystallizes during development. This individuation and differentiation create the ego-self separation, a normal aspect of development. The schism between what is real and what is not in this separation creates problems when not understood properly.

Flow: A concept developed by the psychologist Mihaly Csikszentmihalyi to describe an optimal state of consciousness where the individual feels absorbed in an activity, strong, alert, in effortless control, unself-conscious, and at the peak of their abilities. It correlates with outstanding creativity, performance, and genuine satisfaction.

Fluid intelligence: The ability to think fast and reason flexibly in order to solve recent problems without relying on experience and accumulated knowledge. It allows us to perceive and draw inferences about relationships among variables, and to conceptualize abstract information.

Frozen universe: A metaphor used to describe the individual mind in the present moment, in which neither time nor space have any meaning, and everything experienced just is.

Heuristics: Mental strategies used to form judgments, decide, and find solutions to complex problems quickly and economically, deal with uncertain events, and make the world more predictable.

Incessant rumination: Complex, multifaceted, multilayered, intricate, elaborate, embellished, flexible, and fluent thinking associated with the monkey mind when uncontrolled, but with creative thinking when controlled.

Intuition: The ability to know and understand something instinctively and immediately, with no conscious reasoning. Characterized as the interface between conscious and nonconscious processing.

Left-brain interpreter: An idea proposed by Michael S. Gazzaniga and Joseph E. LeDoux to explain how humans rationalize, reason, and generalize current information to maintain logical consistency with past and future experiences. They assumed this to be a rational, verbal, and left-hemisphere brain function that produces after the fact explanations about behavior.

Mindfulness: A Buddhist meditation practice that enhances an individual's ability to be fully present, aware of their surroundings, what they are doing, and not overly reactive or overwhelmed by circumstances. Its practice changes expectations concerning the mind's rumination by focusing on present circumstances.

Monkey mind: A metaphor for the feral, wild, obsessive part of our mind's nature. It is a Buddhist term referring to a mind that is restless, easily distracted, obsessive, confused, and uncontrollable.

Neuroplasticity: The brain's ability to change its anatomical connections linking sensory experience to emotions and actions because of experience. This means that seeing, hearing, touching, smelling, feeling, and thinking affect the brain's hardware in profound ways.

Nonconscious processing: All the mental activity we are not consciously aware of, and which represents a major aspect of every waking moment of life, exhibiting a level of intelligence that is vast yet unfamiliar.

Observer Mind: A detached perspective that views sensory experiences in a calmer way. It is associated with the real self, Original Mind, and not an aspect of monkey mind.

Original Mind: A Buddhist term describing the mind as having an attitude of openness, eagerness, and lack of preconceptions. It is used to describe the mind at birth.

Predictive brain: Describes the brain's use of gained knowledge of regularities and patterns to make increasingly refined prediction, preparation, anticipation, prospection, or expectation in various domains about the objects and events most likely responsible for the signals it receives from the environment.

Present-moment centering: Bringing one's attention to the immediacy of the moment, whether it involves thoughts of the past, contemplation of the future, or the immediate sensory experience. It is holding these thoughts in awareness.

RUBI: Describes the four stages necessary to transform anxiety into creativity: Recognizing the problem; Understanding the solution; finding Balance; and Implementing answers.

Schizotypy: Alludes to a continuum of personality characteristics and experiences, ranging from normal dissociative, imaginative states to extreme states of mind related to psychosis. The matrix of personality traits includes "positive" ones, such as unusual perceptual experiences, thin mental boundaries between self and other, impulsive nonconformity, and display of magical thinking. It also includes "negative" traits such as cognitive disorganization, physical and social anhedonia, or difficulty experiencing pleasure from social interactions and activities enjoyable for most people.

Self: The first-person and subjective experience we have of ourselves as the object of our own reflective consciousness.

Self-parenting: Consciously choosing the relationship you will have with yourself, as if with a loving parent. It means recognizing the problem of monkey mind as comparable to that of an unruly, disobedient, and undisciplined child; then, addressing the problem by implementing a steady diet of reasonable and loving self-care.

Split-brain patients: individuals suffering from intractable epilepsy who underwent a radical procedure to isolate the two cerebral hemispheres by a deliberate cutting of the fiber connections linking the two.

Sticky thoughts: Thoughts of the past or future that your mind grabs onto and has difficulty letting go no matter how hard you try to shake them, ignore them, or get rid of them. The stickiness of these thoughts affects the smooth flow of information.

Stop Monkey Mind (SMM): The set of exercises which focus on the practice of reducing and stopping obsessive mind rumination. SMM emphasizes awareness of doing so 'at the moment.' It means having a basic conceptual understanding of the problem you are confronting. With this understanding in your background, SMM teaches you to anchor to the present while attentive to the flow of sensory experience.

Virtual me: Another name for the ego-based or created self that arises during individuation. It is what gives rise to the monkey mind.

NOTES

Chapter 1

1. Shodo H. Roshi, "An Eternal Now: Original Mind," June 28, 2010, https://sgforums.com/forums/1728/topics/403706/

2. Walter Isaacson, *Leonardo da Vinci* (New York: Simon & Schuster, 2017).

3. Bridget Balch, "Making Science Serve Humanity: Jennifer Doudna, PhD, Says CRISPR Gene-Editing Technology Should Be Accessible to All," *AAMCNews*, November 8, 2012, https://www.aamc.org/news-insights/making-science-serve-humanity-jennifer-doudna-phd-says-crispr-gene-editing-technology-should-be

4. Jeanna Bryner and Stephanie Pappas, "That's Incredible! 9 Brainy Baby Abilities," *LiveScience*, 2011, https://www.livescience.com/14343-amazing-brainy-baby-abilities.html

5. Natalie Wolchover, "'Peekaboo' Reveals Babies Understanding of Quantum Mechanics," *LiveScience*, 2012, https://www.livescience.com/20803-newborn-babies-quantum-mechanics.html

6. Emma Goksör, Lars Rosengren, and Göran Wennergren, "Bradycardic Response during Submersion in Infant Swimming," *Acta Paediatrica* 91, no. 3 (2002): 307–12. doi:10.1080/08035250252833978

7. Ian Sample, "Struggle to Sleep in a Strange Bed? Scientists Have Uncovered Why," *The Guardian*, April 21, 2016, https://www.theguardian.com/lifeandstyle/2016/apr/21/struggle-to-sleep-in-a-strange-bed-scientists-have-uncovered-why

8. Linda A. Camras and Jennifer M. Shutter, "Emotional Facial Expressions in Infancy," *Emotion Review* 2 (2010): 120–129. doi:10.1177/1754073909352529.

9. Yumiko Otsuka, "Face Recognition in Infants: A Review of Behavioral and Near-Infrared Spectroscopic Studies," in *Special Issue: Face Perception and Recognition*, ed. Ryusuke Kakigi and Masami K. Yamaguchi, *Japanese Psychological Research* 56, no. 1 (2014): 76–90, https://doi.org/10.1111/jpr.12024

10. Lotte Thomsen, Willem E. Frankenhuis, McCaila Ingold-Smith, and Susan Carey, "Big and Mighty: Preverbal Infants Mentally Represent Social Dominance," *Science* 331, no. 6016 (2011): 477–80.

11. Tobia Grossmann, Mark H. Johnson, Sarah Lloyd-Fox, Anna Blasi, Fani Deligianni, Clare Elwell, and Gergely Csibra, "Early Cortical Specialization for Face-to-Face Communication in Human Infants," *Proceedings. Biological Sciences* 275, no. 1653 (2008): 2803–11.

12. Jean-Dominique Bauby, *The Diving Bell and the Butterfly: A Memoir of Life in Death* (New York: Random House, 1998).

13. William James, *The Principles of Psychology* (New York: Holt, 1890).

14. Jean Piaget, *Origins of Intelligence in the Child* (London: Routledge & Kegan Paul, 1936); Jean Piaget, *Science of Education and the Psychology of the Child* (New York: Viking, 1970); Jean Piaget, *Epistemology and Psychology of Functions* (Dordrecht, Netherlands: D. Reidel Publishing Company, 1977).

Chapter 2

1. Elizabeth Gilbert, *Big Magic: Creative Living beyond Fear* (New York: Riverhead Books, 2016).

2. Daniel Smith, *Monkey Mind: A Memoir of Anxiety* (New York: Simon & Schuster, 2013).

3. Jennifer, Shannon, *Don't Feed the Monkey Mind: How to Stop the Cycle of Anxiety, Fear and Worry* (Oakland, CA: New Harbinger Publications, Inc., 2017).

4. Michael Gazzaniga, "The Split Brain in Man," *Scientific American* 217, no. 2 (1967): 24–29, https://doi.org/10.1038/scientificamerican0867-24. Joseph E. Ledoux, Donald H. Wilson, and Michael S. Gazzaniga, "A Divided Mind: Observations on the Conscious Properties of the Separated Hemispheres," *Annals of Neurology* 2, no. 5 (1977): 417–21, https://doi.org/10.1002/ana.410020513

5. Michael Gazzaniga, *Who's in Charge? Free Will and the Science of the Brain* (New York: HarperCollins, 2011).

6. Amos Tversky and Daniel Kahneman, "Judgment Under Uncertainty: Heuristics and Biases," *Science* 185 (1974): 1124–31.

7. David Wolman, "The Split Brain: A Tale of Two Halves," *Nature News Feature* 483 (2012): 260–63.

8. John A. Bargh, "The Modern Unconscious," *World Psychiatry* 18 (2019): 225–26, https://doi.org/10.1002/wps.20625

9. Richard E. Nisbett and Timothy D. Wilson, "Telling More than We Can Know: Verbal Reports on Mental Processes," *Psychological Review* 84, no. 3 (1977): 231–59, https://doi.org/10.1037/0033-295X.84.3.231

10. Linda Ficco, Lorenzo Mancuso, Jordi Manuello, Alessia Teneggi, Donato Liloia, Sergio Duca, Tommaso Costa, Gyula Zoltan Kovacs, and Franco Cauda, "Disentangling Predictive Processing in the Brain: A Meta-Analytic Study in Favour of a Predictive Network," *Scientific Reports* 11, no. 16258 (2021): https://doi.org/10.1038/s41598-021-95603-5

Chapter 3

1. Charlotte J. Beck, *Everyday Zen* (San Francisco: HarperCollins, 1989).
2. Jalāl ad-Dīn Rumi, *The Essential Rumi, New Expanded Edition*. C. Barks, trans. (San Francisco: HarperCollins, 2004).
3. Jaime A. Pineda, *Piercing the Cloud: Encountering the Real Me* (Pennsauken Township, NY: BookBaby, 2020).
4. Kenneth I. Pargament and Annette Mahoney, *Spirituality: The Search for the Sacred*, in Shane J. Lopez and Charles R. Snyder (Eds.), *Oxford Handbook of Positive Psychology*, 3rd ed. (New York: Oxford University Press, 2009), 878–91, https://doi.org/10.1093/oxfordhb/9780199396511.013.51
5. Phillip Kapleau, *The Three Pillars of Zen: Teaching, Practice, and Enlightenment* (New York: Random House, 1989).
6. Nisargadatta Maharaj, *I Am That*, trans., author Maurice Frydman, ed. Sudhakar S. Dikshit (Durham, NC: The Acorn Press, 2012).
7. Wikipedia. Accessed November 22, 2022. Moses, Grandma, https://en.wikipedia.org/wiki/Grandma_Moses

Chapter 4

1. Dee Joy Coulter, *Original Mind: Uncovering Your Natural Brilliance* (Boulder, CO: Sounds True, 2014).
2. Earl K. Miller, "The Prefrontal Cortex and Cognitive Control," *Nature Review Neuroscience* 1 (2000): 59–65, https://doi.org/10.1038/35036228
3. Sigmund Freud, *A General Introduction to Psychoanalysis* (New York: Boni and Liveright Publishers, 1920).
4. Sigmund Freud, *General Psychological Theory: Papers on Metapsychology* (New York: Collier Books, 1963).

Chapter 5

1. Christopher J. Lane, "The Holy Household of Louis and Zélie Martin," *Crisis Magazine*, July 11, 2013, https://www.crisismagazine.com/2013/the-holy-household-of-louis-and-zelie-martin

2. Bruce J. McIntosh, "Spoiled Child Syndrome," *Pediatrics* 83, no. 1 (1989): 108–15, https://pediatrics.aappublications.org/content/83/1/108

3. Dan Kindlon, *Too Much of a Good Thing: Raising Children of Character in an Indulgent Age* (New York: Miramax Books, 2001).

4. Zahra Z. Zahedani, Rita Rezaee, Zahra Yazdani, Sina Bagheri, and Parisa Nabeiei, "The Influence of Parenting Style on Academic Achievement and Career Path," *Journal of Advances in Medical Education & Professionalism* 4, no. 3 (2016): 130–34.

5. Xinwen Bi, Yiqun Yang, Hailei Li, Meiping Wang, Wenxin Zhang, and Kirby Deater-Deckard, "Parenting Styles and Parent–Adolescent Relationships: The Mediating Roles of Behavioral Autonomy and Parental Authority," *Frontiers in Psychology* 9 (2018): 2187, https://doi.org/10.3389/fpsyg.2018.02187

Chapter 6

1. Jonathan Smallwood, "Distinguishing How from Why the Mind Wanders: A Process-Occurrence Framework for Self-Generated Mental Activity," *Psychological Bulletin* 139 (2013): 519–35, https://doi.org/10.1037/a0030010

2. Gerald Edelman, *Wider Than the Sky: The Phenomenal Gift of Consciousness* (New Haven, CT: Yale University Press, 2004).

3. Lorenza S. Colzato, Ayca Ozturk, and Bernhard Hommel, "Meditate to Create: The Impact of Focused-Attention and Open-Monitoring Training on Convergent and Divergent Thinking," *Frontiers in Psychology* 3 (2012): 116, https://doi.org/10.3389/fpsyg.2012.00116. Lorenza S. Colzato, Ayca Szapora, Justine N. Pannekoek, and Bernhard Hommel, "The Impact of Physical Exercise on Convergent and Divergent Thinking," *Frontiers in Human Neuroscience* 7 (2013): 824, https://doi.org/10.3389/fnhum.2013.00824

4. Matthijs Baas, Barbara Nevicka, and Femke S.T. Velden, "Specific Mindfulness Skills Differentially Predict Creative Performance," *Personality and Social Psychology Bulletin* 40, no. 9 (2014): 1092–06, https://doi.org/10.1177/0146167214535813

5. Hugh Delehanty, "The Science of Meditation," *Mindful Magazine*, December 13, 2017, https://www.mindful.org/meditators-under-the-microscope/

6. Hugh Delehanty, "Does Meditation Boost Creativity?" *Mindful Magazine*, June 19, 2017, https://www.mindful.org/does-meditation-boost-creativity/

Chapter 7

1. Sigmund Freud, *General Psychological Theory: Papers on Metapsychology* (New York: Collier Books, 1963).

2. Carl G. Jung and Helton G. Baynes, *Psychological Types* or *The Psychology of Individuation* (London: Kegan Paul Trench Trubner, 1921). Carl G. Jung, *The Undiscovered Self (Present and Future)* (New York: American Library, 1957).

3. Carl G. Jung, *The Archetypes and the Collective Unconscious; Collected Works of C. G. Jung, Vol. 9, Part 1* (Princeton, NJ: Princeton University Press, 1981).

4. Mihaly Csikszentmihalyi, *Flow: The Psychology of Optimal Experience* (New York: Harper & Row, 1990).

5. Mihaly Csikszentmihalyi, *Creativity: The Psychology of Discovery and Invention* (New York: HarperCollins Publishers, 2013).

6. Benjamin Libet, "Unconscious Cerebral Initiative and the Role of Conscious Will in Voluntary Action," in *Neurophysiology of Consciousness. Contemporary Neuroscientists*, (Boston: Birkhäuser, 1993), https://doi.org/10.1007/978-1-4612-0355-1_16

7. Ayn Rand, *Atlas Shrugged* (New York: Dutton, 1957).

8. Sigmund Freud, *Civilization and Its Discontents* (James Strachey, trans., 2017; IndieBooks, 1930).

9. Francis Crick and Christoph Koch, "A Framework for Consciousness," *Nature Neuroscience* 6 (2003): 119–26, https://doi.org/10.1038/nn0203-119

10. Brian Earl, "The Biological Function of Consciousness," *Frontiers in Psychology* 5 (2014): 697, https://doi.org/10.3389/fpsyg.2014.00697

11. Bernard J. Baars, "Some Essential Differences between Consciousness and Attention, Perception, and Working Memory," *Consciousness and Cognition* 6 (1997): 363–71, https://doi.org/10.1006/ccog.1997.0307

12. Jean-François Martel, "Consciousness in the Aesthetic Imagination," *Metapsychosis: Journal of Consciousness, Literature, and Art*, July 11, 2016, https://www.metapsychosis.com/consciousness-in-the-aesthetic-imagination/

13. Claude J. Bajada, Matthew A. L. Ralph, and Lauren L. Cloutman, "Transport for Language South of the Sylvian Fissure: The Routes and History of the Main Tracts and Stations in the Ventral Language Network," *Cortex* 69 (2015): 141–51.

14. Courtney E. Ackerman, "Pollyanna Principle: The Psychology of Positivity Bias," 2019, PositivePsychology.com, https://positivepsychology.com/pollyanna-principle/

15. Paul Rozin and Edward B. Royzman, "Negativity Bias, Negativity Dominance, and Contagion," *Personality and Social Psychology Review* 5, no. 4 (2001): 296–320, https://doi.org/10.1207/S15327957PSPR0504_2

Chapter 8

1. Francis Crick, *The Astonishing Hypothesis: The Scientific Search for the Soul* (New York: Touchstone, 1994).

2. Barbara K. Lipska and Elaine McArdle, *The Neuroscientist Who Lost Her Mind: My Tale of Madness and Recovery* (Boston: Houghton Mifflin Harcourt, 2018).

3. Mariam Arain, Maliha Haque, Lina Johal, Puja Mathur, Wynand Nel, Afsha Rais, Ranbir Sandhu, and Sushil Sharma, "Maturation of the Adolescent Brain," *Neuropsychiatric Disease and Treatment* 9 (2013): 449–61. doi:10.2147/NDT.S39776

4. Carl G. Jung and Helton G. Baynes, *Psychological Types, or The Psychology of Individuation* (London: Kegan Paul Trench Trubner, 1921).

5. William James, *The Principles of Psychology* (New York: Holt, 1890).

6. George G. Campion and Grafton Elliot-Smith, *The Neural Basis of Thoughts* (London: Kegan Paul and Co., Ltd.; New York: Harcourt, Brace and Co., 1934).

7. Malcolm Macmillan, *An Odd Kind of Fame: Stories of Phineas Gage* (Cambridge, MA: MIT Press, 2002).

8. Amy F. T. Arnsten, "The Neurobiology of Thought: The Groundbreaking Discoveries of Patricia Goldman-Rakic 1937–2003," *Cerebral Cortex* 23, no. 10 (2013): 2269–81.

9. Patricia S. Goldman-Rakic, "Circuitry of Primate Prefrontal Cortex and Regulation of Behavior by Representational Memory," in R. Terung, ed., *Comprehensive Physiology, Supplement 5, Handbook of Physiology: The Nervous System, Higher Functions of the Brain*, 2011, https://doi.org/10.1002/cphy.cp 010509.

10. Rengin B. Firat, "Opening the 'Black Box': Functions of the Frontal Lobes and Their Implications for Sociology," *Frontiers in Sociology* 4, no. 3 (2019), https://doi.org/10.3389/fsoc.2019.00003.

11. David Ferrier, *The Functions of the Brain*, 2nd ed. (London: Smith Elder, 1886).

12. Andrea Bari and Trevor W. Robbins, "Inhibition and Impulsivity: Behavioral and Neural Basis of Response Control," *Progress in Neurobiology* 108 (2013): 44–79, https://doi.org/10.1016/j.pneurobio.2013.06.005.

13. Robert E. Burke, "Sir Charles Sherrington's The Integrative Action of the Nervous System: A Centenary Appreciation," *Brain* 130, no. 4 (2007): 887–94.

14. Steve Ayan, "The Brain's Autopilot Mechanism Steers Consciousness," *Scientific American*, December 19, 2018, https://www.scientificamerican.com /article/the-brains-autopilot-mechanism-steers-consciousness/.

15. Nora D. Volkow, Joanna S. Fowler, and Gene-Jack Wang, "The Addicted Human Brain: Insights from Imaging Studies," *Journal of Clinical Investigation* 111, no. 10 (2003):1444–51. doi:10.1172/JCI18533. Nora D. Volkow, Gene-Jack Wang, Joanna S. Fowler, Dardo Tomasi, and Frank Telang, "Addiction Beyond Dopamine Reward Circuitry," *Proceedings of the National Academy of Sciences USA* 108(2011): 15037–42, https://doi.org/10.1073/pnas.1019654108.

Chapter 9

1. Stanley Sadie, "Wolfgang Amadeus Mozart," *Encyclopaedia Britannica,* 2020, https://www.britannica.com/biography/Wolfgang-Amadeus-Mozart

2. Beatriz Rivera and Maribel Huertas, "Millennials: Challenges and Implications to Higher Education," *NYU Faculty Research Network,* November 17– 18, 2006, http://www.nyu.edu/frn/publications/millennial.student/Challenges %20and%201mplications.htm

3. J. Paul Hamilton, Madison Farmer, Phoebe Fogelman, and Ian H. Gotlib, "Depressive Rumination, the Default Mode Network, and the Dark Matter of Clinical Neuroscience," *Biological Psychiatry* 15; 78, no. 4 (2015): 224–30, https:// doi.org/10.1016/j.biopsych.2015.02.020.

4. Rebecca E. Cooney, Jutta Joormann, Fanny Eugène, Emily L. Dennis, and Ian H. Gotlib, "Neural Correlates of Rumination in Depression," *Cognitive, Affective, & Behavioral Neuroscience* 10, no. 4 (2010): 470–78.

5. Kristen M. Beystehner, "Psychoanalysis: Freud's Revolutionary Approach to Human Personality," *Personalityresearch.org,* 1998, http://www.personalityre search.org/papers/beystehner.html. Rachel L. C. Mitchell and Veena Kumari, "Hans Eysenck's Interface between the Brain and Personality: Modern Evidence on the Cognitive Neuroscience of Personality," Personality and Individual Differences 103 (2016): 74–81, https://doi.org/10.1016/j.paid.2016.4.009.

6. Yi-Yuan Tang, Britta K Hölzel, and Michael I. Posner, "The Neuroscience of Mindfulness Meditation," *Nature Reviews Neuroscience* 16 (2015): 213–25, https://doi.org/10.1038/nrn3916.

7. Hans J. Eysenck, *The Biological Basis of Personality* (London: Routledge, 1967).

8. Annette Bolte, Thomas Goschke, and Julius Kuhl, "Emotion and Intuition Effects of Positive and Negative Mood on Implicit Judgments of Semantic Coherence," *Psychological Science* 14, no. 5 (2003). doi:10.1111/1467-9280.01456.

9. Natalie Pilard, "C. G. Jung and Intuition: From the Mindscape of the Paranormal to the Heart of Psychology, *Journal of Analytical Psychology* 63, no. 1 (2018):65–84, https://doi.org/10/1111/1468-5922.12380. Robert L. Hotz, "A Wandering Mind Heads Straight toward Insight," *Wall Street Journal,* June 19, 2009.

10. Daniel Kahneman and Amos Tversky, "On the Psychology of Prediction," *Psychological Review,* Vol. 80, no. 4 (1973): 237–51. Daniel Kahneman, Paul Slovic, and Amos Tversky, *Judgment under Uncertainty: Heuristics and Biases* (London: Cambridge University Press, 1982).

11. Sunny Bonnell, "4 Leaders Who Won by Following Their Instincts (Despite Being Told They Were Crazy)," *Inc.,* January 2018, https://www.inc .com/sunny-bonnell/how-to-follow-your-instincts-in-business-even-when -people-say-youre-crazy.html.

12. Elizabeth Bates, Jeffrey Elman, Mark H. Johnson, Annette Karmiloff-Smith, Domenico Parisi, and Kim Plunkett, *Rethinking Innateness: A Connectionist Perspective on Development* (Cambridge, MA: MIT Press, 1996).

13. Justin Sebastian, "3 Types of Thinking—One of Which Is the Root of All Suffering. On How Incessant Thinking Causes Most of Our Problems," *Medium*, 2017, https://medium.com/@jayseb11/3-types-of-thinking-one-of-which-the-monkey-mind-is-the-root-of-all-suffering-2f0138ffe99a.

14. Albert Ellis, *Reason and Emotion in Psychotherapy: Comprehensive Method of Treating Human Disturbances: Revised and Updated* (New York: Citadel Press, 1994); "Rational Emotive Behavior Therapy," *Encyclopedia of Psychotherapy* 2 (2002):483–87; *Rational Emotive Behavior Therapy: It Works for Me—It Can Work for You* (Amherst, NY: Prometheus Books, 2004).

15. Martin E. P. Seligman, "Positive Psychology: A Personal History," *Annual Review of Clinical Psychology* 15 (2019): 1–23, https://doi.org/10.1146/annurev-clinpsy050718-095653; Martin E. P. Seligman and Mihaly Csikszentmihalyi, "Positive Psychology: An Introduction," in Flow and the Foundations of Positive Psychology (Dordrecht, Netherlands: Springer, 2014), 279–98.

16. Jessica R. Andrews-Hanna, Jay S. Reidler, Jorge Sepulcre, Renee Poulin, and Randy L. Buckner, "Functional-Anatomic Fractionation of the Brain's Default Network," *Neuron* 65, no. 4 (February 25, 2010): 550–62, https://doi.org/10.1016/j.neuron.2010.02.005. Marcus E. Raichle, "The Brain's Default Mode Network," *Annual Review of Neuroscience* 38 (2015): 433–47, https://doi.org/10.1146/annurev-neuro-071013-014030.

17. Howard Gardner, *Frames of Mind: The Theory of Multiple Intelligences* (New York: Basic Books, 1983).

18. Raymond B. Cattell, *Intelligence: Its Structure, Growth, and Action* (New York: North-Holland, 1987).

19. Emily C. Nusbaum and Paul J. Silvia, "Are Intelligence and Creativity Really So Different? Fluid Intelligence, Executive Processes, and Strategy Use in Divergent Thinking," *Intelligence* 39, no. 1 (2011): 36–45, https://doi.org/10.1016/j.intell.2010.11.002.

20. Mihaly Csikszentmihalyi, *Creativity: The Psychology of Discovery and Invention* (New York: HarperCollins Publishers, 1996).

21. Scott B. Kaufman, "The Real Link between Creativity and Mental Illness," *Scientific American*, October 3, 2013, https://blogs.scientificamerican.com/beautiful-minds/the-real-link-between-creativity-and-mental-illness/. Scott B. Kaufman and Elliot S. Paul, "Creativity and Schizophrenia Spectrum Disorders across the Arts and Sciences," *Frontiers in Psychology* 5 (2014): 82–85.

22. Simon Kyaga, Mikael Landen, Marcus Boman, Christina M. Hultman, Niklas Langstrom, and Paul Lichtenstein, "Mental Illness, Suicide and Creativity: 40-Year Prospective Total Population Study," *Journal of Psychiatric Reearch* 47, no. 1 (2013): 83–90, https://doi.org/10.1016/j.jpsychires.2012.09.010.

23. Wikipedia. Accessed November 22, 2022. West, Kanye, https://en.wiki pedia.org/wiki/Kanye_West.

24. James C. Kaufman and Ronaldo A. Beghetto, "Beyond Big and Little: The Four C Model of Creativity," *Review of General Psychology* 13 no. 1 (2009): 1–12, https://doi.org/10.1037/a0013688.

25. Andrei A. Vakhtin, Sephira G. Ryman, Ranee A. Flores, and Rex E. Jung, "Functional Brain Networks Contributing to the Parieto-Frontal Integration Theory of Intelligence," *Neuroimage* 103 (2014): 349–54, https://doi .org/10.1016/j.neuroimage.2014.09.055.

26. Roger E. Beaty, Mathias Benedek, Robin W. Wilkins, Emmanuel Jauk, Andreas Fink, Paul J. Silvia, Donald A. Hodges, Karl Koschutnig, and Aljoscha C. Neubauer, "Creativity and the Default Network: A Functional Connectivity Analysis of the Creative Brain at Rest," *Neuropsychologia* 64 (2014): 92–98.

27. Arne Dietrich, *How Creativity Happens in the Brain* (New York: Palgrave Macmillan, 2015).

28. Mathias Benedeck, Emanuel Jauk, Markus Sommer, Martin Arendasy, and Aljoscha C. Neubauer, "Intelligence, Creativity and Cognitive Control: The Common and Differential Involvement of Executive Functions in Intelligence and Creativity," *Intelligence* 46 (2014): 73–83, https://doi.org/10.1016/j.intell .2014.05.007.

29. Donald A. Treffert, "Brain Gain: A Person Can Instantly Blossom into a Savant—and No One Knows Why," *Scientific American,* July 25, 2018.

Chapter 10

1. Jonathan Smallwood and Jonathan W. Schooler, "The Science of Mind Wandering: Empirically Navigating the Stream of Consciousness," *Annual Review of Psychology*, Vol. 66 (2015): 487–518.

2. Daniel L. Schacter and Donna R. Addis, "The Cognitive Neuroscience of Constructive Memory: Remembering the Past and Imagining the Future," *Philosophical Transactions of the Royal Society of London B: Biological Sciences* 362, no. 1481 (May 29, 2007): 773–86. https://doi.org/10.1098/rstb.2007.2087. Nathan Spreng and Brian Levine, "The Temporal Distribution of Past and Future Autobiographical Events across the Lifespan," *Memory & Cognition* 34, no. 8 (2006): 1644–51, https://doi.org/10.3758/bf03195927.

3. Donna R. Addis, Ling Pan, Mai-Anh Vu, Noa Laiser, and Daniel L. Schacter, "Constructive Episodic Simulation of the Future and the Past: Distinct Subsystems of a Core Brain Network Mediate Imagining and Remembering," *Neuropsychologia* 47, no. 11 (September 2009): 2222–38, https://doi.org/10.1016/a.neuropsychologia.2008.10.026.

4. Matthew A. Killingsworth and Daniel T. Gilbert, "A Wandering Mind Is an Unhappy Mind," *Science*, Vol. 330, no. 6006 (November 12, 2010): 932, https://doi.org/10.1126/science.1192439.

5. Judson A. Brewer, Kathleen A. Garrison, and Susan Whitfield-Gabrieli, "What about the 'Self' Is Processed in the Posterior Cingulate Cortex?" *Frontiers in Human Neuroscience* 7 (2013): 647, https://doi.org/10.3389/fnhum.2013.00647.

6. Jay Bennett, "The Centuries-Long Quest to Measure One Second," *Popular Mechanics*, March 24, 2017, https://www.popularmechanics.com/technology/a25785/quest-measure-second-nist/.

7. George Smith, "Newton's Philosophiae Naturalis Principia Mathematica," *The Stanford Encyclopedia of Philosophy* (Winter 2008), ed. Edward N. Zalta, https://plato.stanford.edu/archives/win2008/entries/newton-principia/.

8. Jim Holt, *When Einstein Walked with Gödel: Excursions to the Edge of Thought* (New York: Farrar, Straus and Giroux, 2018).

9. Nisargadatta Maharaj, *I Am That*, trans., author Maurice Frydman, ed. Sudhakar S. Dikshit (Durham, NC: The Acorn Press, 2012).

BIBLIOGRAPHY

Ackerman, Courtney E. "Pollyanna Principle: The Psychology of Positivity Bias." 2019. PositivePsychology.com. https://positivepsychology.com/polly anna-principle/

Addis, Donna R., Pan, Ling, Vu, Mai-Anh, Laiser, Noa, and Schacter, Daniel L. "Constructive Episodic Simulation of the Future and the Past: Distinct Subsystems of a Core Brain Network Mediate Imagining and Remembering." *Neuropsychologia* 47, no. 11 (September 2009): 2222–38. https://doi.org/10.1016/a.neuropsychologia.2008.10.026

Andrews-Hanna, Jessica R., Reidler, Jay S., Sepulcre, Jorge, Poulin, Renee, and Buckner, Randy L. "Functional-Anatomic Fractionation of the Brain's Default Network." *Neuron* 65, no. 4 (February 2010): 65, no. 4 (2010): 550–62. https://doi.org/10.1016/j.neuron.2010.02.005

Arain, Mariam, Haque, Maliha, Johal, Lina, Mathur, Puja, Nel, Wynand, Rais, Afsha, Sandhu, Ranbir, and Sharma, Sushil. "Maturation of the Adolescent Brain." *Neuropsychiatric Disease and Treatment* 9 (2013): 449–461. doi: 10.2147/NDT.S39776

Arnsten, Amy F. T. "The Neurobiology of Thought: The Groundbreaking Discoveries of Patricia Goldman-Rakic, 1937–2003." *Cerebral Cortex* 23, no. 10 (2013): 2269–81.

Ayan, Steve. "The Brain's Autopilot Mechanism Steers Consciousness." *Scientific American.* December 19, 2018. https://www.scientificamerican .com/article/the-brains-autopilot-mechanism-steers-consciousness/

Baars, Bernard J. "Some Essential Differences between Consciousness and Attention, Perception, and Working Memory." *Consciousness and Cognition* 6 (1997): 363–71. https://doi.org/10.1006/ccog.1997.0307.

Baas, Matthijs., Nevicka, Barbara, and Velden, Femke S. T. "Specific Mindfulness Skills Differentially Predict Creative Performance." *Personality and Social Psychology Bulletin* 40, no. 9 (2014): 1092–1106. https://doi.org /10.1177/0146167214535813

Bajada, Claude J., Ralph, Matthew A. L, and Cloutman, Lauren L. "Transport for Language South of the Sylvian Fissure: The Routes and History of the Main Tracts and Stations in the Ventral Language Network." *Cortex* 69 (2015): 141–51. https://doi.org/10.1016/j.cortex.2015.05.011

Balch, Bridget. "Making Science Serve Humanity: Jennifer Doudna, PhD, Says CRISPR Gene-Editing Technology Should Be Accessible to All." *AAMCNews*. November 8, 2012. https://www.aamc.org/news-in sights/making-science-serve-humanity-jennifer-doudna-phd-says-crispr -gene-editing-technology-should-be

Bargh, John A. "The Modern Unconscious." *World Psychiatry* 18 (2019): 225–26. https://doi.org/10.1002/wps.20625

Bari, Andrea, and Robbins, Trevor W. "Inhibition and Impulsivity: Behavioral and Neural Basis of Response Control." *Progress in Neurobiology*, Vol. 108 (2013): 44–79. https://doi.org/10.1016/j.pneurobio.2013.06.005

Bates, Elizabeth, Elman, Jeffrey, Johnson, Mark H., Karmiloff-Smith, Annette, Parisi, Domenico, and Plunkett, Kim. *Rethinking Innateness: A Connectionist Perspective on Development*. Cambridge, MA: MIT Press, 1996.

Bauby, Jean-Dominique. *The Diving Bell and the Butterfly: A Memoir of Life in Death*. New York: Random House, 1998.

Beaty, Roger E., Benedek, Mathias, Wilkins, Robin, W, Jauk, Emanuel, Fink, Andreas, Silvia, Paul J., Hodges, Donald A., Koschutnig, Karl, and Neubauer, Aljoscha C. "Creativity and the Default Network: A Functional Connectivity Analysis of the Creative Brain at Rest." *Neuropsychologia* 64 (2014): 92–98. https://doi.org/10.1016/j.neuropsychologia.2014.09.019

Beck, Charlotte J. *Everyday Zen*. San Francisco: HarperCollins, 1989.

Benedeck, Mathias, Jauk, Emanuel, Sommer, Markus, Arendasy, Martin, and Neubauer, Aljoscha C. "Intelligence, Creativity and Cognitive Control: The Common and Differential Involvement of Executive Functions in Intelligence and Creativity." *Intelligence* 46 (2014): 73–83. https://doi.org /10.1016/j.intell.2014.05.007

Bennett, Jay. "The Centuries-Long Quest to Measure One Second." *Popular Mechanics*. March 24, 2017. https://www.popularmechanics.com/technol ogy/a25785/quest-measure-second-nist/

Beystehner, Kristen M. "Psychoanalysis: Freud's Revolutionary Approach to Human Personality." *Personalityresearch.org*. 1998. http://www.personality research.org/papers/beystehner.html

Bi, Xinwen, Yang, Yiqun, Li, Hailei, Wang, Meiping, Zhang, Wenxin, and Deater-Deckard, Kirby. "Parenting Styles and Parent–Adolescent Relationships: The Mediating Roles of Behavioral Autonomy and Parental

Authority." *Frontiers in Psychology* 9 (2018): 2187. https://doi.org/10.3389/fpsyg.2018.02187

Bolte, Annette, Goschke, Thomas, and Kuhl, Julius. "Emotion and Intuition Effects of Positive and Negative Mood on Implicit Judgments of Semantic Coherence." *Psychological Science* 14, no. 5 (2003). doi:10.1111/1467-9280.01456

Bonnell, Sunny. "4 Leaders Who Won by Following Their Instincts (Despite Being Told They Were Crazy)." *Inc.* (January 2008). https://www.inc.com/sunny-bonnell/how-to-follow-your-instincts-in-business-even-when-people-say-youre-crazy.html

Brewer, Judson A., Garrison, Kathleen A., and Whitfield-Gabrieli, Susan. "What about the 'Self' Is Processed in the Posterior Cingulate Cortex?" *Frontiers in Human Neuroscience* 7 (2013): 647. https://doi.org/10.3389/fnhum.2013.00647

Bryner, Jeanna, and Pappas, Stephanie. "That's Incredible! 9 Brainy Baby Abilities." *LiveScience* (2011). https://www.livescience.com/14343-amazing-brainy-baby-abilities.html

Burke, Robert E. "Sir Charles Sherrington's The Integrative Action of the Nervous System: A Centenary Appreciation." *Brain* 130, no. 4 (2007): 887–94.

Campion, George G., and Elliot-Smith, Grafton. *The Neural Basis of Thoughts.* London, UK: Kegan Paul and Co., Ltd.; New York: Harcourt, Brace and Co., 1934.

Camras, Linda A., and Shutter, Jennifer M. "Emotional Facial Expressions in Infancy," *Emotion Review* 2 (2010): 120–29. doi:10.1177/1754073909352529

Cattell, Raymond B. *Intelligence: Its Structure, Growth, and Action.* New York: North-Holland, 1987.

Colzato, Lorenza S., Ozturk, Ayca, and Hommel, Bernhard. "Meditate to Create: The Impact of Focused-Attention and Open-Monitoring Training on Convergent and Divergent Thinking." *Frontiers in Psychology* 3 (2012): 116. https://doi.org/10.3389/fpsyg.2012.00116

Colzato, Lorenza S., Szapora, Ayca, Pannekoek, Justine N., and Hommel, Bernhard. "The Impact of Physical Exercise on Convergent and Divergent Thinking." *Frontiers in Human Neuroscience* 7 (2013): 824. https://doi.org/10.3389/fnhum.2013.00824

Cooney, Rebecca E., Joormann, Jutta, Eugène, Fanny, Dennis, Emily L., and Gotlib, Ian H. "Neural Correlates of Rumination in Depression." *Cognitive, Affective, & Behavioral Neuroscience* 10, no. 4 (2010): 470–78.

Coulter, Dee Joy. *Original Mind: Uncovering Your Natural Brilliance.* Louisville, CO: Sounds True, 2014.

Crick, Francis. *The Astonishing Hypothesis: The Scientific Search for the Soul.* New York: Touchstone, 1994.

Crick, Francis, and Koch, Christoph. "A Framework for Consciousness." *Nature Neuroscience* 6 (2003): 119–26. https://doi.org/10.1038/nn0203-119

Csikszentmihalyi, Mihaly. *Creativity: The Psychology of Discovery and Invention.* New York: HarperCollins, 1996.

———. *Flow: The Psychology of Optimal Experience.* New York: Harper and Row, 1990.

Delehanty, Hugh. "Does Meditation Boost Creativity?" *Mindful Magazine.* June 19, 2017. https://www.mindful.org/does-meditation-boost-creativity/

———. "The Science of Meditation." *Mindful Magazine.* December 13, 2017. https://www.mindful.org/meditators-under-the-microscope/

Dietrich, Arne. *How Creativity Happens in the Brain.* New York: Palgrave Macmillan, 2015.

Earl, Brian. "The Biological Function of Consciousness." *Frontiers in Psychology* 5, (2014): 697. https://doi.org/10.3389/fpsyg.2014.00697

Edelman, Gerald. *Wider Than the Sky: The Phenomenal Gift of Consciousness.* New Haven, CT: Yale University Press, 2004.

Ellis, Albert. "Rational Emotive Behavior Therapy." *Encyclopedia of Psychotherapy,* Vol. 2 (2002): 483–87.

———. *Rational Emotive Behavior Therapy: It Works for Me—It Can Work for You.* Amherst, NY: Prometheus Books, 2004.

———. *Reason and Emotion in Psychotherapy: Comprehensive Method of Treating Human Disturbances: Revised and Updated.* New York: Citadel Press, 1994.

Eysenck, Hans J. *The Biological Basis of Personality.* London: Routledge, 1967.

Ferrier, David. *The Functions of the Brain,* 2nd ed. London: Smith Elder, 1886.

Ficco, Linda, Mancuso, Lorenzo, Manuello, Jordi, Teneggi, Alessia, Liloia, Donato, Duca, Sergio, Costa, Tommaso, Zoltan Kovacs, Gyula, and Cauda, Franco. "Disentangling Predictive Processing in the Brain: A Meta-analytic Study in Favour of a Predictive Network." *Scientific Reports* 11, no. 16258 (2021). https://doi.org/10.1038/s41598-021-95603-5

Firat, Rengin B. "Opening the "Black Box": Functions of the Frontal Lobes and Their Implications for Sociology." *Frontiers in Sociology* 4, no. 3 (2019). https://doi.org/10.3389/fsoc.2019.00003

Freud, Sigmund. *Civilization and Its Discontents* (James Strachey, trans. 2017) IndieBooks, 1930.

———. *A General Introduction to Psychoanalysis*. New York: Boni and Liveright Publishers, 1920.

———. *General Psychological Theory: Papers on Metapsychology*. New York: Collier Books, 1963.

Gardner, Howard. *Frames of Mind: The Theory of Multiple Intelligences*. New York: Basic Books, 1983.

Gazzaniga, Michael. "The Split Brain in Man." *Scientific American* 217, no. 2 (1967): 24–29. https://doi.org/10.1038/scientificamerican0867-24

———. *Who's in Charge? Free Will and the Science of the Brain*. New York: HarperCollins, 2011.

Gilbert, Elizabeth. *Big Magic: Creative Living Beyond Fear*. New York: Riverhead Books, 2016.

Goksör, Emma, Rosengren, Lars, and Wennergren, Göran. "Bradycardic Response during Submersion in Infant Swimming." *Acta Paediatrics* 91, no. 3 (2002): 307–12. doi:10.1080/08035250252833978

Goldman-Rakic, Patricia S. "Circuitry of Primate Prefrontal Cortex and Regulation of Behavior by Representational Memory." *Comprehensive Physiology. Supplement 5. Handbook of Physiology, the Nervous System, Higher Functions of the Brain*. R. Terjung, ed., 2011. https://doi.org/10.1002/cphy.cp010509

Grandma, Moses. https://en.wikipedia.org/wiki/Grandma_Moses. Accessed November 21, 2022.

Grossmann, Tobias, Johnson, Mark H., Lloyd-Fox, Sarah, Blasi, Anna, Deligianni, Fani, Elwell, Clare and Csibra, Gergely. "Early Cortical Specialization for Face-to-Face Communication in Human Infants." *Proceedings of the Royal Society: Biological Sciences* 275, no. 1653 (2008): 2803–11.

Hamilton, J. Paul, Farmer, Madison, Fogelman, Phoebe, and Gotlib, Ian H. "Depressive Rumination, the Default Mode Network, and the Dark Matter of Clinical Neuroscience." *Biological Psychiatry* 78, no. 4 (August 15, 2015): 224–30.

Holt, Jim. *When Einstein Walked with Gödel: Excursions to the Edge of Thought*. New York: Farrar, Straus and Giroux, 2018.

Hotz, Robert L. "A Wandering Mind Heads Straight toward Insight." *Wall Street Journal*, June 19, 2009.

Isaacson, Walter, *Leonardo da Vinci*. New York: Simon & Schuster, 2017.

James, William. *The Principles of Psychology*. New York: Holt, 1890.

Jung, Carl G. *The Archetypes and the Collective Unconscious (Collected Works of C. G. Jung Vol. 9, Part 1)*. Princeton, NJ: Princeton University Press, 1981.

——. *The Undiscovered Self (Present and Future)*. New York: American Library, 1957.

Jung, Carl G., and Baynes, Helton G. *Psychological Types* or *The Psychology of Individuation* (London: Kegan Paul Trench Trubner, 1921).

Kahneman, Daniel, Slovic, Paul, and Tversky, Amos. *Judgment under Uncertainty: Heuristics and Biases*. London: Cambridge University Press, 1982.

Kahneman, Daniel, and Tversky, Amos. "On the Psychology of Prediction." *Psychological Review* 80, no. 4 (1973): 237–51.

Kapleau, Phillip. *The Three Pillars of Zen: Teaching, Practice, and Enlightenment*. New York: Random House, 1989.

Kaufman, James C., and Beghetto, Ronaldo A. "Beyond Big and Little: The Four C Model of Creativity." *Review of General Psychiatry* 13, no. 1 (2009): 1–12. https://doi.org/10.1037/a0013688

Kaufman, Scott B. "The Real Link between Creativity and Mental Illness." *Scientific American*. October 3, 2013. https://blogs.scientificamerican.com /beautiful-minds/the-real-link-between-creativity-and-mental-illness/

Kaufman, Scott B., and Paul, Elliot S. "Creativity and Schizophrenia Spectrum Disorders across the Arts and Sciences." *Frontiers in Psychology* 5 (2014): 82–85.

Killingsworth, M. A., and Gilbert, Daniel T. "A Wandering Mind Is an Unhappy Mind." *Science* 330, no. 6006 (November 12, 2010). https://doi .org/10.1126/science.1192439

Kindlon, Dan. *Too Much of a Good Thing: Raising Children of Character in an Indulgent Age*. New York: Miramax Books, 2001.

Kyaga, Simon, Landen, Mikael, Boman, Marcus, Hultman, Christina M., Langstrom, Niklas, and Lichtenstein, Paul. "Mental Illness, Suicide and Creativity: 40-Year Prospective Total Population Study." *Journal of Psychiatric Rearch*. 47, no. 1 (2013): 83–90. https://doi.org/10.1016/j .jpsychires.2012.09.010

Lane, Christopher J. "The Holy Household of Louis and Zélie Martin." *Crisis Magazine*, July 11, 2013. https://www.crisismagazine.com/2013 /the-holy-household-of-louis-and-zelie-martin

Ledoux, Joseph E., Wilson, Donald H., and Gazzaniga, Michael S. "A Divided Mind: Observations on the Conscious Properties of the Separated Hemispheres." *Annals of Neurology*, 2, no. 5 (1977): 417–21. https://doi .org/10.1002/ana.410020513

Libet, Benjamin. "Unconscious Cerebral Initiative and the Role of Conscious Will in Voluntary Action." *Neurophysiology of Consciousness*.

Contemporary Neuroscientists. Boston, MA: Birkhäuser, 1993. https://doi
.org/10.1007/978-1-4612-0355-1_16

Lipska, Barbara K., and McArdle, Elaine. *The Neuroscientist Who Lost Her Mind: My Tale of Madness and Recovery*. Boston: Houghton Mifflin Harcourt, 2018.

Macmillan, Malcolm. *An Odd Kind of Fame: Stories of Phineas Gage*. Cambridge, MA: MIT Press, 2002.

Maharaj, Nisargadatta. *I Am That*. Maurice Frydman (Trans., Author). Sudhakar S. Dikshit (Ed.). Durham, NC: The Acorn Press, 2012.

Martel, Jean-François. "Consciousness in the Aesthetic Imagination." *Metapsychosis: Journal of Consciousness, Literature, and Art*. July 11, 2016. https://www.metapsychosis.com/consciousness-in-the-aesthetic-imagination/

McIntosh, Bruce J. "Spoiled Child Syndrome." *Pediatrics* 83, no. 1 (1989): 108–15. https://pediatrics.aappublications.org/content/83/1/108

Miller, Earl K. "The Prefrontal Cortex and Cognitive Control." *Nat Rev Neurosci* 1 (2000): 59–65. https://doi.org/10.1038/35036228

Mitchell, Rachel L. C., and Kumari, Veena. "Hans Eysenck's Interface between the Brain and Personality: Modern Evidence on the Cognitive Neuroscience of Personality." *Personality and Individual Differences* 103 (2016): 74-81. https://doi.org/10.1016/j.paid.2016.04.009

Nisbett, Richard E., and Wilson, Timothy D. "Telling More than We Can Know: Verbal Reports on Mental Processes." *Psychological Review* 84, no. 3 (1977): 231–59. https://doi.org/10.1037/0033-295X.84.3.231

Nusbaum, Emily C., and Silvia, Paul J. "Are Intelligence and Creativity Really So Different? Fluid Intelligence, Executive Processes, and Strategy Use in Divergent Thinking." *Intelligence* 39, no. 1 (2011): 36-45. https://doi.org/10.1016/j.intell.2010.11.002

Otsuka, Yumiko. "Face Recognition in Infants: A Review of Behavioral and Near-Infrared Spectroscopic Studies." *Special Issue: Face Perception and Recognition*. R. Kakigi and M. K. Yamaguchi, eds., *Japanese Psychological Research* 56, no. 1 (2014): 76–90. https://doi.org/10.1111/jpr.12024

Pargament, Kenneth I., and Mahoney, Annette. "Spirituality: The Search for the Sacred." In *Oxford Handbook of Positive Psychology*, 3rd ed., 878–891. S. J. Lopez and C. R. Snyder, eds. Oxford, UK: Oxford University Press, 2009. https://doi.org/10.1093/oxfordhb/9780199396511.013.51

Piaget, Jean. *Epistemology and Psychology of Functions*. Dordrecht, Netherlands: D. Reidel Publishing Company, 1977.

———. *Origins of Intelligence in the Child*. London: Routledge & Kegan Paul, 1936.

———. *Science of Education and the Psychology of the Child*. New York: Viking, 1970.

Pilard, Nathalie. "C. G. Jung and Intuition: From the Mindscape of the Paranormal to the Heart of Psychology." *Journal of Analytical Psychology* 63, no. 1 (2018): 65–84. https://doi.org/10.1111/1468-5922.12380

Pineda, Jaime A. *Piercing the Cloud: Encountering the Real Me*. New Jersey: BookBaby, 2020.

Raichle, Marcus E. "The Brain's Default Mode Network." *Annual Review of Neuroscience* 38 (2015): 433–47. https://doi.org/10.1146/annurev-neuro -071013-014030

Rand, Ayn. *Atlas Shrugged*. New York: Dutton, 1957.

Rivera, Beatriz, and Huertas, Maribel. "Millennials: Challenges and Implications to Higher Education." *NYU Faculty Resource Network*. November 17–18, 2006. http://www.nyu.edu/frn/publications/millennial .student/Challenges%20and%201mplications.html

Roshi, Shodo H. "An Eternal Now: Original Mind." June 28, 2010. https:// sgforums.com/forums/1728/topics/403706/

Rozin, Paul, and Royzman, Edward B. "Negativity Bias, Negativity Dominance, and Contagion." *Personality and Social Psychology Review* 5, no. 4 (2001): 296–320. https://doi.org/10.1207/S15327957PSPR0504_2

Rumi, Jalāl ad-Dīn. *The Essential Rumi, New Expanded Edition* (Barks, C., trans.). San Francisco: HarperCollins, 2004.

Sadie, Stanley. "Wolfgang Amadeus Mozart." Encyclopaedia Britannica, 2020. https://www.britannica.com/biography/Wolfgang-Amadeus-Mozart

Sample, Ian. "Struggle to Sleep in a Strange Bed? Scientists Have Uncovered Why." *The Guardian*. April 21, 2016. https://www.theguardian.com /lifeandstyle/2016/apr/21/struggle-to-sleep-in-a-strange-bed-scientists -have-uncovered-why

Schacter, Daniel L., and Addis, Donna R. "The Cognitive Neuroscience of Constructive Memory: Remembering the Past and Imagining the Future." *Philosophical Transactions of the Royal Society of London: Biological Sciences*. 362, no. 1481 (May 29, 2007): 773–86. https://doi.org/10.1098 /rstb.2007.2087

Sebastian, Justin. "3 Types of Thinking—One of Which Is the Root of All Suffering. On How Incessant Thinking Causes Most of Our Problems." *Medium* (2017). https://medium.com/@jayseb11/3-types-of-thinking -one-of-which-the-monkey-mind-is-the-root-of-all-suffering-2f0138f fe99a

Seligman, Martin E. P. "Positive Psychology: A Personal History." *Annual Review of Clinical Psychology* 15 (2019): 1–23. https://doi.org/10.1146 /annurev-clinpsy050718-095653

Seligman, Martin E. P., and Csikszentmihalyi, Mihaly. "Positive Psychology: An Introduction." *Flow and the Foundations of Positive Psychology*, 279–98. Dordrecht, Netherlands: Springer, 2014.

Shannon, Jennifer. *Don't Feed the Monkey Mind: How to Stop the Cycle of Anxiety, Fear & Worry*. Oakland, CA: New Harbinger Publications, Inc., 2017.

Smallwood, Jonathan, and Schooler, Jonathan W. "The Science of Mind Wandering: Empirically Navigating the Stream of Consciousness." *Annual Review of Psychology* 66 (2015): 487–518.

Smith, Daniel. *Monkey Mind: A Memoir of Anxiety*. New York: Simon & Schuster, 2013.

Smith, George. "Newton's *Philosophiae Naturalis Principia Mathematica.*" *The Stanford Encyclopedia of Philosophy*. (Winter 2008 Edition). Edward N. Zalta, ed., https://plato.stanford.edu/archives/win2008/entries/newton -principia/

Spreng, R. Nathan, and Levine, Brian. "The Temporal Distribution of Past and Future Autobiographical Events across the Lifespan." *Memory & Cognition* 34, no. 8 (2006): 1644–51. https://doi.org/10.3758/bf03195927

Tang, Yi-Yuan, Hölzel, Britta K., and Posner, Michael I. "The Neuroscience of Mindfulness Meditation." *Nature Reviews Neuroscience* 16 (2015): 213–25. https://doi.org/10.1038/nrn3916

Thomsen, Lotte, Frankenhuis, Willem E., Ingold-Smith, McCaila, and Carey, Susan. "Big and Mighty: Preverbal Infants Mentally Represent Social Dominance." *Science* 331, no. 6016 (2011): 477–80.

Treffert, Donald A. "Brain Gain: A Person Can Instantly Blossom into a Savant—and No One Knows Why." *Scientific American*, July 25, 2018. https://blogs.scientificamerican.com/observations/brain-gain-a-person -can-instantly-blossom-into-a-savant-and-no-one-knows-why/

Tversky, Amos, and Kahneman, Daniel. "Judgment under Uncertainty: Heuristics and Biases." *Science* 185 (1974): 1124-31.

Vakhtin, Andrei A., Ryman, Sephira G., Flores, Ranee A., and Jung, Rex E. "Functional Brain Networks Contributing to the Parieto-Frontal Integration Theory of Intelligence." *Neuroimage* 103 (2014): 349–54. https://doi.org/10.1016/j.neuroimage.2014.09.055

Volkow, Nora D., Fowler, Joanna S., and Wang, Gene-Jack. "The Addicted Human Brain: Insights from Imaging Studies." *Journal of Clinical Investigation* 111, no. 10 (May 2003):1444-51. doi:10.1172/JCI18533

Volkow, Nora D., Wang, Gene-Jack, Fowler, Joanna S., Tomasi, Dardo, and Telang, Frank. "Addiction: Beyond Dopamine Reward Circuitry." *Proceedings of the National Academy of Sciences USA* 108 (2011): 15037–42. https://doi..org/10.1073/pnas.1010654108

Waxman, Stephen G. 2017. "Chapter 18: The Reticular Formation." *Clinical Neuroanatomy,* 28th ed. https://neurology.mhmedical.com/content.aspx?bookid=1969&sectionid=147037558. Accessed: September 19, 2022.

Wikipedia. Accessed November 22, 2022. West, Kanye, https://en.wikipedia.org/wiki/Kanye_West

———. Accessed September 18, 2022. Moses, Grandma. https://en.wikipedia.org/wiki/Grandma_Moses

Wolchover, Natalie. "'Peekaboo' Reveals Babies Understanding of Quantum Mechanics." *LiveScience,* 2012. https://www.livescience.com/20803-newborn-babies-quantum-mechanics.html

Wolman, David. "The Split Brain: A Tale of Two Halves." *Nature News Feature* 483 (2012): 260–63.

Zahedani, Zahra Z., Rezaee, Rita, Yazdani, Zahra, Bagheri, Sina, and Nabeiei, Parisa. "The Influence of Parenting Style on Academic Achievement and Career Path." *Journal of Advances in Medical Education & Professionalism* 4, no. 3 (2016): 130–34.

INDEX

About the Author

Jaime A. Pineda, PhD, is professor of cognitive science, neuroscience, and psychiatry at the University of California, San Diego. For twenty-eight years, he directed the Cognitive Neuroscience Laboratory, where he explored the relationship between mind and brain. He is the author of many widely cited papers in animal and human cognitive and systems neuroscience. He is the editor of the academic book *Mirror Neurons*, and author of *The Social Impulse: The Evolution and Neuroscience of What Brings Us Together*. For over twenty years, he has also been interested in spiritual matters. He has published two books of poetry: *Quieting of a Mind* and *Dawning of a New Mind*. These focus on mind-brain relationships, with an emphasis on spirituality, mysticism, environmentalism, and social activism. Most recently, he published his autobiography, *Piercing the Cloud: Encountering the Real Me*, in which he explores how true seeing, hearing, feeling, and thinking can quiet the overactive monkey mind and allow silence to become the fountain of creative thought. From such silence, there is the emergence of a new perception and awareness: an awareness of unity infused with intrinsic joy and filled with a deep and uncompromising dedication to what is true and real while exuding love and empathy toward others. Professor Pineda resides in San Diego, California, with his wife, Jane, and dog, Darcy.

Printed in the USA
CPSIA information can be obtained
at www.ICGtesting.com
LVHW090302111123
763606LV00004B/172